I Arise! 2024

A devotional book for women

Day by day, from one heart to another

Category: Christianity

ISBN: 9798863701059

Cover design by: Inspirational Journals

Graphic design by: Ashani Allen

Edited by: Jackie Jacobs

Proofreading Team:
Carol Lord-Paul
Deveen Smith
Vera Walters

CONTENTS:

ACKNOWLEDGEMENTS

God alone is worthy of all praise. We thank Him for His guidance and inspiration with the, ***'I Arise!'*** 2024 project. We are always mindful that, *'...without (Jesus) we can do nothing'* (St John 15:5).

We take this opportunity to thank everyone who helped to make this edition happen; whether your contribution was great or small, we appreciate you.

We remember our pioneering mothers of Bethel National Women's Council who were so focused. They laboured tirelessly and effectively with less tools than we have available to us today - they have a sure reward. Their work continues through each of us and will never be forgotten.

INTRODUCTION

Welcome! Can you believe it? Another year has passed and it's time for, ***'I Arise!'*** 2024, an international daily devotional book for women written for you, by you and about you.

Again women from different age groups, nationalities, cultures, etc., have joined together to support each other with God's Word. ***I Arise!*** has become a writing board for many women. This year we have several remarkable, page-turning testimonies shared of God's faithfulness. Testimonies that may move you to tears as you read real personal accounts in November's *'Give Thanks'* section such as, ***'No Limits'***; '***Tragedy to Triumph***'; ***'Same God'***. We have also repeated some of the testimonies published in our 2022 edition for those who did not get to read them the first time around, and for anyone who would just appreciate a reminder of what our God can do.

Do you feel like nobody knows your name? This is not something new for women; going back to Bible days there were many whose names were rarely or never mentioned. Read about some of them in March, which is Women's History month, and be edified. Read about the daughters of Zelophehad, Mary – mother of John Mark, Jehoshabeath, and others.

We've *'bitten the bullet'* and included sensitive writings concerning Dinah, the only daughter of Jacob and Leah, and also Lot's relationship with his two daughters.

A Support Directory is provided at the back of this book should you need professional help as a result of anything you read or are going through now or in the future.

Thank you to our professional medical team for pages of advice.

Ladies, we AWAKEN; we Arise! God is with us!

Bethel National Women's Council

January

Lead Me Lord

*MONDAY 1st

...cause me to know the way wherein I should walk... - Psalm 143:8

LEAD ME LORD, I WILL FOLLOW – Reading: Psalm 143:1-12

'***W****here He may lead me I will go, for I have learned to trust Him so...'.* My wife and I have learned that singing songs with beautiful melodies is one thing, but when the words of those songs become the reality of your life then it takes on a whole new meaning.

As people of God, our desire is always to submit to the will of God and follow where He leads. Romans 8:14 tells us, *'...those that are led by the Spirit are sons of God'.* It takes great faith to follow the Lord not only when He leads us through peaceful seasons and quiet times, but the Lord will also challenge and stretch our faith in times of adversity and uncertainty.

Despite it all we follow, we trust, we embrace every season, and delight in the LORD knowing always that He will direct our paths.

As we embark upon this new year, let us boldly proclaim our trust in our God by trusting His leadership, confident in His care, and say with all that is within us...LEAD ME LORD.

With a childlike faith and the courage to embrace the unknown we cry with words that cannot be heard, knowing that the Divine Interpreter knows the language of the heart. He knows our frailty, He knows exactly how much we can bear and so we say, *'Lead me Lord, I will follow, lead me Lord, I will go. You have called me, I will answer, lead me Lord I will go'*!

Dexter E. Edmund, Presiding Bishop
& First Lady Yolanda Edmund
BUCJC Apostolic UK & Europe

New Year's Day

TUESDAY 2nd

And he led them forth by the right way, that they might go to a city of habitation
Psalm 107:7

FAITH ON TRIAL – Reading: Psalm 107:1-15

This Christian walk with God is definitely one of trust, humility, faith and dependency. Many times this walk will challenge and stretch our belief-system, but if we can remain focused and faithful, we will see the plans of God unfold right before our eyes.

I can recall a time in my life when I was at a crossroad in my job, I felt it was time for a change and was ready for something new that would challenge and stretch me further. This unrest led me to pray, I needed God's guidance on how to move forward. We are encouraged by the words in Proverbs 3:6 that we should, *'acknowledge God in all our ways and he will direct our pathway'*. It was during this time of seeking for God's guidance and direction that it was impressed in my spirit to start looking for a new job.

I remember the Scripture clearly that rested in my spirit at the time, *'faith without works is dead'*, meaning faith requires action. I started job hunting and it was not long after that I saw an exciting opportunity at a well-established educational institution. This job would definitely challenge me and take me out of my comfort zone. I was ready for this challenge. I quickly applied and waited patiently for a response and to my surprise I was shortlisted for the job.

Oh, there was such an excitement in my spirit, I knew God was leading me and this was the answer I was looking for. I knew this was the door He was opening up for me. I was reassured and convinced that this job was mine. I told my work colleagues, *'God has given me this job'*.

The day arrived for the interview and I was prepared and ready to answer any questions deemed necessary to secure this position. The room was filled with other professionals, some of whom were a lot more educated and experienced than myself, but that didn't intimidate me because I knew God had given me a Word.

The interview had two stages and I got to the final stage - at this point it was only three of us left. I successfully completed all stages and was reassured that they would be in touch with me.

I left there that evening with a sense of confidence and peace of mind. On the following day, I received a phone call from the institution commending me for my excellent interview skills but, unfortunately, someone more experienced and qualified than me got the position. I was devastated, discouraged and confused. I knew I had heard the voice of God reassuring me that the job was mine. I began to question what I'd heard - did I hear God correctly? Was it my own thoughts? Was God leading me or was it my own desperation to move on? For days these thoughts played on my mind; I prayed, I cried, I questioned myself. A few days had passed and I was at home meditating when I heard the voice clearly saying, *'The job is yours, the lady that they have given the job to will give it back. I have given you that job and they will be in touch to offer you the job'*. Oh, this was even more specific but this time I kept what I heard in my heart. Still struggling and doubting, but I dared not repeat it.

Four weeks had now passed since I applied for this position, still struggling with doubting questions, I kept rehearsing what I heard from the Lord, *'The job is yours'*.

It was just over a month since the interview when I received a phone call from the institution stating, *'Because you were the next best candidate at the interview, we would like to offer you the position. The lady who we offered the job to, got another job which she has accepted'*.

I could not believe my ears; did I hear right? I wanted to scream, shout, jump around the office! I was given 24 hours to decide whether I wanted the job. I rang them the next day and said yes. My work colleagues who had mocked and jeered me were in shock and disbelief. My salary doubled; my status changed overnight. God is amazing!

God was indeed leading me all the way. What I didn't realise was that my faith, my trust, my dependency on Him was on trial. God proved to me that day that His word is final. His methods might not make sense to us at the time but rest assured, He is leading us *'in the right way' (Psalm 107:7)*, and if we are patient for long enough, we will inherit the promises of God.

Name withheld

WEDNESDAY 3rd

...the journey that thou takest shall not be for thine honour; for the LORD shall sell Sisera into the hand of a woman... - Judges 4:9

LET HIM LEAD, HE KNOWS THE WAY - Reading: Judges 4:1-15

N*o one ever sought the Father*
And found He was not there
And no burden is too heavy
To be lightened by a prayer
No problem is too intricate
And no sorrow that we face
Is too deep and devastating
To be softened by His grace.

No trials and tribulations
Are beyond what we can bear
If we share them with Our Father
As we talk to Him in prayer.
And men of every colour
Every race and every creed
Have but to seek the Father
In their deepest hour of need.

God asks for no credentials
He accepts us with our flaws
He is kind and understanding
And He welcomes us because
We are His erring children
And He loves us everyone
And He freely and completely
Forgives all that we have done
Asking only if we're ready
To follow where He leads
Content that in His wisdom
He will answer all our needs.

(Helen Steiner Rice)

As we reflect on the words of Helen Steiner Rice today, may the resistant struggle within ourselves to remain where we are yet do God's will, be surrendered completely. May we trust that He has the compass for our future and humbly follow where He leads.

Name withheld

*THURSDAY 4th

Shall I pursue? Shall I overtake? – 1 Samuel 30:8

READY TO GO, READY TO STAY - Reading: 1 Samuel 30:1-19

I often have fond memories of the adult brethren during testimony service as a youth, *'Pray for me that comes what may, I will continue with this man Jesus'*. In other words, *'Whatever may come my way, it will not get the better of me'*. At times trouble does get the better of us, especially when it reaches our own doorsteps.

Look at David's behaviour in the horrific situation at Ziklag; we could have been reading the above Scripture differently where David took matters into his own hand. However, we aren't. Instead, we are left with a timely principled Word for the age; *'And David inquired at the LORD, saying, Shall I ...?'.*

It is right to ask of the Lord for His leading. It is a wise and good thing to know and understand the wisdom of this truth, so that we can possess a non-pre-emptive approach to the Lord.

Thus, ready to go as well as ready to stay; reflecting a prayerful heart that is saying, *'O LORD, I know...it is not in man that walketh to direct his steps' (Jeremiah 10:23).* I come to you as I want to be led.

Pastor Josephine Lewis

***World Braille Day**

FRIDAY 5th

The steps of a good (person) are ordered by the LORD - Psalm 37:23

JESUS, OUR HOPE IN DESPAIR – Reading: Psalm 37:23-28

In times of despair, many people look to their political leaders for leadership, but the people of God look to Him, and trust Him for leadership.

Jesus is our hope. He knows our feelings and how fragile we are. He understands that oftentimes we are battle-worn, and battle-fatigued. He too was human and wants us to know that He understands the humdrum that comes with long days, and lonely nights. Although our trailblazer, He was tempted in all points like us but He overcame all.

Jesus pioneered our salvation through the world you and I face daily. He is unchanging and His love unconditional. He is champion of the cause for our survival; a covenant-keeping God. Over time human relationships change, health changes, customs change, but God remains the same. He is God who ruled the earth last night, and He is the same who rules today.

Not only does God comfort us during the storms of life, but He is able to still the storm. Philosophers debate the meaning of life, but we need a Lord who declares the meaning of life. Friends can hold your hand at your deathbed, but you need God who defeated the grave.

When we search through the Scriptures, we find many ways in which God led His people, and He is still leading us today.

Dr Una Davis

SATURDAY 6th

Teach me to do your will, for you are my God; your Spirit is good. Lead me in the land of uprightness - Psalm 143:10 (NKJV)

SEEKING GUIDANCE – Reading: Psalm 143:1-12

If you are like me, no matter what stage of your faith journey you are in, you have struggled with knowing and doing God's will. This is due, in part, to the fact that most of our life, we strive for independence and self-reliance. It's difficult to turn over our lives for another to direct.

In this psalm, David is being pursued by his enemy, he is oppressed and, in his own words, he is overwhelmed and helpless. As we look at his prayer posture in this situation, it is clear that seeking guidance involves great humility and trust, both of which are born out of true intimacy with God.

Humility is being willing to admit you don't know (what or how), and that you need help. Hear David as in humility, he surrenders to God, *'...in your sight no one living is righteous...my spirit is overwhelmed within me; my heart within me is distressed...I spread out my hands to you...O Lord...my spirit fails!' (vv:2, 4, 6, 7)*. Ultimately, David turns to God because he trusts Him. He trusts the nature, ability and character of the One he seeks help and guidance from; this trust is grounded in relational experiences. He states, *'I remember the days of old; I meditate on all that you have done...cause me to hear your lovingkindness in the morning, for in you do I trust...' (vv:5,8)*.

What's important to understand, however, is that David's humble, trusting response didn't develop overnight. It is the inevitable result of seasons growing in intimacy with his God. Intimacy is about knowing and being known. In Hebrew, the root word for *'know'* is '***yada'***, and it includes perceiving, attuning, learning, understanding, and experiencing. Therefore, when you know someone in the biblical sense, you know them intimately; not just physically, you know who they are, and why you trust them, you cherish them, and you want to be uniquely vulnerable with them.

As David closes his prayer, he declares, *'I lift up my soul to you... teach me to do your will,* ***For you are my God***;' (vv:6,8,10). *'You are mine'*, he says of God; this is intimate covenant language. I am tied to you. I know you and am known by you. And, in complete confidence, he surrenders his will (soul) and declares what he knows about God, and why he trusts only Him to lead his life: *'**Your Spirit is good**'*.

AT (Canada)

SUNDAY 7th

...Get thee out of thy country...unto a land that I will show thee...- Genesis 12:1

GOD'S MOVE – Reading: Genesis 12:1-7

Even in our readiness for a God-led move we can still feel a little inadequate. There are so many variables and unknowns. No wonder the Word says that without the essentiality of faith, pleasing God is impossible.

Though we will not have all the answers right there, in Genesis 12:1 we're given some prompts of how to proceed with a move of God. A move blessed by God is preceded with a clear word to *'Go!'* from God. Ask ourselves how does the Lord speak to me? How is it confirmed, and does it line up with His Word and the peace of God?

It takes a step towards the unknown from our 'country', safety, known, business as usual. God's move is uncomfortable. We may be ready and willing, but let's not expect it to be easy and joyous. Many called felt ill-prepared, but they loved God's will and His clear word to, *'Go!'*, more than their own inadequacy or comforts.

A move requires understanding that the new land is the one God not only plans but shows us. In our steps of faith, we begin to see unfolding what God has in store. But we have to do something. Faith without works is dead! His move gives not only vision but precision. Meaning, a vision begins our steps but we actualise that vision by doing the work and stepping out. Often it is as we go that God confirms what we had in our hearts.

Some benefits to others will come of our 'move'. Though it may begin with us, we should prayerfully trust that any move of God will not be self-serving for us. If our move is self-serving, let's ask for a heart to truly serve. Let's not allow fear and uncertainty to convince us God is not with us. But let it drive us to a confirmed certainty that, *'Lord, I must know you have spoken'.*

Ahead is a great adventure for you, my sister and, like any, it can test our resilience and faith. It can be arduous and even have moments of tears and fears. Be assured that if we are following hard after Him, He will bless and not curse what we do, because after all, we are on HIS move!

Joy Lear-Bernard

MONDAY 8th

Arise, take thy wife, and thy two daughters, which are here; lest thou be consumed in the iniquity of the city - Genesis 19:15

GOD IS ALWAYS LEADING – Reading: Genesis 19:1-16

Like Lot and his family, there are times when catastrophe hits and you are in danger, but that's when you can rely on the sure mercies of God to be especially active.

God is leading even when all that you know and have been assured of throughout your whole life is now crumbling and unstable. God is leading even when you are comfortable - longing to stay - and not wanting to move. God often uses the *'prickly challenges'* in your *'nest of life'* to discomfort you just enough to cause you to fly and soar to heights you never thought imaginable!

Could it be that where you are right now is a threat to your life? Could it be that the sense of urgency in your spirit is God ringing the alarm bell to alert you that it's time to move?

Trust and believe that God is leading you from catastrophe and danger to a place of calm, peace, and safety. Have a renewed sense of assurance in Him because He will not lead you into any darker paths than He Himself has gone. Never forget, God is the best leader because He leads you through the many dangers, toils, and snares, as well as all the ups and highs in life. Even better yet, God will lead you from this side of glory to the other, all the way from earth to heaven!

Minister Kay Dawkins/ MinK

TUESDAY 9th

Arise, and go down to the potter's house...Jeremiah 18:2

ON THE POTTER'S WHEEL - Reading: Jeremiah 18:1-6

The word of God teaches the believer to understand spiritual matters using natural examples.

To undertake a key lesson, our Sovereign Lord is the potter and Israel the clay. Jeremiah was instructed to get up and go to the potter's house to observe God at work. He watched intensely as the potter moulded and shaped the clay, to the point it became spoiled in his hand as the clay was not taking the shape that the potter was aiming to achieve. To remedy this, the potter broke and reworked the clay because the intention was to transform the clay into a vessel fit for purpose.

The lesson taught by our Sovereign Lord was not only for the children of Israel, but also for our learning today. God's chosen people, Israel, should have been the light to other nations, but had become hard-hearted and stiff-necked. They would not take heed to the Word of God spoken through His prophet, Jeremiah. They had become idolatrous in their behaviour by replacing God with other gods.

The lesson for believers today: God is our Sovereign Potter and believers in Christ are His clay. We are placed on His wheel for moulding, knocking off those brittle edges to shape us for His purpose. Similar to Israel, we also become marred in His hand, e.g., when we become bitter, or cannot forgive others, or maybe ungrateful, or fleshy. Our Sovereign Lord then brings us to a place of brokenness, for it is only at that place we are ready to acknowledge, confess our sins, and repent. God who is faithful and just will forgive us and purify us from all unrighteousness (1 John 1:9-10).

With skill and care, Jesus Christ (the Potter) puts our broken lives back together again. God sees our potential and the vessel that we can become which is clean, empty and available for His use.

Missionary Audrey Simpson

WEDNESDAY 10th

If your presence go not with me, carry us not up thence – Exodus 33:15

I JUST WANT YOU – Reading: Exodus 33:12-23

O to be led by the only wise God, who knows all things and has declared Himself *'I AM …'*. He's able to accomplish all things, numerous possibilities are in His joyous and precious presence. His leading is essential and efficacious. A shepherd who guides us in our weakness and insufficiency. We cannot make this journey alone, so we surrender and submit to the All Sufficient One.

Our confidence, hope and trust, must be wholly placed in Jesus. His way is excellent and far superior to ours. For not only does He know the way, but He is The Way, providing access and strategic means to achieve on our behalf according to His will. He is omnipresent so is everywhere at the same time. Therefore, we're never alone, and cannot get lost if we follow Him.

It's impossible for God to lie because He is truth. He utters and it's done. His Word is alive and powerful. He easily commands things into being. He is life and the hope of eternal life. He is the breath that we breathe as we live and move, and our very existence is in Him.

O Father! Show us the way and lead us to stay close beside you, to abide in your presence and never wander. Moses said to the LORD, *'Unless you are with me, I'm not going' (Exodus 33:15)*. Having experienced the pleasure and power of God's manifestations, Moses valued God being with him, God's attendance and appearance. God's companionship and Him showing up to and being in everything. An angel's leading was not good enough, Moses insisted on only being led by God.

Wherever God's presence leads, my answer must always be *'Yes Lord'*.

Sis Jx

THURSDAY 11th

...the LORD went before them by day...and by night...- Exodus 13:21

WILDERNESS EXPERIENCE: THE LORD KNOWS BEST – Reading: Exodus 13:17-22

We often say that we are going through a 'wilderness experience', but what do we really mean?

A natural wilderness has no food, water or sustenance. You have to travel through rough land in the middle of nowhere, drawing on your own inner strength.

A spiritual wilderness is where we feel alone, far from God, hungry, thirsty, and drained of spiritual energy.

Sometimes we find ourselves in a spiritual wilderness (which is what we really mean). We don't understand how we got there, why we are there, and don't know which way to go. Do we turn back or continue in the hope that one day we'll be victorious? We blame Satan, but rarely stop and think that maybe God put us in the wilderness for our own good.

The LORD deliberately took the children of Israel into the wilderness because He didn't want them to fear and return to Egypt. The wonderful thing was that although He took them through the wilderness, which was longer and harder than the way of the Philistines, God didn't leave them there! He was with them in the daytime and in the nighttime. Our omnipresent God is with us 24/7 (even in our wilderness moments), whether He put us there or whether we ended up there by our own doings.

All that we need to do is ask Him to lead us, then listen and follow the still small voice, especially when the way seems strange. Believe Him when He said in Hebrews 13:5 *'... I will never leave thee nor forsake thee'.*

If God knew what was best for the children of Israel, then He knows what is best for us – even if it means going through the wilderness.

Lady Pam Lewin

FRIDAY 12th

In the year the king Uzziah died I saw also the Lord... - Isaiah 6:1

WHO & WHAT WILL YOU SEE THIS YEAR? – Reading: Isaiah 6:1-13

Isaiah 6:1 is a familiar verse of Scripture to most of us, *'In the year that king Uzziah died I saw also the Lord sitting upon a throne, high and lifted up, and his train filled the temple'.*

On this 12th day of a new year, you may have already broken any new year resolutions you'd made. However, seeing God in His fulness and awesomeness should not be a one-off event. The more that we see is the more we should want to see. The more we get of Him should be the more that we desire Him.

Very often we start the year with a great pledge of, '*I'm going to serve God better this year than last. I'm going to fast and pray more, study my Bible more'.* But what gets in the way?

It is only when we identify our hindrances that we will truly see the LORD.

JEJ

SATURDAY 13th

...being warned of God in a dream...they departed...another way – Matthew 2:12

A WAY OF ESCAPE – Reading: Matthew 2:1-18

The account of the wise men visiting Jesus at His birth, is a familiar one. Worthy of note is their obedience to God to establish a different route back home. They were warned and they heeded the warning.

Warnings are messages or signs of impending danger from which we need to escape. Joseph was also warned to take Mary and Jesus and flee to Egypt. Knowing of the clear and imminent danger that Herod posed, God made a way of escape. He wasn't about to allow Herod to derail His plan of salvation by destroying the Messiah! After all, the world had long awaited Jesus' arrival for redemption.

We too experience situations from which we need a way of escape. The enemy lays hidden snares and entices us with temptations daily, but God has made that way for us. In 1 Corinthians 10:13, we are told that, He, *'will with the temptation also make a way to escape...'*.

When we ask our Heavenly Father to lead us, we can be sure that we will escape the traps of the enemy. God has equipped us with the weapons of our warfare so that we not only escape but we gain the victory.

Hallelujah!

Sister Barbara Hendrickson (Nevis)

SUNDAY 14th

... (the jailer) rejoiced, believing in God with all his house – Acts 16:34

GOD-LED – Reading: Acts 16:16-40

When we ask God to lead us, we sometimes have in mind what a route led by God looks like. It could be having everything we need not far away, no obstacles from beginning to end, everybody loving us and speaking well of us. An easy life is what many of us see as evidence of being God-led.

We read in Acts 16 of Paul and Silas being stripped and harshly beaten for rebuking and casting out an evil spirit of divination present in a young girl, i.e., she was a fortune-teller. Her spiritual deliverance meant the loss of a valued income-stream for her employers. As a result, Paul and Silas were thrown into prison.

We often focus on Paul and Silas praising God whilst incarcerated, and the earthquake at midnight. But what I'd like us to also see today is that, as a result of their humiliation, i.e., public beating and then cast into prison, the jailer and his family received salvation. Joseph, son of Jacob, also fulfilled some of his purpose in prison. The bigger picture hidden from Joseph was that in prison he would connect with the butler who would *eventually* mention Joseph's name to the Pharaoh so that *eventually* Joseph would be promoted to be Pharaoh's deputy and thus be able to save lives in the seven-year famine.

Just as John writes of Jesus, *'and He must needs go through Samaria'* in John 4:4, we learn that in the will of God, what I call the three Ds, i.e., delay, diversion, disappointment, are for a purpose. I doubt that praying and praising God first came into the minds of Paul and Silas when being cruelly beaten or whilst being thrust into the inner prison still bleeding from the beatings. But God knew what the ultimate outcome would be.

God-led means purpose-led: *'He leadeth me, O blessed thought! O words with heavenly comfort fraught! Whate'er I do, where e'er I be, still tis God's hand that leadeth me. Sometimes mid scenes of deepest gloom, sometimes where Eden's bowers bloom. By waters still, o'er troubled sea, still 'tis God's hand that leadeth me.' (He Leadeth Me – JH Gilmore)*

JEJ

MONDAY 15th

Except the LORD build the house, they labour in vain that build it – Psalm 127:1

TOTAL DEPENDENCE ON CHRIST, THE MASTER BUILDER – Reading: Psalm 127:1-5

Building a house requires a good plan and adequate resources.

Without these, there will be no knowledge of the total cost and hours needed to complete the building. Sometimes we see uncompleted structures because financial resources have dried up and, as a result, there are insufficient funds to purchase materials and pay salaries. On the other hand, there may be magnificent buildings successfully completed, but the owners may not be able to protect them from foundational problems and disasters, despite the expertise of building and environmental specialists.

Despite contingencies, builders are often faced with unforeseen surprises of all kinds. Human beings do not have the capacity to plan for all the uncertainties in our world, neither do we have the capacity and power to always watch over our homes, families, jobs, or ministries. God is the ultimate Planner, Watchman, Decision Maker, and Preserver. He neither slumbers nor sleeps. He is the only dependable one to establish and guarantee success. Anything attempted without the Master Planner will fail.

The Scripture (*'unless the LORD build the house...'*) is reminding us of our frailty and, therefore, our need for divine leadership. We must depend on God who is the Master Builder with the blueprint. He has all the resources as well as knowledge of the future. The building is not limited to the church or a dwelling place, it extends to our lives. Unless God is in control of every aspect of our lives, our planning will be in vain. To have and enjoy a successful future, whether it be in the form of our church, home, education, career, marriage, relationships, family, and ministry, we need the Master Builder to lead us as we make our decisions. Human ability is likely to fail but God never fails! David knew that he needed divine leadership and prayed, *'Show me your ways, O LORD; and teach me your paths'* and *'Lead me in thy truth and teach me...' (Psalm 25:4-5a)*. Before we take another step in planning and building our lives, let's stop to pray:

'Lord, I am depending on you; please take control of all I am and have'.

Overseer Joy Henry

TUESDAY 16th

And the angel of the Lord spoke unto Philip, saying, Arise and go... - Acts 8:26

GO, EVEN WHEN YOU DON'T UNDERSTAND – Reading: Acts 8:26-40

I remember, while living in London, I was unemployed for several years. I frequently visited the Job Centre, applied for jobs, attended interviews, only to receive a letter that I was unsuccessful. Little did I know that God was working His purpose out for His glory. I continued to visit the Job Centre and on one occasion noticed there were jobs for nurses and midwives in Derby; I had a strong urge to apply. I knew it was God's leading because I did not previously want to go into nursing or midwifery. But I applied for the midwifery course, attended the interview, and was told I would get a reply within two weeks.

Two weeks passed with no reply; I was almost convinced that I was not successful. But one Tuesday night during our prayer service, whilst praying, I saw in the spirit an angel entering the room. He wore a long white garment and had a letter in his hand. He walked up to the noticeboard, placed the letter there and left. I went to the noticeboard in the spirit to read the letter. The letter had three paragraphs most of which were blurred except for the first few words which stated, *'Dear Miss Smith, I am pleased to tell you...'*. When the letter finally arrived from the Job Centre, the format was exactly how I saw it that Tuesday night. God is worthy of praise!

On my last Sunday with the brethren in London, I believed and expressed that I would be away for the duration of the course but would return. But as I was about to go through the door after saying my goodbyes, the Lord spoke and said, ***'You're not coming back!'***.

I didn't even need a map. During prayer, I was given specific instructions... *'Go to Elephant and Castle, there you will see a sign for the M1; follow it and it will take you to Derby'*.

I had now been in Derby for several months but did not understand my purpose for being here...why was I here? I tried to pinpoint the reason but to no avail. There was one thing I knew and that was, God was taking me in a direction which I did not understand. At the end of our day service, a sister told me she saw me in a dream before I came to Derby and in the dream, she was told that I was coming to help the Church. Thank you, Jesus, for opening my understanding.

About two years had elapsed, my midwifery training was going well, I loved the church, I even loved the City of Derby. One morning while praying, the Lord told me to leave the course. I was so shocked I replied out loud and in haste, *'No, I can't leave!'*. I desperately needed answers. How can I tell brethren and family that the same God who told me to do this course, was now telling me to leave? I did not understand.

After pondering the matter for some time, I suddenly remembered Abraham, how God told him that he would have a son in his old age, only to be told he had to offer his son as a sacrifice. But Abraham believed God. This was a great encouragement to me. I left midwifery and settled in another job. God has been so faithful.

So, my encouragement to you is, '*Trust in the LORD with all thine heart; and lean not unto thine own understanding. In all thy ways acknowledge him, and he shall direct thy paths'* (Proverbs 3:5-6).

Deveen Smith

WEDNESDAY 17th

I have set the LORD always before me…Psalm 16:8

BEFORE… – Reading: Psalm 16:1-11

Before I sleep, have I prayed?
Before I fully awake, have I prayed?
Before I reach for the mobile phone
Have I prayed that the messages I have received
Have not disturbed God's spirit when my phone was at rest?

Before I speak to you
Have I just checked my conversation -
Will it be spoken with God's love?

And as you leave me to go your way
Have I left you with God's fire burning bright
Or is it a conversation we should not be having
And after it, do we need to just pray?

Before I go to my work today
Have I given God time
Before work tries to have all of my day?

Before I eat, is there a big thank you?
I have food in my cupboard
Which is sufficient for today.

Before I give my opinion on things
Just remind me, God, I was not good when I was wallowing in my sins.

Before you saved me
I looked one way
But since you saved me
You're making a beautiful woman out of me.

Before I wonder about my past
And what it had in store for me
Yes, I can reflect on it
But right now in my life.
The woman then, today is not me!

Before I look at others
Let me know you are my Saviour
You have made great promises to me
No matter what, they must come now or later.

Lord let me remember
That there is always a 'Before'
A pause, and an action that
Carefully goes 'Before' me
Thank you for my 'Befores'.

Praise, praise God.

Sister Jennifer Henry

THURSDAY 18th

...Who will go for us? Then said I, Here am I; send me – Isaiah 6:8

BRAVING THE UNKNOWN – Reading: Isaiah 6:1-13

Acknowledging that you need to be led is an incredibly vulnerable position to be in. It means admitting that you don't know where you're going or how to get there, and that you are relying on the knowledge and capabilities of another person to get you there. What if you know *where* you have to get to, but don't particularly want to go there? That makes asking to be led even harder. Why ask for help to get somewhere that you don't want to go?

God commissioned Isaiah to send His people a message of their impending conquest by the Assyrians and Babylonians because of their rebellion against Him. Not exactly *'good tidings of great joy'*; but Isaiah's surrender and desire for the will of God to be done led him to exclaim, *'Here I am! Send me' (Isaiah 6:8),* in answer to God's call for a messenger to His people. The Word was piercing, and the judgment seemingly terrible, but there was also a message of hope and deliverance through a coming Redeemer.

Once you are confronted by the glaring realisation of your own weakness and sin (just as Isaiah was), your only relief is found in complete submission to the holiness and will of God. In His mercy and kindness, He purifies you to be used as His vessel and gives courage for the journey. If you stay close to Christ, the journey and the destination will always be beautiful.

B E McKenzie

FRIDAY 19th

...He leadeth me beside the still waters – Psalm 23:2

CHOPPY STILL WATERS – Reading: Psalm 23:2; Jonah 1:1-17; 3:1-3

'He leadeth me, O blessed thought...' – a lovely song but what about when God is leading me to where I don't want to go?

Jonah had this problem. God sent him on a mission to Nineveh but he didn't want to go so went in the opposite direction. His disobedience put not just his life in jeopardy, but also the lives of the other passengers en route to Tarshish.

God is like a strict parent. They mean what they say and don't treat their children as friends or equals; ***'No!'*** means no, ***'Sit down!'*** means sit down, and ***'Go!'*** means go. Jonah finally submitted to instructions when he was in the belly of the fish – what a prayer service he had in there (Jonah 2:1-4)!

We often wrestle with the surrender of our will to God's as though He doesn't know what He is doing, or like He won't take care of us where we've been sent. Sometimes our sea is tempestuous simply because we are outside of the Will of God. See that as soon as the mariners threw Jonah overboard, the water became calm (Jonah1:15).

He leads me beside the still waters because, even in the worst of storms, as long as I'm going in the right direction, which is God's direction, all is well – *'on the stormy seas, He speaks peace to me, how the billows cease to roll' (Blessed Quietness – M P Ferguson).*

JEJ

SATURDAY 20th

Look not behind thee...escape to the mountain – Genesis 19:17

LOT & FAMILY: A WASTED OPPORTUNITY – Reading: Genesis 19:1-29

As I thought about what else could be said on our January theme of, *'Lead Me Lord'*, Lot and his family came to mind.

They were comfortable living in Sodom despite its sin-infested, immoral environment. So settled that neither Lot nor his wife wanted to move when they were urgently bidden to depart. Fully accustomed to and accepting of the corrupt culture of Sodom, they lingered, to the extent that an angel had to take Lot, his wife and daughters, by their hand, *'the LORD being merciful'* (Genesis 19:16), and pull them out of Sodom. Life in Sodom had affected and infected them all.

The urgent warning, *'Escape for your life…look not behind thee' (v 17)* had fallen on deaf ears. Yes, their bodies left Sodom but their hearts remained. One of the shortest Bible verses is, *'Remember Lot's wife' (Luke 17:32).* I'm wondering what plans God had for Lot and his family which never materialised because they were not fully persuaded in their heart to leave Sodom. Everything that we read about this family after their exit from Sodom is grievous. Surely God wanted better for them, not worse, otherwise why would He have insisted that they leave? Maybe they couldn't embrace by faith the plan of God because they resented His interrupting plans of their own.

The lesson of Lot gives a clear illustration of what can happen when we are reluctant to be led away from our comfort zone. Lot first went to Zoar - it was near to Sodom, small, a plain - rather than going straight to the mountain as instructed. Again, God extended mercy to him, for Abraham's sake (Genesis 19:29), and gave him time to move to the mountain before the destruction of Zoar.

Lot, his wife, his daughters, have gone down in history for all of the wrong reasons, the root cause being pining for the familiar, i.e., Sodom. We learn then that in order to be led/purposefully follow, and to not waste God-given opportunities, we must, *'forget those things which are behind and reach (stretch/strain) forward to what lies ahead…'. (Philippians 3:13).*

JEJ

SUNDAY 21st

...I will send you to Jesse...for I have provided me a king among his sons
1 Samuel 16:1

WE CANNOT MAKE IT ALONE – Reading: 1 Samuel 16:1-13

Israel's first king, i.e., Saul, fulfilled the people's desire (1 Samuel 8:6-10), but was still selected by God (1 Samue 9:15-17).

They no longer wanted to be led by God, the King of kings, they had no desire to be spiritually led. Instead, they asked for a carnal king whom they could see. But Saul, the democratic king, didn't have a heart to follow God's lead.

Ironically, just as Israel had rebuffed Spiritual Leadership, Saul became defiant to spiritual instructions which resulted in him being rejected by the LORD. Although Samuel, the priest, mourned over Israel's lusting after a king like the other nations, yet he continued to mourn over Saul when Saul was rejected by God.

Israel's situation was unfortunate, and was evidence of their disloyalty to Jehovah. Israel failed to accept Theocratic Leadership, where God Himself rules and reigns. He is fair and just, loving, merciful, forgiving and could supply all of their needs. Yet Israel gave up on Him who is Alpha and Omega, the beginning and the end; He whom the wind and waves obey, and before whom all of creation bows. Their preference was a weak, finite, insecure man who was destined to mess up.

Nevertheless, God reserved Himself a man who was like-minded, of godly qualities, a true worshipper, with a heart to be led of God. *'Lead me, O LORD'*, was a cry David made throughout his reign because David was *'a man after God's own heart' (1 Samuel 13:14)* who loved being in the presence of God.

LORD, lead me with by your mighty hand, show me the way to go, because I can't make it alone.

Sis Jx

MONDAY 22nd

…man looketh on the outside, but the LORD looketh on the heart – 1 Samuel 16:7

TRUST & OBEY – Reading: 1 Samuel 16:1-13

Samuel was led by God to anoint a new King. He was told where to go but not whom to anoint; he had to trust God's leading.

Has the Lord ever led you to a place where you knew it was the Lord's will but didn't know what the outcome would be?

Well, over 30 years ago my husband and I were led to Luton; a place I hadn't heard of at the time. We left our jobs and sold our home in the middle of a recession when houses were not selling. The Lord provided us with a new home and jobs - but no childcare for our two young children. We continued with the move because we knew it was the will of God.

The school was sorted, but still no childcare. I asked our new neighbour if she knew of a local childminder with two vacancies; she said no, but then offered to look after our children as her children went to the same school. She looked after them before and after school – what a God!

I thank God that, like Samuel, we listened to the Lord's voice; He had it all under control. Everything was already in place, all we had to do was follow His lead - trust and obey.

Jesse presented all but one of his sons to Samuel, but the LORD said 'no' to each one. Samuel had to ask if there were any more children because he knew that the LORD had told him to go to Jesse's house, but He rejected the sons presented. Sure enough, there was another son, David, who became King of Israel.

There are times when we don't understand what God is doing or where He is leading us – we just need to trust and obey, for there's no other way!

Lady Pam Lewin

TUESDAY 23rd

Abraham said unto him, Beware thou that thou bring not my son thither again
Genesis 24:6

LEAVING ALL BEHIND TO FOLLOW – Reading: Genesis 24:1-67

Eliezer a senior servant in Abraham's household, whose name means *'God is my help'* is also in typology the Holy Ghost who is selfless and faithful.

After he cemented the oath, he asked a very important question., i.e., if the woman is not willing to return with him, should he bring Isaac to her? The instruction was clear as crystal, the answer is no. Many believers in Christ fail to follow instructions due to not having a spirit-filled heart and are left facing the consequences.

When we read the Scripture and see, *'beware, thou that thou bring not my son thither again' (Genesis 24:6)*, what is the reason why the word *'beware'* is used? This is a word of warning for Eliezer to take heed/be alert of the risk of danger to Isaac if he was to go back to the family in Padanaram. Similarly, the Holy Ghost leads us and guides believers into all truth.

The family home was many hundreds of miles away. Isaac, as a man, could succumb and be tempted to settle there with his extended family and his new wife. The writer of Hebrews 11:15 states if Isaac was aware of his original roots, he might have seized the opportunity to return. This situation of looking for a wife was the ideal opportunity for him to return to the family home, especially with the instruction not to marry a Canaanite woman.

Isaac was the son of promise and it was ordained by God that he should not leave the promised land, not even to choose a wife. The chosen wife was to come to him.

Looking back at the life of Abraham, God called him out of a land of idol worship. He was required to leave his country, kindred and family for God to show him a land. By faith, he was obedient to the call. Here we see Abraham who had lived a full life, desire to see his son marry before he died. He is called a Friend of God and a Father of Faith, who had a close relationship with God. Therefore, Abraham knew the importance of not going back to be entangled in sin (2 Peter 2:20). As the father, Abraham gave godly instructions to continue the progressive revelation of Jesus Christ. Isaac's wife, Rebekah, is a type of the Church.

Missionary Audrey Simpson

*WEDNESDAY 24th

...thou shalt eat no bread, nor drink water...in this place – 1 Kings 13:17

GOD CAN STOP EVENTS SUDDENLY – Reading: 1 Kings 13:1-34

God can stop events suddenly in our day
As Christians we have our days planned
But our God has our lives mapped out.

When our eyes first open from that great morning sleep
In that comfy bed
Do we smile and thank Him for another day immediately
Or do instead we roll over and say' I will take five more minutes'?

Whether we have slept extremely well
Or been up all night with the baby
Or perhaps we have been unable to sleep
Because we are ill or life's issues are spinning around in our heads

We can say, 'This is the day the LORD has made
And we shall rejoice in it
But let's just take some time out
And see if we are really rejoicing in it.

When there's no brethren.
When you are in the car or any other mode of transport
That will take you near or far, at work at home
We need to rejoice! Let's celebrate our God.

When you feel tested and God intervenes suddenly with, 'for now, don't go that way today'
For today I need your attention
I am asking you to slow down
You are serving me in Spirit and Truth.

But I need time with you, you are not near
But spiritually afar and I need you to grow
God requires our attention; He is the centre of our joy.

When God tells us just to slow down
He wants to talk to us
And sometimes He will put issues there
Or put us really down.

Then suddenly, whatever the test this day
We will have to pray, praise, and rest
But glory be to God if suddenly we do as He bids.
Our life will be better! We can hear from Him!

We will be stronger when we slow down and spend valuable time with Him
God will open doors, we will see Him and His glory
The sudden stopping of events was to remind us who is Sovereign
God wants to keep us on His track.

Sister Jennifer Henry

International Day of Education

THURSDAY 25th

...the LORD said...by the three hundred men that lapped will I save you... - Judges 7:7

VICTORY BELONGS TO GOD – Reading: Judges 6:33-40; 7:1-25

How many times have we struggled to manage challenges in our lives only to realise that God will lead us if we depend on him? One thing is certain, change is all around us and only God is constant, an embedded guarantee in our lives.

The Bible identifies a man, Gideon, chosen as deliverer for Israel. Scripture tracks him down at a wine press, hidden from sight of the invading Midianites (Judges 6:12).

The background story: The nation had entered Canaan, the land promised by God to the children of Israel. Under leadership of Joshua, son of Nun, each tribe had been apportioned sections of the land for settlement following God's command concerning the conquest of Canaan to possess it. God led Israel to claim the land He had promised them (Numbers 14:8). Israel initially obeyed and fought against the Canaanites, capturing some regions, however in some cases when Israel didn't drive out the occupants, they made treaties with them (Judges 1:28-35). This move inevitably influenced a mix with the Canaanite lifestyle. The children of Israel wandered away from serving God, then when Joshua died, Israel forsook God. Their actions opened a door of invasion from the unconquered people within the land, and the outside nations (Judges 2:1-5).

The Crisis: The Midianites had invaded the country. They terrorised and ravaged everything Israel worked for. They were on lockdown whilst the Midianites stole and plundered all their livelihood. It was desperation on every angle, until the people cried unto God (Judges 6).

Testing times put our faith under trial and the truth is, at times it can be a struggle to walk with the Lord. Through the maze of uncertainties, challenges, pressing through discouragements, or rerouted by the impulse of our own ideas only to be corrected by God; we journey through a wilderness of the unknown. The distraction of voices we hear, we may ponder, *'Was that the Lord speaking to me or my own thoughts?'.* We need to recognise His voice, His lead and guidance to live an abundant life. Lead me Lord...

We are declared, to be *'more than conquerors'* (Romans 8:37). God will graciously guide us confirming each step of faith, even when we place a *'fleece'* request before Him (Judges 6: 36-40). Lead me Lord...

Look at Sovereign God simplify a crisis - Gideon gathered men from the northern tribes to organise an army of 33, 000 soldiers. The army of the Midianites was 135,000 strong. Yet the Lord wanted 'His' army reduced to **total dependence** on God. It was too many for God to work with! Only 3% of the original quoted number qualified as soldiers to go into battle. Israel was stripped of any self-confidence in their own effort against the enemy who were at least 135,000 strong in number! The vulnerability of a reduced army led to a victory **no one could claim but God.** The enemy had not reduced their numbers; at face value it was a suicide mission! God decreased Gideon. It was not by might or by power that Gideon conquered, but by the instruction and leading of God. Lead me Lord.
CDP

FRIDAY 26th

For where two or three are gathered together in my name, there am I in the midst of them - Matthew 18:20

LED TO WEEP & PRAY – Reading: Matthew 18:15-20

Matthew 7:8 says, *'Everyone who asks receives'*.

There is power in corporate prayer, *'One (person) will chase a thousand, and two put ten thousand to flight' (Deuteronomy 32:30).*

It was Monday night prayer meeting, I finished work at 6pm and prayer service starts at 7pm. I was tired and thought that maybe I would not go to church, but there was an inner push that I could not resist, so I went. I got down on my knees and began to pray.

Soon into the prayer, I found myself weeping and couldn't control the tears. I felt a burden for my children that I could not understand. I started to cry aloud and did not care who was hearing that I was bawling. I started to speak the Word of God over my daughter and her family, reminding God of His promises towards His children. I was crying in desperation. I cried and used the words of Bartimaeus, *'Jesus, son of David, have mercy on me' (Mark 10:47).*

When we finished praying, one of the mothers of the church who was in the seat behind me, asked me if my daughter was alright. I answered yes, so she was wondering why I was crying and mentioning her name to God in the way that I did. I myself did not know why I was crying like that in desperation to God.

Then my phone rang, I went around the back to take the call. My daughter was crying on the phone. She said that she and her husband were driving and had minutes to escape their car as the car exploded, it went up in fire! The car was burnt out, only the structural frame remained. My daughter watched their possessions burn as they were unable to retrieve them from the car. She said, *'I usually have my children strapped in the car. God would have it that tonight they were not with us as we would not have been able to get them out of the car in time'*!

The car had just passed its MOT, we couldn't understand what would cause it to go up in flames. Then I remembered the burden I was feeling during prayer, and understood why I was crying like that. I explained to my daughter the burden I had felt, and that God had delivered her and family out of the hands of the enemy. Surely I can say, *'God is our refuge and strength, a very present help in trouble' (Psalm 46:1).*

'The LORD is my strength and my shield; my heart trusted in him, and I am helped: therefore my heart greatly rejoiceth; and with my song will I praise him. The LORD is their strength, and he is the saving strength of his anointed' (Psalm 28:8).

Name withheld

SATURDAY 27th

Except these abide in the ship, ye cannot be saved – Acts 27:31

STAY ON BOARD – Reading: Acts 27: 27-44

During Paul's journey to Rome, he encounters an experience on board a ship. The weather conditions were boisterous and it seemed likely they could be shipwrecked should they continue on their journey.

The correlation of this incident reminds me of the struggles we experience in our lives. Around us are the storms of life, and it seems inevitable that we will be 'shipwrecked' as we journey with the Lord. However, we need to remember that God is sovereign, and in control. No matter the storms, the pressure of high winds, yet the vessel we journey in is held by God's hands.

The key thing we are reminded of is to *'stay in the vessel' (Acts 27:31)*. By doing so we allow God to lead us, asking the Holy Spirit to direct our course, navigate the path on which we are journeying. Allow the gifts of the Holy Spirit to discern the conditions around us and be confident that God's got this!

Minister Hedy

SUNDAY 28th

For I know the plans that I have for you, declares the LORD – Jeremiah 29:11 (ISV)

LOVING MY ENEMIES – Reading: Jeremiah 29:1-14

Too often we find ourselves praying for our enemies, but not in the way that the Lord has commanded. It is easy for us to get angry at circumstances which are beyond our control, feel betrayed by the actions of others, feel abandoned by the seeming lack of a timely response from God, and other similar destructive emotions.

In times like these, we need to go back to the Scriptures and measure ourselves against the Living Word. God has commanded us to pray for the peace, safety, and prosperity of our enemies – especially given that we are required to co-exist with them in this world. How we behave in times of adversity is a direct reflection of our relationship with God.

While we may not see His mighty hand at work, we cannot afford to believe that we have been abandoned. The battle is not won by those who refuse to obey their commander-in-chief just because we disagree with the vision and therefore the instructions given. When that is our behaviour, the lesson is repeated again and again until we finally learn to accept that God is ever present, even when we cannot see it.

If it appears that trouble and sorrow are our constant companions, let us examine ourselves and our relationship with those we have declared to be our enemies. Do we pray for them to receive God, or do we pray that they receive the just recompense of their actions?

Only when we learn what it is to love our enemies, as Christ loves us, will we reap the rewards of 'plans God has for us'.

Pastor Londy Esdaille (Nevis)

MONDAY 29th

Lead me, O LORD...make thy way straight before my face – Psalm 5:8

WHOSE LEAD WILL YOU FOLLOW TODAY? Reading: Psalm 5:1-8

When going on a long journey, or sometimes even a short one where I am unsure of the route, I will put the details into my sat nav and follow its directions.

Sometimes, as I'm following the route laid out before me and the road around me, I wonder if it's taking me to the right destination. There have been occasions that I've decided that it can't be right and either stopped to check or gone off the designated route – it doesn't always end well.

Following the Spirit's lead should be the simplest thing to do, we know that God will never lead us the wrong way, we know that He is always right. We know, but yet we allow elements of doubt when we are in unfamiliar territory, *'Lord, do you really want me to say or do that?'*.

Following the lead of God takes faith and trust - not only in Him but in our relationship with Him.

Life comes with challenges, and following the lead of God doesn't mean that things will always go easy or to plan. I encourage you and myself to know that even during our challenging moments or periods, God is there.

As we live our lives in faith, building our relationship with Him, allowing Him to order our steps, following His lead, we are stronger. Know that with His guidance we will be stronger having reached our destination. We will complete our journey being able to declare that He will never leave us or forsake us.

Today, listen for His voice, for His direction and guidance – you can't go wrong.

Christine Knight

TUESDAY 30th

...He leadeth me in the paths of righteousness for His name's sake - Psalm 23:3

I'LL SURRENDER TO BE LED – Reading: Psalm 23:1-6

When we search through the Scriptures, we find many ways in which God led His people and is still leading today.

Some examples of His leading are through dreams, visions and even a small voice. For instance, Joseph regarding Mary and her pregnancy (St Matthew 1:20), Moses with the children of Israel through the wilderness by pillar of cloud by day and pillar of fire by night (Exodus 13:21).

St Paul had several visions (Acts 16:9-10; Acts 18:9-11). Peter had a vision concerning the Gentiles (Acts 10:9-15), and Cornelius had a vision to send for Peter (Acts 10:1-6). Jesus Himself was led by the Spirit into the wilderness (Luke 4:1).

But God does not have to use dreams and visions; His written Word is our rule for faith and practice along with the indwelling Holy Spirit which illuminates the Word for His will for our lives.

Following God's leading means letting go of our will and agenda, giving up the things we hold so dearly which will not direct us to where God wants us to be.

King David in Psalm 23 describes us being led by the still waters. These waters are calm, peaceful, safe, where saints can rest. These waters are not stagnant or tempestuous. God leads us in the paths of righteousness: a holy path, a good path, straight and perfect, not crooked, dangerous, contrary or futile.

There is no danger of wandering, nor risk of getting lost, as long as God is leading the way. Though there will be difficulties, trials and troubled times, they will not destroy us. Where God leads there will be no lack of provision.

'(Jesus) like a shepherd lead us, much we need thy tender care'. (D Thrupp/H Lyte).

Missionary M Fraser

*WEDNESDAY 31st

Arise, and go into the city, and I'll tell you what to do – Acts 9:6

TO BE SIMPLY LED – Reading: Acts 9:1-19

For three days Saul was struck blind and without any food or water - right at the beginning of his new walk with God. Saul learned quickly that his insufficiency more than his strength would make way for the powerful three-day miracle that is the centre and pinnacle of all ministry.

Saul, or Paul as he was also known, was a strong powerful threatening man. He used that strength to literally seek out and persecute Christians. I have always been intrigued by his Damascus Road experience, and truly believe we all need a Damascus Road experience in exchange for the sight Jesus gives us of new life in Him.

To be led by Jesus, we must see Him and nobody else. The Scripture reminds us to trust in the LORD with all our heart and lean not on our own understanding. And here we see that very depiction in a humble Saul. His ability to see and keep his own physical strength meant nothing in the moment of encounter with the Lord Jesus. In that moment, as he began to truly be led, he could no longer direct himself.

For us to be led by God we may well feel stripped of our own 'sight'. Our own understanding is limited and redundant until we know how to walk humbly in faith. Paul's sight was recovered to him as he began to obey.

What do we have that we rely on? What gifts and ability might God use for His glory? What ability, understanding, knowledge do we quickly use to replace faith in seeking God's ultimate authority? We know it is easy to do what 'seems right to a man' but Jesus showed us with Saul that our being led by Him cannot rely on our summations; but on His Sovereignty.

'Lead us Lord, we relinquish our sight and hold on to faith in your leading. Humbly we ask that you will show us how to use our best as we acknowledge that without you that best is never enough. We trust you. Lord, teach us to wholly trust. In Jesus name. Amen'.

Joy Lear-Bernard

****National Hot Chocolate Day***

HYSTERECTOMY

Hysterectomy is a surgical procedure that involves the removal of a woman's uterus (womb).

The uterus is a reproductive organ that plays a crucial role in the menstrual cycle and pregnancy, hence, a woman will no longer have periods or become pregnant after a hysterectomy. Hysterectomy may be performed for a variety of reasons, including to treat gynaecological conditions such as fibroids, endometriosis, abnormal uterine bleeding, uterine prolapse and cancers.

The main types of hysterectomy are: Total hysterectomy; Subtotal hysterectomy; Total hysterectomy with bilateral salpingo-oophorectomy and radical hysterectomy.

Hysterectomy may be performed via different methods, including abdominal hysterectomy, vaginal hysterectomy, and laparoscopic hysterectomy. The method used will depend on the patient's condition, the reason for removing the womb and the surgeon's preference. Abdominal hysterectomy involves making an incision (cut) in the abdomen, while vaginal hysterectomy is performed through the vagina. Laparoscopic hysterectomy involves the use of small incisions in the abdomen and a laparoscope - a small camera that allows the surgeon to see inside the body.

Recovery period after a hysterectomy may vary depending on the method used and the patient's overall health. Generally, women who undergo vaginal or laparoscopic hysterectomy have a shorter recovery period than those who undergo abdominal hysterectomy. Most women are able to return to normal activities within four to six weeks after surgery.

After care following a hysterectomy includes managing pain and discomfort, preventing infections, and resuming normal activities gradually. Pain medication may be prescribed to manage pain and discomfort after surgery. It is important to keep the incision site clean and dry to prevent infections. Women should avoid heavy lifting and strenuous activities for several weeks after surgery. If the ovaries are removed (oophorectomy) along with the uterus during the surgery, then hormone replacement therapy (HRT) with oestrogen may be necessary, due to a surgical induced menopause.

It is important to note that hysterectomy is a major surgical procedure with potential risks and complications. Patients should discuss the risks and benefits of the procedure with their doctor before deciding to undergo surgery.

SUMMARY: Hysterectomy is a surgical procedure that involves the removal of the uterus. There are 4 main types. It may be performed for a variety of reasons and can be done using different methods. Recovery period and after care following a hysterectomy will depend on the type, the method used and the patient's overall health. It is important to carefully discuss the risks and benefits of the procedure with your doctor before deciding to undergo surgery.

Dr Carol S. Ighofose BSc (Hons); MBChB; MRCGP

february
My Saviour's Love

THURSDAY 1st

Throw all your worry on him, because he cares for you – 1 Peter 5:7 (ISV)

THROW IT DOWN – Reading: 1 Peter 5:1-11

Have you ever felt that you don't have the capacity to take on even one more problem? You don't want another meeting, another phone call, another text, another letter or another email. You've reached your maximum – in fact, your problems are now having problems!

There's a solution to that feeling of gloom which any one of us can experience depending on the season of our lives, *'Casting all of your cares upon (Jesus); for He careth (with deepest affection) for you' (1 Peter 5:7).* His tender heart has been moved with compassion watching you struggling under your heavy load, seemingly about to break. Peter is not the only one who gives us this counsel in Scripture; David says something similar in Psalm 55:22, *'Cast your burden upon the LORD, and he shall sustain thee: he shall never suffer the righteous to be moved'.* I like the Amplified Bible's version of this, it breaks it down very well, *'Cast your burden on the LORD (release it) and he will sustain and uphold you; He will never allow the righteous to be shaken (slip, fall, fail)'.*

I do recognise that for different reasons some of us as ladies are fiercely independent, and feel that we can deal with absolutely anything that comes our way. But we can't! *'Hear the blessed Savior, calling the oppressed, O, ye heavy laden, come to me and rest. Come, no longer tarry, I your load will bear. Bring me every burden, bring me every care' (Hear the Blessed Savior… – Charles Price Jones).*

How about today taking that rucksack of burdens off your back and throwing it down at Jesus' feet. Let Him deal with the contents – He wants to!

JEJ

FRIDAY 2nd

Who is a God like unto thee, that pardoneth iniquity…? Micah 7:18

MY SAVIOUR'S PERFECT LOVE – Reading: Micah 7:1-20

'Such love, such wondrous love, that God should love a sinner such as I, how wonderful is love like this...' (Such Love - C. Bishop)

In this chapter, we see a world in chaos (much like today's world). Micah warns Israel that God's judgment and destruction will come, but also reassures them that there is hope for those that follow God's will.

We serve a great, big, wonderful, merciful, gracious, and forgiving God. When we didn't know Him, our lifestyles were an abomination to Him. When we ignored/ignore His words and warnings, He still loved/loves us (but not our sinful ways!). It doesn't matter what we were/are, if we repent and turn to Him, He will forgive us and grant us His promise of eternal life. God doesn't remain angry forever, instead, He shows His love by having compassion and forgiveness.

Those of us that are parents know that when our children do wrong, we do not remain angry with them for long; instead, we scold and forgive them (even when we know that they have already been taught and shown the correct way). Why? Because we love them. That's how God is with us. In fact, He went further because Scripture says in John 3:16 *'For God so loved the world, that he gave His only begotten son, …'*. Jesus died on Calvary bearing the weight of our sins – that's love!

If you have fallen by the wayside, repent and return to God – He loves and will forgive you.

Lady Pam Lewin

*SATURDAY 3rd

The LORD did not set his love upon you, nor choose you, because you were more...
Deuteronomy 7:7

HE LOVED ME IN SPITE OF – Reading: Deuteronomy 7:1-11

Have you ever seen an outwardly 'stunning' woman with a 'plain' man as her husband or partner, and wondered, *'how did he manage to get a woman who looks like that?'* Or have you seen a really good-looking guy (in your opinion) with a woman who is not what many would consider to be attractive, and asked yourself, *'Gosh, how did that happen?'*! Depending on how either party feels about themselves, they too may have wondered, *'What does he see in me?'* or, *'What does she see in me?'.*

It's love! This goes beyond the exterior, *(which is fearfully and wonderfully made - Psalm 139:14)*, and sees the pearl within.

C H Gabriel must have been thinking along those lines, considering himself to be an undeserving recipient of God's love when he wrote:

I stand amazed in the presence
Of Jesus the Nazarene
And wonder how He could love me
A sinner, condemned, unclean!

How marvellous, how wonderful
And my song shall ever be
How marvellous, how wonderful
Is my Saviour's love for me.

Love like this humbles us all.

JEJ

***Carrot Cake Day**

*SUNDAY 4th

The LORD disciplines those he loves – Proverbs 3:12 (NIV)

FATHERLY DISCIPLINE – Reading: Proverbs 3:7-12

Can we read the book of Proverbs without feeling the sense of fatherly wisdom being passed down like honey to the lips of children? Proverbs 3 is no different. It lovingly lists instructions to a 'son' on obedience, faithfulness and love, and their importance and many benefits thereof.

It is God's love that urges us to live obedient and surrendered lives. It reads so simply and yet verse 12 gives us insight of how complex our response as children can be towards this Fatherly warning, *'My son, don't despise the LORD's discipline and do not resent his rebuke'*.

Something in a child, no matter how loved they are, has a tendency to resent being shaped. Our sometimes subtle resistance to the prompts of the Holy Spirit, is still a leaning away from the love of the Father. Unpopular by today's standards but let's for a moment remember that love is synonymous with discipline, shaping, correction. With this in mind, let us truly respect how our Father implores us, His children, to not despise God's love, don't resent His love.

When we feel our childish hands tugging away from His ways to wander off on our own - in our thoughts and deeds - remember we are tugging against love, against favour and a good name, our resentment is against peace and prosperity.

If we still feel daily correction from God, we should be thankful that He is each day showing signs of His love. Let's thank Him for leading us to paths of safety, prosperity and peace.

Joy Lear-Bernard

World Cancer Day

MONDAY 5th

For whom the LORD loveth he correcteth – Proverbs 3:12

CORRECTION, THAT'S LOVE – Reading: Proverbs 3:7-12

I would never commend a 'good' teacher who is willing to leave a student misinformed or unenlightened. We're thankful during our tests when an incorrect answer is highlighted, so that we begin to live to our full potential of understanding and pass our next tests.

How much more does a loving father do this for his own child? Correction in Proverbs is synonymous with love and delight. A sign of how much God loves our sonship is that He shapes and corrects us. It's a personal connection where He has access to our trusting hearts and we to His guidance.

Love will correct. There's a sense of deep endearment that we have so close a relationship that He can show us personal things that are not right in us. And then in turn He Himself empowers us to change. Our prayers towards our Father should be one of thankfulness that because you love me, you won't leave me as I am.

A day of reckoning will separate us from the righteous judge because of our sin. But He is pained enough now to extend His hand so that we can be presented before Him as His children, spotless and looking like our Abba Father.

Every new parent who holds their precious baby does so with deep delight. It isn't long before baby is cleaned up, simply because of the love the parent has. Dirty nappies aside that baby is perfectly loved, enough to do for them what they cannot do for themselves. Our Father is neither unkind or neglectful. He cleans up His children who trust in His fatherly hands to do so.

Let God take delight in loving us enough to shape us. To clean us up as a father does and make us to be the very best we can be as a reflection of His glory.

Remember sometimes love looks just like correction.

Joy Lear-Bernard

TUESDAY 6th

But God is rich in mercy because of his great love for us – Ephesians 2:4 (GNW)

UNCONDITIONAL LOVE – NO CHARGE – Reading: Ephesians 2:1-10

On the calendar, February has been celebrated as the month of love. Shops are stacked with merchandise in preparation of 14th February. *'Say it with flowers!'*, or chocolates, red roses, love hearts, presumed cherubs, romantic dinners, cards and presents. Yes, it's the official month to pour out the heart, even for a day, to declare affection to one's sweetheart. The origin of this celebration is layered, shrouded in certain rites and festivals. However, many dismiss its history for the opportunity to celebrate with their special love, before it's back to the hustle and bustle of life.

The greatest love story there will ever be is the agape love of Almighty God for humankind. It's beyond our finite comprehension that, *'God, who is rich in mercy, for his great love wherewith he loved us' (Ephesians 2:4):* Let's pause a moment; there's the riches of precious stones, metals, money, etc. Stock markets across the world, trades in these commodities, and more. Yet there is not a World Bank or IMF for mercy. But God has an endless stock supply. There are songs about love, ballad serenades of heart to heart, setting the ambiance of the moment.

But God has set the bar of His unconditional love far beyond one day in a month. His supernatural presence is love, powerful to save the fallen state of humankind. Rich in unmentioned mercies, rich enough to redeem us, to buy us back from sin's penalty of death. There is a supernatural force that only the Lord Jesus' love is - unconditional. It's because of love that we have been saved from eternal death. The message of the gospel of salvation that the Lord Jesus, the very image of the invisible God, would empty Himself of Himself (kenosis), subject Himself to His own laws for humanity, enter this world legally by childbirth, for the purpose to die for humankind. Love us back to life by death on a cross, an instrument of condemnation. How wonderful is my Saviour's love!

CDP

WEDNESDAY 7th

...(nothing) shall be able to separate us from the love of God, which is in Christ Jesus our Lord – Romans 8:38-39

LOVE THAT WILL NOT LET ME GO – Reading: Luke 15:11-32

There are more songs written about love than on any other subject. Solomon says, *'Love is strong as death...many waters cannot quench love, neither can floods drown it' (Song of Solomon 8:6-7).*

God's love is the greatest kind of love - by far superior to the love that humankind can ever express. It is perfect, 100% unconditional, and constant. God continues to love us when we don't love Him back, and embraces us even if we do not love ourselves. Remarkably, He first loved us ***'while we were yet sinners'*** *(Romans 5:8).* Pause and absorb that for a moment.

As we read this page in the privacy of our home, or some other quiet place, each of us can reflect on times when we really 'messed up' and wondered whether God would keep on loving us in spite of...We can relate to the parable of The Prodigal Son when he was away in a far country, and there wasted his substance in riotous (reckless/foolish) living. When he could disgrace and degrade himself no longer, he remembered home and the love of his father.

The father's love received him back as a son, not a servant. The father's love said, *'change his clothes and feed him'*. The father's love said, *'Let's celebrate the return of my son's conscience which was dead and is alive again. Let's rejoice that after a diversion from the plans I had for him, he's back on track' (Luke 15:21-24).*

Really, the father's first sighting of his son's return was not when the son was on his way back, but when he gave him his portion. The father could have insisted that his son stayed home but instead released him to learn! Likewise, God can stop us from making mistakes and wrong turns, but serving God and loving Him has to be a freewill offering. So, our Father waits for us to come to ourselves and return to Him through His love that draws and will not let us go.

JEJ

THURSDAY 8th

...I have come that they may have life, and have it to the full – John 10:10 (NIV)

THE LOVE THAT GIVES LIFE – Reading: John 10:1-21

O how wonderful, O how marvellous, is my Saviour's love for me!

The unconditional love of our Saviour gave us the opportunity to be restored from death to life.

My Saviour's love is pure, genuine and infinite. We could never do anything to deserve His love. *'For God so loved the world that He gave his only begotten Son, that whosoever believeth in him should not perish, but have everlasting life'* (John 3:16).

Just think - Jesus gave His sinless life to give us abundant life - wow! We were so undeserving of this ultimate sacrifice because of our sinful state. Our heavenly Father didn't just breathe life into Adam when he created him from the dust (Genesis 2:7), but God also breathed His love into Adam. He gave him life and everything he would ever need, but his disobedience plunged the whole world into sin.

The enemy's aim is to destroy us; he is that thief that cometh to steal, kill and destroy. But Jesus, our Saviour, came that all of us could have life, and not just life, but abundant life (John 10:10). This current life is temporal, it is the Saviour's love that is sustaining us through life. Yes, His love gives life. Thank you, Jesus!

Min. Genevieve Dinnall

FRIDAY 9th

...His compassions fail not – Lamentations 3:22

UNSURPASSABLE LOVE – Reading: Lamentations 3:18-26

Try as hard as I might, there is no earthly language or words on mortal tongue that can adequately describe the love of my Saviour: our LORD Jesus Christ.

His love is incomparable in that it is without equal in quality and in extent. It excels way beyond the love of a spouse, a beloved child, a close sibling, or the dearest of friends. IT IS MATCHLESS, beyond comparison, and unsurpassable. Love divine, all loves excelling!

Throughout my lifetime, over fifty years, my Saviour's love has been inexhaustible. Yes! It's unable to be used up or run out because His love exists in abundance. Oh, the riches of His love, it far outweighs the purest of gold.

What blows my mind, even to this very day, is how He could love me so! I can't fully understand or grasp its height, depth, and breadth. I most definitely cannot comprehend or explain it. It's unfathomable.

Dear Reader, herein is Love: in that Christ died for us, *'...scarcely will a man lay down his life for a good person...' (Romans 5:7)*, yet Christ gave His life for me when I was His enemy. *'I have found Him whom my soul loveth' (Song of Songs 3:4).*

The only thing I can really say to you in closing is that this kind of love is better felt than told!

Name withheld

SATURDAY 10th

We love him because he first loved us – 1 John 4:19

IRRESISTIBLE LOVE – Reading: 1 John 4:7-21

Our love story with Christ Jesus started with Him making the first move.

There's a saying which you may have heard, *'When I was not thinking of Him, He was thinking of me'.* God did not 'woo' us with words, but with actions. His ultimate demonstration of love was His death and resurrection, '*For God so loved the world that He gave His only begotten Son…' (John 3:16).*

Day by day we continue to see signs and symbols of God's love all around us, and by what He speaks to us, with the things He reveals to us of Himself, and those special favours which He grants just to us. There is something about the love of God which penetrates and softens the hardest of hearts, even the *'move me if you can!'* kind of heart.

I think of Saul and how he used to fiercely persecute the church. He would beat Christians, he was merciless even to women (Acts 9:1-2), but when God dipped His pen of love in Saul's heart, we heard Saul say, *'Who are you, Lord?'* (v5) followed by, *'Lord, what will you have me to do?'* (v6); and then, *'I count all things but loss for the excellency of the knowledge of Christ Jesus my Lord' (Philippians 3:8).*

The person who is 'in love' may try to hide it but there are usually some tell-tale signs, e.g., an unusual glow on their face; distracted with thoughts of their beloved, anxious to hear from that special person again. It's the same when our heart has been captivated by the love of God. Someone wrote it this way:

'When God dips His pen of love in my heart
And He writes my soul a message He wants me to know
His spirit all divine fills this sinful soul of mine
When God dips His love in my heart.

Well I said I wouldn't tell it to a living soul,
How He brought salvation and made me whole
But I found I couldn't hide such a love as Jesus did impart!
For He makes me laugh and He makes me cry, sets my sinful soul on fire
When God dips His love in my heart.'
(When God Dips His Pen of Love in my Heart – C Derricks)

JEJ

SUNDAY 11th

Because your love is better than life, my lips will glorify you – Psalm 63:3 (NIV)

IT WAS LOVE! – Reading: Psalm 63:3

Psalm 63:3 depicts David as a fugitive in the desert of Judah. David was deeply distressed and was very thirsty. He was in a dry land where there was no food or water. Yet he refused to refrain from praising and glorifying God.

David declares the love of God as better than life so his lips will always glorify his God. The thirst we have in common with David is worth looking into. We thirst for different things at different times but most of all we thirst to love and be loved. In life, things may not always turn out the way we wish. We may give and do not receive anything in return. We may love and may not be loved. But there is a God whose love to us is from everlasting to everlasting. His love is unconditional and without limits.

David received a blessing when he cried out to God; similarly, these blessings can be yours also. You will see the glory of God manifested in your life. To know God's love is better than life, it is better than the love of any other individual. So, praise Him with singing lips and meditate on Him day and night. Everyone who asks can and will receive (Matthew 7:8) the love of God that is better than this present life.

Evangelist Dezrene Beezer

MONDAY 12th

…Love one another as I have loved you – St John 13:34

FOLLOW MY EXAMPLE – Reading: St John 13:31-38

LOVE is the one word that we all believe we have a good understanding of, i.e., what is required to demonstrate it.

It is easy to talk a good talk, but all too often when we are deeply wounded, hurt, treated unfairly, the love that was first shown loses its vigour or disappears altogether.

Jesus did not merely ask His disciples to love, but to love *'as I have loved you' (John 15:12)* i.e., follow my example.

This Agape love, which Jesus demonstrated, is so selfless and sacrificial. It knows no limits. It refuses to stop giving, its end product is never-ending joy and peace.

For God so loved that He gave of Himself and wants to take us on a journey of discovery.

Let us submit to His will, it is only then that we can truly follow His example.

Deveen Smith

TUESDAY 13th

The LORD thy God in the midst of thee is mighty; he will save… – Zephaniah 3:17

WHAT A LOVE! Reading: Zephaniah 3:9-20

Zephaniah's name meaning, *'God has hidden'*, is streaked with His divine love.

Amazing love in the face of one of the most intense, impending judgments prophesied against national Israel and surrounding nations. Judgment was at hand back then, including future ones, and rightly and justly so.

On the other hand, the strong call for repentance and promise of protection for the remnant of national Israel, where the remnant would be hidden, reveals the intents of God's heart. Know assuredly that when God pronounces judgment, it is 'His heartbeat' that our hearts are turned to Him so that He can save us; even *hide us* from the wrath of His judgment reserved against ungodliness (Romans 1:18).

As regenerated believers in Christ, chastening is expected, for, *'whom the Lord loveth He chasteneth; even scourgeth us' (Hebrews 12:6)*. Why? That we should not be condemned with the unbelieving at the White Throne Judgment (Revelation 20:11-15).

Our Saviour delights in saving not condemning! He wants to express joy over us with strong emotions, sing, spin around and dance with great rejoicing. Yet in His holiness, we see His: **indignation and fire of His jealousy. Oh, how our Saviour wants to save us and to sing over us!** What a love!

Pastor Josephine Lewis

WEDNESDAY 14th

Don't be afraid, because I am with you. Don't be intimidated; I am your God...
Isaiah 41:10 (GW)

HE'S YOUR GOD – Reading: Isaiah 41:1-10

We all have at some stage in our lives been afraid. Fear is not something which we have to be taught, it comes naturally. We therefore need to know how to manage fear so that it does not control and manage us. Uncontrolled fear can be very debilitating indeed.

We can feel fear when we need to have a conversation with who we see as a difficult person, or about a difficult matter. We can feel fear when we have to give a public presentation – we may imagine all of the things that could go wrong. Sometimes we feel fear when we look at the size of a personal problem and contrast it with our ability to get it solved. Anxiety takes over and can cause loss or increase of appetite, loss of sleep, absentmindedness, irritability, etc., as we become consumed with constantly wondering, *'What am I going to do?'.*

A Word of Comfort comes to us today from Isaiah 41:10, *'Fear thou not; for I am with thee: be not dismayed; for I am thy God; I will strengthen thee; yea, I will help thee; yea, I will uphold thee with the right hand of my righteousness'.*

On a day which the world celebrates as Valentine's Day, there isn't a man who can make a promise to a woman in any way close to what God declares in Isaiah 41:10! I've selected three takeaways from this verse, but there are more: 1) God will not abandon you in your crisis; 2) Note His endearing and rather intimate statement concerning relationship – *'I am **your** God'*; 3) Picture God with His arm around your waist, bracing you up, whilst He fights and wins your case with His strong right hand.

Every woman reading this page today should celebrate that God is not just everybody's, He is also personally and lovingly **yours**!

JEJ

THURSDAY 15th

Keep yourselves in the love of God...- Jude:21

FAITH ONCE DELIVERED – Reading: Jude:1-25

Jude, the brother of our Lord Jesus Christ, wrote both with warnings and encouragements. Set at a similar time as today, Jude warned against false teachers who wanted to tamper with the truth of Jesus Christ which was established by sheer love from Him. Some tried to bring the grace of God into disrepute, but the love of our Saviour is the genesis of *'the faith'* for which Jude instructed us to earnestly contend. In other words, this *precious 'common salvation'* that we have, was birthed by the love of God - Jesus Christ the author and finisher of our faith.

All because of God's love for Adam's fallen race, He became our Saviour. A saviour is one who rescues or saves you from danger. Jesus saved us with His life. He was motivated by love with no strings attached of which, as Jude wrote, ungodly men wanted to pollute this salvation with false narratives.

The beloved saints of God are encouraged to stay true and strong in the faith, to defend the truth and uphold sound teaching. Called to be spiritually built up, through studying the Word and with fervent prayers, in order to maintain the love of God in heart and in action. For Jesus has gone through much suffering for us to have this great salvation. Any effort to change it in any way must be challenged!

God's love is amazing. Love moved Him to die even for those who rejected Him, and some will never believe that He died. Yet He died and rose again, regardless, for the whole world.

Sis Jx

FRIDAY 16th

...my kindness shall not depart...neither shall the covenant of my peace...
Isaiah 54:10

STEADFAST LOVE – Reading: Isaiah 54:1-17

In this chapter we see that marriage is used as a metaphor to describe God's covenant relationship with Israel. Within this covenant, God tells Israel that if they commit adultery (violate His laws), although there would be judgment, His lovingkindness towards them would remain (Psalm 89:30-34).

A simile is used when God reminds Israel about the promise He made to Noah after the flood (Genesis 8-9). God is explaining to Israel the relevance of both covenants, i.e., the marital metaphor speaks of a mutual obligation to remain faithful to this relationship. But if Israel failed, although there would be judgment for sin as there was in the time of Noah, God promised not to utterly destroy them.

Israel did sin and God told them that it was only for a short period of time He hid his face from them. God did this because of His mercy and grace - really His judgment should have exceeded what Israel received. Instead, God expresses the sincerity of His love by telling Israel that just as He promised never to send another flood, He would bring them peace, everlasting kindness and mercy once their relationship had been restored (Isaiah 54:8-9).

Mountains and hills can mean obstacles; God promised Israel that He would remove them, but His love, His covenant of peace, would never depart from His chosen nation (Isaiah 54:10).

You may have sinned which resulted in God hiding His face from you. The mountains in your life may have left you thinking there is no way back to God, but a broken and a contrite heart God will not despise (Psalm 34:18; Psalm 51:17; Isaiah 57:15). God is faithful and just to forgive, to heal and restore. God's redemptive plan is still being activated in our lives today. That's Agape love, the highest level of love. A song writer says, *'The steadfast love of the Lord never ceases, His faithfulness never comes to an end'*. So, no matter how low you have fallen, just as Israel experienced God's love and redemptive intervention, so can you.

Rachel Lewin

*SATURDAY 17th

But thou art a God full of compassion, and gracious – Psalm 86:15

MY SAVIOUR LOVES ME TOO! – Reading: Psalm 86:1-17

Looking through Psalm 86, David extols God's love for him and us in a prayer of thanksgiving.

Each verse is a blessing:

1. He hears us
2. He preserves us
3. He is merciful
4. He causes us to rejoice
5. He forgives us
6. He attends to us
7. He answers us
8. He is unique
9. He loves us all
10. He is God all by himself
11. He is truthful
12. His name is everlasting
13. He is our deliverer
14. He protects us
15. He is compassionate, gracious and long suffering
16. He gives us strength
17. He helps us and comforts us

I think David was a complex person, from his childhood he had to deal with adversity - but God had His hand on him. David killed a lion and a bear. He struck the Philistine giant Goliath dead with one stone - God had his hand on him.

King Saul hated David and often tried to kill him - but God had his hand on him. Even though David's harp-playing was the only thing that would soothe Saul, Saul still hated David - but God had His hand on him.

David was far from perfect; he was a fearsome warrior. He was also a loving friend to Jonathan and mourned his death and the death of Jonathan's father, King Saul. David showed mercy to Mephibosheth.

David was also a worshipper, dancer, and the sweet Psalmist of Israel. A man of great passion, he had many wives and concubines. God called him a man after my own heart (1 Samuel 13:14 and Acts 13:22). Through it all, David had the assurance that God loved him. And our dear Lord Jesus came through David's family line.

God has His hand on us too as we go through life, He is constant. He loves you!

Beverley V Galloway

***Random Acts of Kindness Day**

SUNDAY 18th

Behold, what manner of love the Father has bestowed upon us... - 1 John 3:1

HONOURED TO BE CALLED THE SONS OF GOD - Reading: 1 John 3:1-10

In the context of the Scripture, the word *'sons'* is neutral gender and refers to both males and females.

As a child, many people in my neighbourhood knew my dad. I didn't know them but, because I looked like my father, they would approach me and ask, *'Are you Rudi's daughter? You look just like him!'*. I was always proud to say, 'yes', because I loved my father.

Now, let's take it to the spiritual. Before I knew Christ, I couldn't say that I'm His child, because I didn't know Him, but now that I know Him (glory, hallelujah), and know that He loves me, I'm privileged to be able to declare that I am a child of God and, guess what? I look like Him because I've been made in His image. Genesis 1:27 states, '*So God created man in his **own** image, in the image of God created he him; male and female created he them.*'

I am a child of God, made in His image, and I hold my head high because I belong to a King. The world does not recognise me because I don't look like them, I don't sound like them, and my mannerisms are not like theirs.

If you are a child of God, and find that you are not liked in the world, don't worry, because they can't relate to the kind of love the Father has bestowed upon you. If you're not a child of God, and wish to experience that love and sense of belonging, then just surrender your all to Him.

Lady Pam Lewin

MONDAY 19th

...Every one that loveth is born of God – 1 John 4:7

THERE IS NO MATCH FOR GOD'S LOVE – Reading: 1 John 4:7-21

The word, 'love' is a primary theme of the Holy Bible and is mentioned several times. The Bible tells us about the love of God for a fallen world.

God's love is pure, it has no strings attached nor any hidden agenda. St Paul also wrote about the love of God which is not envious, not selfish, has no pride, and beareth all things (1Corinthians 13:4, 7-13).

1 John 4:7 is amazing – it speaks about the love of God. John gives us a reminder that we should also love one another, (even those whom we may consider to be unloveable) for every one that loveth is born of God.

The love that my Saviour has, even for me as an undeserving person, is so vast and immeasurable:

'The love of God is greater far than tongue or pen can ever tell
It goes beyond the highest star and reaches to the lowest hell
The guilty pair bowed down with care, God gave His son to win
His erring child he reconciled and pardoned from his sin.

Could we with ink the ocean fill and were the skies of parchment made
Were every stalk on earth a quill, were every man a scribe by trade
To write the love of God above would drain the ocean dry
Nor could the scroll contain the whole though stretched from sky to sky.

Oh, love of God, so rich and pure
How measureless and strong
It shall forevermore endure
The saints and angels' song'.

(The Love of God - Fredrick M.Lehman)

This song bears such a rich message. My Saviour's love will not let me go, He will love me to the end and throughout eternity.

Missionary M Fraser

TUESDAY 20th

...we have known and believed the love that God hath to us. God is love...
1 John 4:16

A LOVE SUPREME – Reading: Ephesians 3:17-19; 1 John 4:16-17

'Love' is probably one of the most overused (and incorrectly used) words in English. We're expected to have a social and intellectual consensus on its meaning, yet its experience and direction are incredibly subjective.

We believe that we show love by being good to others, and convince ourselves that we treat people equally and without bias or discrimination. If we're honest about it our love is conditional, fragile, it wavers, has dependencies, is not universal, and can be exhausted. We're even told now that *'love is love'* (whatever that means). But John's writings completely destroy these inferior concepts of love: he tells us that GOD is love, and that its manifestation is evident in Christ dying for our sins to provide us with salvation.

We as believers are privileged to fully experience the love of God – to swim in its balmy depths, to summit its heights, to be completely engulfed, surrounded and consumed by our Saviour's love. It is so deep, so wide, so marvellous and indescribable; it escapes cognitive reasoning and overwhelms the heart and soul. God commended His love towards us in that, *'while we were yet sinners, Christ died for us' (Romans 5:8).* Jesus laid down His life for His friends (John 15:13) – there is no greater love. Before we loved Him, He loved us – a love so unconditional that it drove Jesus to suffer for our sins. At its summit, the love of God means that we no longer need to be afraid of judgment and wrath because our sins are forgiven. *Such love!*

God's love uplifts and empowers us. When experienced in all its glory, His love is impossible to contain – we cannot *but* love others. That is why it is impossible to say that the love of God dwells within us yet not display that love to others (I John 4:21). John's exhortation to brotherly love is not just an instruction to action, but speaks to the necessity of our submission to and oneness with the Holy Spirit. His love is alive in us and can only be worked through us when we have become the sons of God and are filled with all of His fullness. The greatest testimony to the world of our position as disciples of Christ is our love of one another (John 13:35); and being rooted and established in love (Ephesians 3:17) will produce the most beautiful fruit.

Matched against this definition, any *'love'* that is not the love of God pales in comparison. It is weak, futile, perishable, impure and of no effect. Living in God's Love Supreme is the only thing that can impact this broken world.

The love of God fills us yet empties us of our own self-righteousness; it lifts yet grounds us; it strengthens yet leaves us weak in the shadow of its majesty; and we are covered by this Banner of Love. There is no greater comfort than knowing that we, in all our imperfections, struggles and unworthiness, are known and loved by God.

B E McKenzie

WEDNESDAY 21st

O give thanks unto the LORD; for he is good; for his mercy endureth for ever
1 Chronicles 16:34

GOOD SAMARITANS - Reading: Luke 10:25-37

Have you ever heard these quotations? *'All good things come to an end!'*, and *'Nothing lasts forever!'*. These sayings are often true but not so when it comes to God's mercy and lovingkindness. What would life look like for any of us if when we needed another dose of divine mercy, we were told it was not meant to be forever and it's no longer available?

Let's briefly look at the parable of The Good Samaritan. Imagine that we are the man wounded by bandits and, in our helpless semi-conscious state, are hoping for someone to notice us and come to our aid. We hear the footsteps of the priest coming towards us before he decides to cross the road and blot what he has seen from his memory. We also hear the Levite as he comes up closer than the priest did, takes a good look but is off duty after worship, and decides to cross over. He detaches himself from the problem; this man although a Jew like himself, is a stranger.

Thank God for the 'good Samaritans' we have all encountered at one time or another in our lives. God's hand of mercy operated through them! When we were weak or fell, and it was touch-and-go whether or not we would live or stand up again, they became the hands and feet of God. They were also the mouth of God to resuscitate us with words of life. They lay aside any feelings of self-importance to help clean up the mess, no matter how bloody, and regardless of whether our condition was our own fault or a life circumstance.

The Samaritan, I believe, was a man of wealth. I say this because he had his own beast, he carried his own oil and wine which are not cheap commodities. He also had enough money with him to pay for the victim's hospital care at the inn, and confidently said that he would settle anything in excess of what he had already given, upon his return.

The Good Samaritan was a man of dignity, a man of grace and compassion. It feels right to bring this parable into today's meditation when we're looking at lovingkindness that lasts forever. That's mercy which does not discriminate based on colour, creed, status or gender. Mercy that puts questions of, *'How did this happen?'*, on pause and chastises later when strength has returned; mercy which does not give us the full force of judgment that we truly deserve.

JEJ

THURSDAY 22nd

...there is no God like thee in the heaven, nor in the earth – 2 Chronicles 6:14

AMAZING LOVE: Reading: 2 Chronicles 6:12-21

The Omnipotent God, of unmeasurable powers, is LORD.

That's above all authorities, principalities and powers, whether present, past or future, all are under His feet. For the gods of the nations are idols and the works of man's hand. There's no one that is like Him, none to be compared to the Most High, and we are loved by Him.

My Saviour's love is unconditional, consistent, and everlasting. He promised never to leave or forsake us, but will be with us to the end of the world. From age to age my Saviour's love remains the same. It's because of His great love, tender mercies, and lovingkindness, that we're not consumed. He lovingly and patiently waits for us to turn when we do wrong. Through His amazing love, He secured an escape route for us from the curse, condemnation and wrath to come.

His anger lasts only for a moment, but His favour continues for a whole lifetime. By His love He makes provision both for our spiritual and natural wellbeing. His love spans generations and is evident in every dispensation. His love reaches to people of every tribe and nation, individually and collectively, and always meets us at the point of our need.

Although we needed a Saviour, we didn't know it, but, *'God so loved the world that He gave his only begotten Son…' (John 3:16)*. My Saviour's love extended a universal salvation to a universal audience via the universal message of love!

What kind of love is this, that The Everlasting King would surrender His life to die for all humankind, and for some who don't even want Him, and others who don't even care? My Saviour's love is truly wonderful.

Sis Jx

FRIDAY 23rd

But God demonstrates his own love towards us...while we were still sinners
Romans 5:8 (NKJV)

A DEMONSTRATION OF LOVE – Reading: Romans 5:1-11

Sometimes we find it hard to love each other because of a personality clash. Sometimes it's because of something we've heard or even just imagined. We may say to ourselves, *'I would get on better with Claire if she would just change her ways; I could love her if she would stop doing that thing to annoy me'.*

Let's look at what makes God's love stand out and places it in a class of its own. Christ demonstrated the purity and depth of His love towards us by dying for us while we were sinners. When I picture Jesus hanging on the cross, I see Jesus saying by His actions, *'This is how much I love you although you don't yet love me, and may never love me!'.*

Paul tries to comprehend or reconcile the uniqueness of what Jesus did at Calvary, he wants to understand the logic (but there is no logic to God's love). Whilst trying to fathom, Paul agrees that one might reluctantly, after much deliberation and persuasion, die for someone who is righteous – but that would still be unusual. The NLT Bible writes Romans 5:7 this way, *'Now, most people would not be willing to die for an upright person, though someone **might perhaps** be willing to die for a person who is **especially** good'. 'Might?', 'Perhaps?' 'Especially good'?* As a sinner, how could I possibly be *'especially good'*? Here comes one of Paul's, 'But Gods'! ***'But God** demonstrates his own love for us in (like) this: While we were **still sinners (not at all good)**, Christ died for us (Romans 5:8 NIV).*

I did not and could not do anything to make Jesus Christ love me, He just did.

JEJ

SATURDAY 24th

Greater love has nobody than this...St John 15:13

THE GREATEST LOVE STORY – Reading: St John 15:1-16

The word, 'love' is a primary theme of the Holy Bible, and is mentioned several times. The Bible tells us about the love of God for a fallen world.

Humankind has many different expressions of love, depending on to whom love is being shown. Greek philosophy speaks of at least seven types of love. The romance and passion between husband and wife are commonly known as Eros. This is followed by Storge which is family love, e.g., between parents and children. We have friendship love, known as Philia. We also have Agape love which is God's love for the whole world; it is universal and everlasting unlike any of the other types of love I've mentioned. This is unconditional meaning there are no strings attached to God's love.

When I read this Scripture verse, I am in awe of my Saviour's selfless sacrifice owing to His ultimate concern for the welfare of humankind. My Saviour knew how helpless, hopeless and wretched we had become since sin came from the fall of Adam in the garden of Eden.

To reconcile you and me back into the right relationship with Him, did you know the Son of God had to meet three criteria to fulfil the atoning work on the cross?

He had to be willing.

He had to have the means.

He had to be a man related to whomever needed to be redeemed.

The work of Jesus Christ on the cross was the ultimate evidence of God's love for humankind. Isaiah the prophet graphically outlines the cruelty that was inflicted on Jesus. We grasp how much men despised and rejected Him which resulted in the cruelty that was inflicted on Jesus' body. His face was marred more than any other man; this tells us that Jesus was unrecognisable.

The extent of God's love supersedes all hatred of men. The love of God is seen in his death, even more so in the resurrection, for underserving sinners rebelling against Him - even you and I.

This is the greatest Love Story on earth. I exhort you to be like the Berean brethren (Acts 17:10-11) and see if this is so.

Missionary Audrey Simpson

SUNDAY 25th

I am crucified with Christ – Galatians 2:20

LOVE'S ULTIMATE SACRIFICE – Galatians 2:20

Many of us, when we read of the crucifixion of Jesus for the first time, were left speechless as we could not fathom how someone could allow themselves to go through such agony. Not only that; but would choose, and plan this way to die because of His love of humankind and that He might give us eternal life (St John3:16). What kind of love is this?

Galatians 2:20 states *'I am crucified with Christ: nevertheless, I live; yet not I, but Christ liveth in me':* So, as Jesus gave His life, our life has to be totally surrendered to Him.

We make sacrifices for our families, friends and even strangers. But it is far more challenging to willingly give your all to an individual or a cause and receive nothing in return. It is certainly heart wrenching to give our all only to have it thrown back in our face. When this happens, we often declare we would never do it again! The writer of the book of Hebrews tells us to *'Consider him that endured such contradiction of sinners against himself, lest ye be wearied and faint in your minds'* (Hebrews 12:3).

True sacrifice comes out of LOVE! Love makes sacrifices and never complains. Love surrenders all, and never feels that it is too much. *'Greater love hath no man than this, that a man lays down his life for his friends. Ye are my friends, if ye do whatsoever I command you' (St John 15:13–14).*

Deveen Smith

MONDAY 26th

Yea, I have loved thee with an everlasting love: therefore, with lovingkindness have I drawn thee – Jeremiah 31:3

EVERLASTING LOVE – Reading: Jeremiah 31:1-11

I believe that the Saviour's love is the greatest love alive, there is nothing like it!

His love is greater and more meaningful than any other power in this world. On earth we have experienced love from our families, spouses, and friends, and yet none measure up to my Saviour's love.

God's love expressed through the Saviour always has the ability to do greater works than we can ever imagine to do. Jesus was sent to remove everything from us; all our stains, transgressions and faults, and to make something out of us that would seem impossible to others. His love had to be greater, His love had to be better, and His love had to be superior. To handle the failures of entire generations and still have enough to love every single person on their level is truly a Saviour's love.

Jeremiah makes it plain that the Saviour's love is an everlasting love taking on the nature of the One who first loved. Love is an action word and should never be taken at face value alone. If we are going to experience love at all, we first would need to examine the actions that such a love produced. The Saviour's love resulted in salvation, redemption, crucifixion, and then resurrection. It is through this love that the Saviour brings us into the gifts He has prepared, and now we can all live the abundant life because of everlasting love.

Pastor Chelly Edmund (USA)

*TUESDAY 27th

For God so loved the world, that he gave his only begotten Son...John 3:16

COMPLEX SIMPLICITY OF LOVE – Reading: John 3:1-17

Nicodemus met privately with this incredible teacher, Jesus, who expounded the truth that every single soul needs to be born again. Nicodemus, himself a great teacher, couldn't get his head around the idea and so Jesus likened it to a natural birth bringing forth natural life. But yet Nicodemus lacked understanding because it is the Spirit of God bringing us forth new in the Spirit that completes true new birth.

The explanation encrypted to the simple human mind was powerfully explained by Jesus - Nicodemus, with all your earthly understanding and great teaching, your new life will only come through me being lifted up on that cross, just like Moses lifted the snake in the wilderness. Humankind can only find eternal life through Jesus choosing to die for us.

Jesus' words inspired John to continue the story so much that in chapter 3:16 he shares these famous words, exclaiming just why Jesus would die and bring the miracle of new life, *'For God so loved the world that he gave his only begotten Son, that whosoever believes on him should not perish, but have everlasting life'.*

Jesus shared the metaphor, and John showed us exactly where it was realised and WHY. The story of the cross is one of love, the complexity of a new spiritual birth that confounded the wisest of religious leaders did so with simply His show of love, the passage to eternal salvation through the cross that Jesus bore was an act of love. It still confounds us today yet it is just as powerful. Our Saviour's love.

Joy Lear-Bernard

National Strawberry Day

WEDNESDAY 28th

...as the heaven is high above the earth, so great is his mercy... - Psalm 103:11

GREAT MERCY – Reading: Psalm 103:1-22

I wonder if the writer of this song had just finished reading today's key verse when they penned:

'Love, wonderful love, the love of God to me
Love wonderful love, so rich, so full, so free
Wide, wide as the ocean
Deep, deep as the sea
High, high as the heavens above
God's love to me.'
(Unknown)

The word *'mercy'* can be used interchangeably with lovingkindness or compassion. David, who wrote Psalm 103, must have been having some deep reflective moments when he said God's **great** mercy is as high as the heaven above the earth. Oh, if anyone could testify of great mercy, it was certainly David. It is first for *'mercy'* then *'tender mercies'* that David pleads in Psalm 51:1, after he was confronted by Samuel the prophet regarding his illicit relationship with Bathsheba, and the coldly plotted assassination of her husband, Uriah: *'Have mercy upon me O God, according to thy lovingkindness: according unto the multitude of thy tender mercies blot out my transgressions'*.

Have you ever had to pray a prayer which you thought you would never need to pray? You at no time imagined that situation would or could ever happen to you! I can't read Psalm 51:1 without hearing and feeling the anguish of David's soul as he cried out to God in repentance for the gravity of his sins. If you have done something that you will forever regret, you will grasp not just the depth of David's cry for mercy, but the extent of God's grace.

Now forgiven, and his connection with God restored, David testifies, '*as the heaven is high above the earth, so great is his mercy toward them that love him' (Psalm 103:11)*. I'm sure that David is not the only one who, when they had to appeal to God for mercy, He generously multiplied mercy into great mercy!

JEJ

*THURSDAY 29th

I am the true vine, and my Father is the husbandman – John 15:1

THE BROKEN BRANCH – Reading: John 15:1-15

As she entered where she lived
In her eyesight there was only one
Just that one broken branch
Bowing heavily down, its face to the ground.

She could see
It had fallen all on its own
There were little branches
Attached to it
Then there were numerous bright green leaves flowing around.

This branch had fallen
And what a fall
I knew there had been gusts of wind
But as I looked up
I could not help but ask what was it
That had caused the branch to descend?
As I recall it had stood so tall.

We as Christians as you know
Are branches as is mentioned
In the New Testament Book of John
In its 15th chapter verse 2.

But we are not lone branches
We have branches attached to us
In front, at our side, and behind us
We have our fellow branches
Even under and over us.

The greatest thing is
We are attached to is Jesus
And God is the Husbandman
He takes care of our branches.

But life brings unexpected gusts of winds
Where we feel so many emotions
And pain as well.

But God helps us
As we may make mistakes
Placing others as idols in our lives.

I felt it as I saw the broken branch
I felt it to my very core
I could not lift the broken branch
As its attachments to the other branches
Were no more.

So Lord help us every day
So we be not like that broken branch
Broken off from its fellow branches
Which now lies astray
With fire as its final destination.

Help us as brethren
To pray when we get each other
It could be in a vision, thought, a dream
Or any other means.

But please, dear God, let us cover one another
Cover our brethren in prayer
Cover our brethren with Jesus' blood
Cover our brethren with words that don't hinder
Cover us where there is strife.

Let's cover each other with sound doctrine
Please God help us to speak life
Life to each other so we are strong
So we can stay connected
So that we are not stray branches
But to Jesus and our brethren we belong.

To God be the glory!

Sister Jennifer Henry

National Toast Day

Not Named & Rarely Mentioned Women of the Bible

*FRIDAY 1st

Jesus turned (around); and...said, Daughter, be of good comfort... - Matthew 9:22

GOD KNOWS YOUR NAME – Reading: Matthew 9:18-26

As women we can often feel invisible, like the world is passing us by and no one is taking the time to see us for who we are, or the pain we are sometimes in.

The woman with the issue of blood in Matthew 9:20-22 probably felt this way; but her faith and healing by Jesus is one of the most told stories from the New Testament and is the basis for many a familiar sermon. This woman – with no name, no mentioned occupation or place of residence – has become highly significant in time.

We see that God values and is pleased by faith. This is what gets His attention – not your name, status or education, but your faith. We see many other women in the Bible (unnamed or rarely mentioned) who exercised the same:

- The widow who shared the last of her food with Elijah and experienced the miracle of overflow during famine (I Kings 17)
- Rahab, the prostitute who hid Israelite spies, saved her family during Jericho's invasion, and is in the genealogy of Jesus Christ (Joshua 2-6)
- Miriam, Moses' sister, watched over Moses as he floated down the river in a basket, preserving his life. Once found by Pharoah's daughter, Miriam fetched Jochebed, her own mother to be his wet nurse (Exodus 2)

...and there are a lot more!

Though many may not know your name, God does. Your radical faith in Him excites Him and draws Him close to you. Your faith pleases Him. However small or insignificant you may feel, remember that you are known by God. Just like the woman with the issue of blood He sees you reaching out, pushing through all that life has thrown at you just to touch Him, and feels the purity of your faith in His ability to bring the miracle you need.

B E McKenzie

World Day of Prayer

SATURDAY 2nd

The Syrians... brought away captive out of the land of Israel a little maid – 2 Kings 5:2

THE LITTLE STAR – Reading: 2 Kings 5:1-14

Some of us will be familiar with the lesson in 2 Kings 5 concerning Naaman, who the writer described as: 'great', 'honourable', 'mighty in valour'. Although of high status he was a leper and, in those days, there was no cure for leprosy.

Each time that I've heard a sermon preached on this, the focus has been on either Naaman or Elisha. But in my private reading a few years ago, I saw the lesson from a totally different angle, and went back to the events which led to the remarkable healing of Naaman.

There's a little maid. She is a young Jewish girl who was kidnapped during a raid on Israel by Syrians, and brought over to Syria. By divine order, she is taken into the house of Naaman and his wife to become Naaman's wife's maid. Naaman and his wife are idol worshippers, they do not know Jehovah.

Thank God for the parents of the maid, they must have instilled good teaching into their daughter from the time she was born as the Israelite parents were instructed to do in Deuteronomy 6. It is this teaching that allows the unnamed girl to live in a house with heathen adults and not forget God. I believe that she still said her prayers as taught and, without a scroll, had the Word in her heart, plus she conducted herself in the ways of the LORD - she must have done otherwise the wife of Naaman would never have considered what the maid said (2 Kings 5:3-4).

Note also that, up until this point, no lepers had been healed in Israel (Luke 4:27). Therefore, the maid was not speaking from what she had seen but by innocent faith in God who she knew worked miracles through His servant Elisha. She spoke on the basis of, '*if God can do this (whatever she had seen Him do in the past), He can do that*'. She fearlessly recommends the man of God to her mistress, confident that God will give a solution for Naaman through the prophet.

We never know when our children will have to defend The Faith in our absence, so let's be tireless in teaching and answering their questions. We have only read about Naaman's healing from leprosy, and Elisha's ministry to the Syrian, because of The Little Maid who was bold enough to speak up whilst in a strange place, empowered by her upbringing. To me, she is the key character and Little Star of this story!

JEJ

SUNDAY 3rd

...she put in everything – all she had to live on – Mark 12:44 (NIV)

YOU CAN'T BEAT GOD GIVING - Reading: Mark 12:41-44

The Cost of Living crisis has impacted many of us. We look for ways to reduce what we spend, even on essential items. But one thing that I would encourage us not to do is to cut back on giving to God. Still take out God's portion first, you will not perish (Proverbs 3:9-10).

I have proven over and over again, that when I give to God, although I never give to get it back, He returns it to me somehow – not necessarily as cash but in a way that is most needed. I've been astonished by God's care. I always look upwards, blow Him a kiss and say, *'You're something else!'*.

The key character today Jesus describes as a *'poor widow'* (Mark 12:43). She comes to the temple and brings with her, her all to give as an offering. She could have said that since what she had was so small, why give anything at all. Instead, she gave it from her heart. People sometimes give to impress others while God is left unimpressed. Jesus was sitting near to where the coins were being dropped. Mark reports, *'many that were rich cast in much' (v41),* but Jesus says nothing about their *'much'*.

However, here comes a widow with two mites, all that she has; she makes no announcement that this is all, but Jesus knew. In Jesus-style, He commends someone who others would probably have seen as insignificant and thus ignored. Jesus calls His disciples to come over and observe what has happened. Who has given the most? Not those who gave much – they had plenty left. The one whose contribution equated to the value of a farthing gave the most because it was her all.

It is not recorded in Scripture but I do believe a blessing followed that woman for the sacrifice she made. When it comes to giving to God, not just money but of our time and service, never give Him less if we can give more.

JEJ

MONDAY 4th

(Jesus) answered her not a word – Matthew 15:23

LORD, DID YOU HEAR ME? Reading: Matthew 15:21-28

Today's Scripture introduces us to a Canaanite woman, also known as a Syrophenician woman (Mark 7:26). She is a mother, her daughter is *'grievously vexed with a devil' (Matthew 15:22).*

I think it's interesting that the mother doesn't say, *'Have mercy on my daughter'*, she pleads, *'Have mercy on me, O Lord, thou son of David…'.* The situation in her home was beyond what she could manage on her own. How long her daughter had been like this, we do not know, but the condition was grave enough for this Gentile sinner to go seeking for Jesus.

Although a pagan Canaanite, she knows that the help she needs for her daughter can only be found in Jesus Christ, not in one of her idols. She's a woman of determination, as women often are when it comes to caring for their children. Her fortitude becomes evident when, even though she does not get the kind of response from Jesus which she had expected, i.e., he does not acknowledge her or even that she has spoken, she persists with her request.

Silence from Jesus, then followed by hostility from His disciples, *'send her away…' (v23)*, what would you have done? Or should I ask, what do you do when you're talking to God and He's not talking back? You've been praying about something, maybe for years, and He has answered not a word! What do you do when those who should understand tell you to be quiet, that circumstances can't be as bad as you say?

You do what the Canaanite woman did. Keep on calling: *'Lord, help me' (v25),* and you don't stop until Jesus says, *'O woman, great is thy faith: be it unto you even as you wilt' (Matthew 15:28).*

JEJ

TUESDAY 5th

Now there was at Joppa a certain disciple named Tabitha... - Acts 9:36

TABITHA – WHEN DEATH BRINGS REVIVAL – Reading: Acts 9:32-43

***'A** good name is better to be chosen than great riches, and loving favour rather than silver and gold' (Proverbs 22:1).*

The Bible records the miracle of people being raised from the dead in both the Old and New Testaments.

One notable lady in the New Testament, called Dorcas by her Greek name or Tabitha by her Hebrew name, ministered to the widows in Joppa where she lived. Her name meaning *'Gazelle'* conjures up warm affection of a woman who naturally cared for people. With no official social service benefits, or clothing charities in Joppa, this disciple used her business to help clothe those in need. Her care and errands of duty were known in the community of such that her death caused an outpour of grief and sorrow.

She was a highly regarded disciple, and the only one given a title as a female disciple, *'mathetria'*, in recognition of her tireless labour of love. As a woman in those times, she had found freedom in the gospel to serve people in need. If it were now, she may have been nominated for a Community Enterprise award or receive an OBE.

The sudden death of Tabitha moved the widows to bathe and lay her expired body in the upper room of her home. Imagine a crowd of women mourning this outstanding community figure who had been a help and support to them. She had a good name and was loved by the people for her care and consideration The desperation of the widows and other disciples (v. 38) created an atmosphere for a miracle. There will be times when we refuse to accept a situation as final, God will show up when faith has room to work.

The disciples went to find Peter. Once Peter arrived, he entered the room where Tabitha had been laid; he put out the mourners - we must evict the spirit of heaviness in exchange for the power of God. Peter prayed, called her name, and instructed her to rise. He gave her his hand and lifted her up.

The miraculous set the power of the Word in motion; the buzz of joy, excitement, and praise to God, lifted faith and belief, revival broke out in the city. The next move of the Spirit of God was to manifest His presence at Cornelius' house; his household became the first Gentile converts (Acts 10).

The miracle of God raising Tabitha from the dead had impacted the community. We are the Acts continued.

CDP

WEDNESDAY 6th

...they took Apollos unto them, and expounded the way of God more perfectly – Acts 18:26

THE GOOD MENTOR(S) – Reading: Acts 18:23-28

Priscilla was a hard-working Jewish Christian woman, who worked in the tent making business with her husband, Aquila.

They were well known to the Apostle Paul and were his loyal friends (Paul also was a tent maker) and they assisted him in ministry. Paul sent greetings to them and the church that they held in their home (Romans 16:3-5, & 1 Corinthians 16:19). Priscilla along with her husband demonstrated hospitality, kindness and a passion for God's Word.

We can truly learn a lot from Priscilla and her husband for mentoring. I like the part where they come across the young scholar, Apollos, in the synagogue. He spoke and taught diligently the things of the Lord, knowing only the baptism of John (Acts 18:25).
I love their approach to mentoring; they did not correct or challenge Apollos' teaching publicly. Instead, they took him unto them, and expounded unto him the way of God more perfectly. I believe that they took Apollos home, built a relationship with him, and had a positive impact in his ministry (Acts 18:26-28).

I truly thank the Lord for the mentors that I have had in my life: Mother Chloe Dunn and Bishop Sydney Dunn, Elder Oscar Mclean, and others (too many to mention). These all had different mentoring styles, but they were all good mentors. They understood the Apostolic doctrine and the standard of holy living. They were great examples to me.

I pray that the Lord will continue to lead and inspire good mentors to expound the way of God more perfectly to those willing to learn and grow in the Lord and in their ministry.

Min. Genevieve Dinnall

THURSDAY 7th

And the name of Amram's wife was Jochebed, the daughter of Levi – Numbers 26:59

A WOMAN OF FAITH, COURAGE & INTEGRITY – Reading: Exodus 2:1-10

Jochebed in Numbers 26:59 is the un-named woman mentioned in Exodus 2:1-2.

Jochebed is a Hebrew woman from the tribe of Levi. She was married to Amran who was also from the tribe of Levi. Jochebed had three children, i.e., Aaron, Miriam and Moses.

Jochebed is known for her bravery and ingenuity in saving Moses' life when he was a baby. She knew that Moses' life was in grave danger: she hid him for three months and when she could no longer hide him, she placed him a basket and placed it among the reeds along the banks of the River Nile (Exodus 2:3).

Jochebed's story shows us that, even in adversities and challenges, God will make a way to protect His people from danger. Her bravery and ingenuity in saving Moses' life is an example to all parents who are facing challenging situations with their children. Jochebed also teaches us that it is right to pass on our values and beliefs to our children.

The name Jochebed means '*God's Glory*' (Ref: Universal Dictionay.com) or '*Jehovah is her glory*' (Bible Study Tools). Her name mirrors her faith in God, and her confidence that He would protect her son despite the looming challenges.

Jochebed played an important role in educating Moses about his Hebrew culture and customs. She imparted to him the history of the Jews - their culture, history and relationship with God. This impartation would have been a good foundation for Moses in his early years, and for the plan that God had for him to be the children of Israel's future leader.

Jochebed's story teaches us that even in difficult times, we can still rely on God to protect, guide, and provide for us. Jochebed's quick actions in saving Moses' life were all a part of God's plan.

Jochebed leaves behind a heritage of faith and courage (Hebrews 11:23). Her story is an awesome encouragement to all mothers to follow. We can learn from the story of Moses' mother as it teaches us that God is forever faithful and just. It also teaches us the importance of standing up for what is right even when there is adversity. Jochebed's story ends here, but her inspiration lives on.

Missionary M Fraser

*FRIDAY 8th

...I will be exalted in the earth – Psalm 46:10

BE STILL, I AM GOD – Reading: Psalm 46:10-11; 47:1-9

Six Thousand US Dollars ($6K), was the medical bill for services rendered in 2022. It's now 2023.

I looked at the bill, said, *'Thank you, Jesus'*.

I proceeded to make necessary inquiries, which led to making a payment plan with the creditor.

I continued to pursue making an official filing, believing that the bill was not accurate.

I forwarded all necessary documents to support the case, and forwarded to Head Office via certified mail and facsimile.

Two weeks later, a letter was received that states, *'Balance for Services is zero'*.

HE IS GOD. Thank you, Jesus.

Lady Yolanda Edmund

***International Women's Day**

SATURDAY 9th

…the daughter of Pharaoh came down to wash herself at the river – Exodus 2:5

NAMELESS BUT NOT UNKNOWN – Reading: Exodus 2:1-10

It's not so much one's name that identifies an individual, but the role one has played, and the impact one has on the lives of others. Throughout the Bible we read of women who God used mightily to accomplish great things, but their names are not mentioned, or rarely mentioned.

The roles of women were more important than their names during the patriarchal, Old Testament era. Wives were 'the property' of their husbands. Husbands were brought to the limelight oftentimes by the work undertaken by their wives.

Don't we find the same thing happening in today's world? Isn't it true to say that the patriarchal culture operates even in the Christian church where the names of many faithful, hardworking married women are never mentioned, although the names of their husbands are?

It's important to understand that the names of many individuals will soon be forgotten, but their works continually speak for them centuries after they have departed this life. An old songwriter reminds us that the things we do live after us.

Let us labour not that men should know our name, but that the name of Jesus Christ be exalted in the earth.

Dr Una Davis

*SUNDAY 10th

...and Orpah kissed her mother-in-law; but Ruth clave unto her – Ruth 1:14

ACTIONS SPEAK LOUDER THAN WORDS – Reading: Ruth 1:1-14

Orpah the Moabite is mentioned in the book of Ruth as the wife of Chilion, the son of Elimelech and Naomi. Orpah became a widow after around ten years of marriage, and joined her mother-in-law and her sister-in-law to leave Moab and return to the land of Judah as the famine there had ended.

During the journey Orpah was faced with an ultimatum, either to continue to Judah or return to her family home. Her only words recorded in the book of Ruth was her response, '*Surely we will return with you to your people*' (Ruth 1:10 - NKJV).

Orpah appeared committed to return with Naomi and to be a part of her family. She was confronted with many reasons why she should return home. Naomi had no more sons and was too old to conceive anymore; and even if she did would she wait around until he reached adulthood.

But how committed was Orpah? Was her heart ready to relocate and serve Jehovah, or was it still in Moab? Orpah said the right thing initially, but her actions didn't match her words as she chose to return to her people and her gods. There's a saying, '*home is where the heart is*' and this was true for Orpah.

Jesus said in Matthew 15:8, '*These people draw near to Me with their mouth, and honour Me with their lips, but their heart is far from Me*' (NKJV). Orpah is a reminder that what we do should reflect what we say and true intention of our heart.

Name withheld

Mother's Day (UK)

MONDAY 11th

...the woman came and told her husband, A man of God came unto me – Judges 13:6

FAITH AND OBEDIENCE FROM THE UNNAMED WIFE – Reading: Judges 13:1-25

Manoah's wife/Samson's mother is referred to as 'the woman'. Here we have a woman who could not have children. However, unlike the following childless women:

- Sarah (Gen 18:10-12) - laughed at the thought of having a child in her old age.
- Rachel (Gen 30:1) - complained and gave her husband an ultimatum.
- Hannah (1 Sam 1:10-11) - prayed for a child
- Rebekah (Gen 25:21) - whose husband prayed for her childless situation

the Bible withholds her name and doesn't tell us what, if anything, she did about her situation. One can only assume that she had accepted her circumstances.

One day, whilst minding her own business, she had a visit from an angel telling her that she would have a son who would be a Nazarite for life, and she was to comply with the Nazarite way of living during her pregnancy. Nazarites voluntarily took a vow for a specific period; however, Samson was to be a Nazarite until his death.

So, what can we learn from 'the woman'? Well, she was contented, faithful, and obedient.

- She was obedient to the voice of God and raised her son according to God's will keeping the Nazarite vow during her pregnancy.
- Her faith was strong; she didn't doubt the angel neither did she believe they would die as her husband suggested in Judges 13:22-23.

We must aim to be like 'the woman' because the Lord is looking for us to be obedient, do His will, be faithful, and be committed to Him.

I thank God for those unassuming, unknown, and known mothers who are raising their children as God instructed.

Lady Pam Lewin

TUESDAY 12th

And God remembered Rachel, and God hearkened to her – Genesis 30:22

YOUR TURN WILL COME – Reading: Genesis 30:1-24

Leah and Rachel were sisters but the Scriptures don't record there being a sisterly-bond of any sort between them. They were rivals; they both loved the same man, Jacob, and he loved only one of them in return.

Rachel, who was Jacob's favourite wife, was barren. I can imagine and feel the pain in her heart each time that Leah announced another pregnancy. Moses, who is the writer of Genesis, pens this: *'And God hearkened unto Leah, and she conceived and bare Jacob the fifth son' (Genesis 30:17) 'And Leah conceived again, and bare Jacob the sixth son' (v19) 'And afterwards, (Leah) bare a daughter, and called her name Dinah' (v21).* O my Lord! Am I the only one feeling Rachel's torment?

But finally, at last, after a long time, we read, *'And God remembered Rachel, and God hearkened to her…' (v22).*

The test for Rachel which she may have failed, and applies to all of us, is the ability to genuinely celebrate the achievements and joy of others when God blesses them with what we want and seem to have been denied. Women are not always good at that. Don't we realise that when our turn comes, we will want someone to sincerely rejoice with us too? *'O magnify the LORD with me, and let us exalt His name* ***together****. I sought the LORD and He heard me' (Psalm 34:3-4).*

You don't know when your *'pot will start to boil'* and it'll be your turn for a lifelong desire to be fulfilled, but whilst waiting, have the right attitude and be glad for somebody else!

JEJ

WEDNESDAY 13th

...immediately she was made straight, and glorified God – Luke 13:13

THE WOMAN BENT LOW BY THE SPIRIT OF INFIRMITY – Reading: Luke 13:10-17

Characterised by the Blue Letter Bible as, *'The woman healed on the sabbath day'*, recorded solely in the gospel of Luke, we are presented with an unnamed woman bowed low by what we are told by the ESV Bible was a disabling spirit. Although we understand that not all sickness has a spiritual source, we have to acknowledge that there are some physical ailments which have a spiritual root.

The Message Bible suggests that this woman's condition was arthritis, whilst Pate suggests that her physical disability was *'due to spondylitis ankylopoetica, which produces the fusion of the spinal bones'*. It is in this condition that this woman, having suffered her fate for 18 years, enters the synagogue on the sabbath day. It is in that condition Jesus sees her.

This is comforting, reassuring and empowering. God sees us! We are reminded of Hagar who declared God to be, *'El Roi'*, i.e., *'the LORD who sees me' (Genesis 16:13)*. God sees me in all my circumstances. Nameless, identified by various Bible translations as, *'The woman with the spirit of infirmity'*; *'The crippled woman'*; *'The woman with a disabling spirit'*; *'The woman bent low unable to lift herself up'*. But Jesus sees her.

Our circumstances often have us bent low but we can be assured that Jesus sees us. It's interesting that the scripture talks about the woman being bent low because that implies that she was unable to look up, and it is important that Christians look up, that we are able to look to the hills from whence cometh our help. It's also interesting that the phrasal verb to *'look up'* means that things are getting better, things are improving, things are on the up-and-up. Hence, it is important that as Women of God we have that mindset, that we are able to look up and see things from a positive angle, see things in a clearer way; get a vision – a panoramic view – of things, as opposed to looking down and seeing things in a negative fashion.

It is noteworthy that the woman was nameless, therefore perhaps she felt insignificant. Sometimes we see ourselves as insignificant, we see ourselves as being surplus to requirements. But in all of this we need to be assured that Jesus, the Lord of the Sabbath, sees us!

Jesus wasn't constrained by the legalistic systems of the time. Although it was the sabbath day, and he would later on be reprimanded by those in the synagogue, Jesus took time away from teaching to see this woman, evaluate her condition, determine that the eighteen years of suffering would have cost her dearly and decided, **by His Word**, to loose her from her infirmity, to release her from pain, stigma and shame, and to cause her to be able to straighten herself and indeed to look up.

Her immediate response was to glorify God. That is something, again, that we also ought to be aware of; when the Lord meets us at our very point of need, our immediate response should be to glorify Him.

Lady Shirley Hamilton

THURSDAY 14th

...the daughter of...Herodias came in, and danced, and pleased Herod
Mark 6:22

DON'T COMPROMISE THE MESSAGE – Reading: Mark 6:12-29

We know from the narrative in Malachi 3:1 that John was the one whom the prophet prophesied as the forerunner for Jesus. He was ordained to clear the way before Jesus stepped into His public life. When this was accomplished, John stepped out of the way; Jesus must increase and John must decrease (John 3:30).

Calling sinners to repentance was John's ministry, he was an inclusive preacher whose mission was to preach Repentance. He called out sin whether it was in the street, synagogue or in the palace.

John called to repentance the rich and powerful Herod the Emperor and Herodias who was his brother's wife. Herod was never given the title of King, this was used as a local custom. Herod heard the message but it went through one ear and came out the other. Our Heavenly Father hates sin, Paul informs believers the wrath of God is revealed from heaven against all ungodliness and unrighteousness of men (Romans 1:18-32).

Despite Herod's conviction that John is a holy man, the stage is set where the daughter of Herodias is dancing before him and other officials. This stimulates his carnal nature as she is licentious in the dance, which was ticking all his boxes to the point he offered her half of his kingdom. Checking with her mother about what she would reply, her mother thought of a way to get rid of John the Baptist, and told her to ask for his head.

Now, why on earth would anyone request a dead man's head? Satan, that old dragon, thinks to kill the message, you kill the messenger. However, Jesus is on the scene and growing in popularity. The message is still the same, *'Repent the Kingdom of Heaven is at hand'*. Ladies, *'How shall we escape so great salvation; which at the first began to be spoken by the Lord, and was confirmed unto us by them that heard Him' (Hebrews 2:3)*. The preaching of the Gospel of Jesus Christ will soon be over, I beseech one and all to heed the message!

Missionary Audrey Simpson

*FRIDAY 15th

...Dinah the daughter of Leah and Jacob, went out to see the daughters of the land
Genesis 34:1

YOU ARE NOT ALONE IN YOUR SUFFERING – Reading: Genesis 30:21; 34:1-31

In Genesis 34, we have a rather challenging chapter that narrates the defilement of Dinah, the daughter of Leah and Jacob.

The chapter highlights a number of serious issues and it is obvious that her brothers, Simeon and Levi, in avenging Shechem, deceitfully agreed to an intermarriage that would not take place. Such a marriage would be in violation of God's commandment. God had previously warned against His chosen people marrying the Canaanites. Isaac and Rebekah made it clear to Esau and Jacob that they were not to intermarry with the Canaanites. It is not clear why Jacob did not object to the intermarriage when he knew it would be displeasing to God. It took Simeon and Levi to stop the marriage taking place. Their actions were not godly and were contrary to what God expected of them. God is a God of justice and requires His people to be honest and just (Psalm 82:3; Amos 5: 24). There is a right way to encourage justice. Revenge, resentment, and retaliation cannot be accepted as justice.

It is interesting to note that Jacob did not take action against his only daughter's defilement, her shame and emotional wellbeing. Rather, it seems that he wanted to protect himself, his family and assets and live without fear with the Hivites. Meanwhile, Simeon and Levi were intent on seeking justice for the defilement of Dinah. The action taken was one of vengeance which led to mass murder, and not necessarily to obey God's commandment. Dinah's voice is almost silent in the narrative. There is no reference of Dinah receiving much needed help, particularly when the culture of that time is taken into consideration. To experience rape would have had a lasting emotional impact on her life. We do not know how she felt but one can only imagine the pain, the shock, the dishonour and regrets for *'going out to meet the women of the land' (Genesis 34:1).*

Always seek first to understand than to judge. It is not wrong to assume that this young woman was innocent, and probably lonely, being the only daughter among twelve brothers. She needed someone to instruct her but it appears motherly, fatherly and brotherly instruction and guidance were not available, and so she paid a high price for believing there was safety where danger lingered. Was she foolish in going out? Probably it was unwise to venture out on her own, but that does not justify rape, molestation or abuse. She was created in the image of God and was loved and cherished by God. The Bible speaks clearly of how much God loves His children. He will fight for His people and avenge their enemies (Romans 8:31-34; Isaiah 49:25; Matthew 18:6).

Dinah's is not the only situation of this kind recorded in the Bible. King David's son Amnon raped his sister, Tamar (2 Samuel 13); she was left with the shame of defilement and once again we see the father stepping back and not seeking justice or help for his daughter. Her brother Absalom took revenge and murdered Amnon. These are two biblical stories of innocent women suffering defilement. Yet, the defilement of our sisters continues, not only in the secular world, but in religious establishments. Many of our women are living with secrets of defilement and abuse because no one listened to them. The degree of their suffering and pain have intensified over the years, probably because they were blamed for contributing to the situation, or because *'dirty linen must not be washed in public'* and so the perpetrator is protected and escapes punishment while the victim has no choice but to live with her shame and pain for the rest of her life.

But it is not the end, for God sees. The all-seeing eyes of God do not miss anything. His light penetrates the darkness and one day all will be revealed. Let not your heart be troubled, God will console and He will deliver. God sees and God does not forget. God expects us to forgive the perpetrator and leave vengeance to him. However, it does not mean we should sit still and do nothing. We should speak out against wrongdoing, irrespective of the gender and status of the wrongdoer.

What can we learn from Dinah's experience? Irrespective of age, social status and church position, wisdom must be a principal thing. Be alert, vigilant and sober. Seek to please God rather than human beings. Guard your salvation, it is priceless. Seek help and advice. There are no secrets to be kept when your salvation is in danger. Avoid mental and emotional ill-health by speaking to someone in confidence. Do not be a slave to fear. It is time to get rid of those secrets and release healing into your body so that spirit, soul and body can be healed completely. God offers holistic healing that transforms lives. God cares for you. Cast all your cares on to him. Trust Him for your healing. He is the Great Physician.

'For I know the thoughts I have for you…thoughts of peace and not of evil, to give you an expected end' (Jeremiah 29:11).

Overseer Joy Henry

Please see the Support Directory at the back of this book if you have been affected by today's reading and need professional support

SATURDAY 16th

...(Peter) came to the house of Mary the mother of John, whose surname was Mark: where many were gathered together praying – Acts 12:12

MARY'S HOUSE OF PRAYER – Reading: Acts 12:1-19

Mary the mother of John Mark is a woman whose name is written in the New Testament for her good works. The question is how much do we know about this outstanding woman? We know she was an active Christian in Rome who willingly gave up her home to be used as a place of worship. The apostle Paul sent greetings, *'as to one who worked hard for you'* (Romans 16:6).

The Bible reveals that she is a close family member to Barnabas, (Colossians 4:10), who was moved to sell his land and gave the proceeds to support the early Church. Mary Mark was instrumental in the early Church; she gave up her house as one of the meeting places to enable brethren to fellowship. When believers heard the news of Peter's arrest, they stood in the gap, sought the Lord, and made their petition of deliverance to God. It is therefore not an accident that, after Peter was escorted from prison by the Angel of the Lord, he made his way to Mary Marks's house. We can conclude there was a special relationship between the two individuals. Peter had mentored Mary's son, John Mark, and refers to him as his son in 1 Peter 5:13.

We know from the Scripture that John Mark was a travelling companion with Barnabas and Paul. It has been suggested that, due to the persecution and famine at that time, John Mark was worried about the welfare of his mother (Mary Mark), and this could have been the reason why he withdrew from the missionary journey of Paul and Barnabas.

Missionary Audrey Simpson

SUNDAY 17th

Felix came with his wife Drusilla, which was a Jewess…- Acts 24:24

DRUSILLA HEARD BUT DID NOT CHANGE – Reading: Acts 24:22-27

Soon after birth, each of us was given a name, an identity. Our name captures our uniqueness and the individuality of who we are.

There are women in the Bible whose names are not mentioned at all, it is like they have no identity. Then there are others whose names are rarely mentioned.

Drusilla is mentioned only once. She was the daughter of Herod Agrippa I. She was a Jewess whose name means, *'watered by the dew'*. Her siblings were her brother Herod Agrippa II, and her sisters Bernice and Marianne (*ref. Bill Allan*). She was betrothed by her father by the age of 6 years to Callinius the Prince of Commangene, a descendant of Antiochus Epiphanes (*ref. Bill Allan*).

Drusilla was afterwards married to Felix and was present with him when Paul spoke to them of righteousness, temperance and judgment. Though Felix trembled, was afraid, and asked Paul to leave until a more convenient time, there was no mention about Drusilla's response.

Drusilla heard the message of salvation from Paul but failed to understand the importance of it. As a result, she dismissed Paul's message as being irrelevant and failed to make the necessary life-changes. Instead of allowing Jesus Christ to free her from the burden of sin, she left in the same sinful condition in which she came.

Just like Drusilla, we are each responsible for our soul and the choice to enjoy our long eternity with Jesus, or to be separated for eternity. Her story serves as a message for us all today. If we hear the message of salvation, we should not harden our heart but use the opportunity to accept Christ.

Missionary M Fraser

MONDAY 18th

...his wife sent unto (Pilate), saying, Have nothing to do with this just man–Matt 27:19

POWERLESS TO STOP INJUSTICE – Reading: Matthew 27:15-26

Another unnamed woman who is only mentioned in the book of Matthew and referred to as *'his wife'.*

Why is Pilate's wife mentioned? Well, I believe it's because she tried to stop injustice from being done because of a dream she had (i.e., the killing of an innocent man named Jesus). She was fearful of the dream and maybe also of her husband, Pilate, because she didn't speak to Pilate face-to-face, but instead sent him a note advising him to have nothing to do with Jesus. But she was powerless to stop injustice.

What she didn't realise was that Jesus had to die and that man, even though they thought they had killed Him, couldn't kill Him. Jesus said in John 10:18 (NLT), '*No one can take my life from me. I sacrifice it voluntarily. For I have the authority to lay it down when I want to and also to take it up again. For this is what my Father has commanded'.*

When injustice is before us, we can either ignore it or be like *'his wife'* and try to stop it from happening. Sometimes fear stops us from doing what is right. However, we should stand for the right, speak up for what is right and see the power of God at work.

'....The Lord is my helper, and I will not fear what man shall do unto me' (Hebrews 13:6 KJV)

Lady Pam Lewin

TUESDAY 19th

...Simon's wife's mother was taken with a great fever – St Luke 4:38

WHO WAS SHE? – Reading: St Luke 4:38-41

Jesus was in Capernaum - He had escaped being thrown down a hill by passing through the midst of a wrathful crowd who had been listening to him in the synagogue (Luke 4:28-31). Jesus came to do good, however He was met with hostility on many occasions. Nonetheless, the fame of Jesus was sweeping through Galilee.

Jesus came to Peter's home. Peter's mother-in-law lay sick with a great fever. This no doubt had the household tending to her needs; they knew that Jesus could heal her and told him about her condition.

Jesus had been ministering all day. Yet with the simple touch of His hand (Mark 1:31), He rebuked the fever (Luke 4:39) and it not only left her, but immediately she arose and ministered unto them.

Usually, a recovery period would be needed after a great fever, but the ability for Peter's mother-in-law to minister was also restored. Another miracle from Jesus!

Many of us can testify of God's healing virtue, we share to give glory to Jesus and to encourage others too. This woman's experience is in the Holy Bible for all to see, that's the God that we serve! Although she is not named but she will never be forgotten.

That evening many others came to Peter's house as word of the Lord being there spread, and the testimony of this woman was told.

Peter's mother-in-law is not named but was healed and restored. Who was she?

Beverley V Galloway

WEDNESDAY 20th

...let us make our father drink wine, and we will lie with him, ... – Genesis 19:32

DELIVER US FROM EVIL – Reading: Genesis 19:30-38

The Bible does not confirm the names of Lot's two daughters. However, we read about them in Genesis 19 and quickly learn about a taboo subject which still exists today in the 21st Century.

Incest is the name given to this type of sexual relationship between close family members. Would you be tempted to go to this extreme measure for fear of your family becoming extinct? These two sisters hatched a criminal plan to carry on their family lineage (Genesis 19:32).

When we closely examine the events, many will agree that Lot was not a willing or conscious participant in the incest. He was intoxicated, and whilst in this state of drunkenness, he was seduced by each of his daughters. Given the circumstance, we may come to the conclusion that Lot was forced twice. After the manual of the priest was written (Leviticus), God's law prohibited this type of sexual behaviour between close family, i.e., father, daughter, brother, and sister (Leviticus 18:6-18).

Before the law, there were many incestuous relationships which were not deemed as incest, and were seen as a necessity to ensure that the earth was replenished with other humankind, e.g., Adam and Eve's children married each other. As the population grew, this extended out to marrying your cousin. Abraham married Sarah, his half-sister (Genesis 20:12), and Amram took Jochebed his father's sister (i.e., his aunt) for his wife (Exodus 6:20).

Today the Bible clearly instructs humankind **not** to approach anyone of his close relatives to uncover their nakedness (incest). See again Leviticus 18:6-18. This type of aberrant behaviour occurs in some cases when power is exercised over another person. This is sexual abuse. It is illegal; it is going against the Word of God. If you have been, or are being abused in this way, ask God to give you the courage to speak up and tell someone to get the help and support needed. It is said that an abuser is often a person who has themselves been abused. The added danger of silence is that, if you do not disclose the perpetrator, he/she may go on to abuse others.

Women of God, please do not remain enslaved victims of this practice. Remember that we are victorious through Christ who is able to deliver us from anything and everything, and strengthens us to walk worthy in our calling.

Missionary Audrey Simpson

Please see the Support Directory at the back of this book if you have been affected by today's reading and need professional support

THURSDAY 21st

...Ananias, with Sapphira his wife, sold a possession... – Acts 5:1

HONESTY, THE ONLY POLICY - Reading: Acts 5:1-11

It's only *'a small white lie'!* It's just *'a slight exaggeration'*!

In the book of Acts we read of a husband and wife called Ananias and Sapphira. They were both members of the early Apostolic Church. Who knows, they may have been filled with the Holy Ghost as this event occurred during the dispensation of Grace, i.e., the Church Age, after the Day of Pentecost.

They sold a personal possession and held back part of the money. That was their choice to make. It reads as though the idea to withhold part of the sale proceeds, and pretend that it was all, was that of Ananias (Acts 5:1-2). But Sapphira was aware or *'privy'* to her husband's decision. We do not read that she rebuked her husband by telling him that deception is sin.

Instead, they colluded to lie about the amount of profit made from the sale of their land. They tried to make it seem as though, just like the other brethren who had sold what was theirs and given everything, they too had done the same. Husband and wife rehearsed their storyline so that, if questioned, they would both say the same thing; nobody would possibly guess the truth...

However, in their plotting and scheming, Ananias and Sapphira made no allowance for the spirit of discernment which was very active in the anointed man of God, Peter.

Sadly, this couple's last service attended ended with instant death (literally) and burial of them both.

Mothers, daughters, wives, sisters, aunties, everyone: Telling lies is never a solution. Honesty is not the best policy; it is the only policy.

JEJ

(I Arise! 2022)

FRIDAY 22nd

The daughters...speak right: thou shalt surely give them a possession of an inheritance...Numbers 27:7

I WILL NOT BE SILENT – Reading: Numbers 27:1-11

'Why should our father's name disappear from his clan because he had no son? Give us property among our father's relatives' (Numbers 27:4 – NIV).

The book of Ecclesiastes 3 tells us of the importance of seasons and times. There is an appointed time for everything. We are told that there is a time to be silent and a time to speak up. We know the power of our words can either bring life or death. So, the question we must ask ourselves is when do we speak and when do we remain silent. It is often in those moments of decision where we should humbly seek the guidance and wisdom of our Heavenly Father. The Word tells us that in all our getting, get understanding and wisdom is the principal thing (Proverbs 4:7).

In the book of Numbers 27, we are introduced to five tenacious and intentional sisters named Mahlah, Noah, Hoglah, Milcah, and Tirzah, called the daughters of Zelophehad. Their father had died and it was customary in those days to give the inheritance (properties) to the sons and not the daughters. The era had ended, the season was changing, and the children of Israel were coming out of the wilderness and entering into the promised land. These five women understood what time it was and were ready to seize the moment and claim what rightfully belong to them.

With great courage and boldness, they stepped into an arena where only certain men sat. They presented their petition before Moses, the priest, leaders and congregation. This was a revolutionary and pivotal move in the history of Israel. Moses listened keenly to their request and placed their petition before the Lord, and the Lord granted their request.

They were willing to risk their reputation, status, and image in order to fulfil destiny and change the course of history. They were trailblazers, pioneers and history makers. What is God calling you to do today? Are you going to remain silent? Is it the time for you to rise up, stand up, and claim your inheritance? The next generation is depending on you. I will not be silent.

Name withheld

SATURDAY 23rd

And I went unto the prophetess; and she conceived – Isaiah 8:3

QUIETLY VALUED – Reading: Isaiah 8:1-22

The prophetess' significant role was to warn of the swift destruction to Israel's enemy, as well as being a servant of God. She was unnamed due to the time, cultural biases, and religious practices of the day.

Generally chauvinistic, unfair behaviour that treated women unequally, was normal within society back then, hence bias and under-representations of women are reflected throughout the Bible.

The book of Judges shows various incidences of women not named: Samson's father, Manoah, is named but his mother, who had supernatural visitations and was given a promise of a son by divine intervention, her name is not known. She had two encounters with the angel of the LORD, yet she's only referred to as, *'the woman'* (Judges 13:3, 6,9,10). In chapter ten, Jephthah's daughter is unnamed.

In Exodus 12:37, a record of Israel's deliverance from Egypt, there are six hundred thousand men on foot but the number of women is not mentioned. Jesus fed five thousand men (Matthew 14:21) and four thousand men (Matthew 15:38), but neither of these figures include women.

Howbeit, Jesus treated women somewhat differently to the status quo. He highlighted women, giving them identity. For example, Jesus declared a memorial, '*wheresoever this gospel shall be preached throughout the whole world…'* (Mark 14:9) for the woman who anointed his head with the contents of her alabaster box in the house of Simon the leper (Mark 14:3). John reveals that it was Mary who, on another occasion, wiped Jesus' feet with her hair (John 11:2; 12:3).

Women in Jesus' inner circle are named, and played major parts following His resurrection. They were the first witnesses and proclaimers of the Gospel, i.e., the good news of His death, burial and resurrection.

Overall, though anonymous or silent in many cases, yet every woman is valuable in Scripture.

Sis Jx

SUNDAY 24th

O give thanks unto the LORD; for he is good – Psalm 136:1

100 YEARS OF LIVING! – Reading: Psalm 136:1-26

I give God thanks who took me from my mother's home in Jamaica to England. I've had many ups and downs, but through it all God has been good to me. I have reached to the age of 100 years old, an age which I never thought that I would see - my husband never lived to see 100.

Living to this age is very hard, I have had many sicknesses but God has taken care of me. I also thank God for my children, and rest of the family, who have helped to look after me so that I don't have to be in a Care Home. They are very good to me. I am blessed to see God using so many of my children and offspring in ministry.

I can truly say that after all the things I've been through I still have joy. Sometimes my experiences made me feel like I was Daniel in the Lion's Den, but God delivered me. I trust Him. God is my refuge and fortress. He's everything to me.

One of my favourite songs is:

My hope is built on nothing less
Than Jesus' blood and righteousness
I dare not trust the sweetest frame
But wholly lean on Jesus' name

On Christ the solid Rock I stand
All other ground is sinking sand
All other ground is sinking sand
(The Solid Rock – E Mote)

I always ask God for mercy and forgiveness. When I walk through the valley of the shadow of death, He comforts me. I will continue to hold fast until He chooses to call me home; I do not know when that will be.

God bless you, brethren.

Mother Alice Lewin

MONDAY 25th

...take unto thee a wife of whoredoms...so he went and took Gomer
Hosea 1:2-3

WHEN LORD GOD HURTS – Reading: Hosea 1:1-11

Allow the thought: our Lord God can feel hurt from those He is in covenant relationship with.

God is a covenant keeper; such is His character that He is faithful in everything, He is flawless. His unconditional love is untainted by sin. It takes depth of love to rescue a troubled marriage.

Emotional infidelity or extramarital affair, the gut-wrenching pains of betrayal and confusion can leave a trail of devastation on both cheater and cheated. Conflicting feelings, of the aggrieved and the guilty, raise questions about the relationship. Some husbands and wives reach out for mediation or counselling, but for others, it is beyond capacity to cope. Deep wounds of anguish and/or numbness, only God can reach.

In Hosea, God expressed His anger and jealousy for Israel. Strong metaphors hit home comparing Israel's behaviour to a *'backsliding heifer'* (Hosea 4:16). It is enough to make one cringe, but understand that this striking imagery brings home the pains God felt.

Comparisons of their wayward behaviour to a marital relationship: they were unfaithful, having lovers, i.e., they depended on other nations, obtained military assistance from other countries, forsaking their commitment and to trust God.

Israel is now divided into two kingdoms (following the revolt of Jeroboam from under King Rehoboam; 1 Kings 11:26 to Chapter 12). Hosea's ministry began about two hundred years after the separation. Judgment was coming; unknown to Israel, Assyria would invade their land. Hosea was the first prophet to warn Israel to amend their ways.

Prosperity and economic boom in Israel created a pride and disregard for the Word of God. Connections with merchants brought luxuries into the kingdom. A Laodicean attitude of success and affluence eventually influenced a neglect of God. Israel turned to copy the practice of Baal worship and other gods of the surrounding nations, also their lifestyle had become immoral.

At God's command, Hosea had to marry a woman described as, *'a wife of whoredoms'* to portray the state of the people. Hosea married Gomer; she became pregnant with his children. Their three children were: *Jezrell, meaning, 'God scatters', Lo-Ruhamah, 'not pitied'; and Lo-Ammi, 'not my people'.* Their names were symbolic of the condition of the people. Gomer played around with other lovers and ended up in trouble as result. Hosea had to buy her back from a slave market (Hosea 3:1-3).

About Gomer, there is no record of her thoughts or reasons why she had other lovers. Only that she was the daughter of Dibliam, *meaning, 'double cakes, two cakes'*. Why double though? Is it double mindedness, like Lot's wife? Just a thought…

The grief in the LORD's heart is in the rawness of Hosea 2:2-4. Such was the blatant disregard of Israel to Him. Their adulteries of worshipping other gods and dependency on pagan nations for support was an insult to Him. He is Elohim, their Jehovah Jireh; all they needed He had supplied. Yet, because of His faithfulness, God reached out to His people as the faithful, loving, forgiving LORD of covenant, promising Israel that they will call Him *'Ishi'*, meaning, *'My husband or my man'* (Hosea 2:16).

God is still reaching out to humanity despite the maligned flaws we have carried. Jesus, the Word made flesh, is the answer to heartbreak. He has absorbed every judgment we deserved by extending His mercy by the blood of the New Covenant in Jesus Christ shed for you and me.

He is the lover of my soul.

From one who knows

TUESDAY 26th

...tell me, what hast thou in the house?... – 2 Kings 4:2

THE ANSWER IS WITH YOU – Reading: 2 Kings 4:1-7

Today we are looking at a woman who was in debt. She was a widow and had two sons; she could see no way to clear the liability left by her late husband. This was indeed a serious matter because, if she couldn't settle the financial obligation, her sons would be taken away by the creditors to be bondmen, i.e., slaves, and she might never see them again.

She brought her case to the man of God, Elisha, hoping that he would have a solution, but Elisha's reply took her by surprise, *'What hast thou in the house?' (2 Kings 4:2).* A strange question because if she had something in the house which could have been used as payment, she would surely have already considered this. The widow's answer of, *'I have nothing in the house except a pot of oil'*, was all that Elisha needed to hear. '*...nothing apart from...*', means that you don't have nothing, you do have something. Nothing is not nothing if it's followed by *'apart from'*. Sometimes our answer is in something that we overlook and consider to be unimportant. We then seek help from a far place when the remedy is staring us in the face. There's a 'pot of oil' that we walk past every day; what might yours be?

The pot of oil can also be symbolic of the anointing. There are times in our lives when we experience a major difficult event or a series of crises; life feels like it's been turned upside down and, like the widow, we feel destitute perhaps mentally, emotionally, spiritually, and physically. Notwithstanding, if we still have a pot of oil, i.e., the anointing, we've retained something of great value. Whilst it is understandable that we would lament over what we have lost, still we need also to thank God for what is left!

JEJ

*WEDNESDAY 27th

...as we went to prayer, a certain damsel...met us – Acts 16:16

THE NAMELESS WOMAN – Reading: Acts 16:16-23

At the time of our birth, we were given a name, an identity by which to be identified. Our names capture the uniqueness of our individuality, of who we are as human beings created in the image of God.

However, there are certain women in the Bible whose names are rarely mentioned or not mentioned at all. They appeared to not have an identity, only being defined by their disease, disability, or circumstance.

The damsel or young unmarried woman mentioned in Acts 16-16-18 is one such woman; she is known as possessed by an evil spirit. She was owned by several masters who all capitalised from her gain and misery. Apostle Paul was grieved because her state was one of bondage and delusion. Grieved because of what she did for the exploitation of others, Paul rebuked the evil spirit and it left her immediately.

There is no mention that when the evil spirit left the damsel she was spiritually converted; we would hope though that she had turned her life over to Jesus and accepted Him as her Saviour. The Lord is no respecter of persons. He loves each one with His perfect love, not desiring that anyone should perish but that all should have eternal life.

Just like this nameless damsel, there are times when we may even feel lost within the crowd, undervalued and abused. Marginalised, put down, belittled and undermined, only valued to do menial tasks, and used for the promotion of others. But be reassured, women of God, Ephesians 2:10 tells us that, *'ye are His workmanship, created in Christ Jesus for good works which God prepared beforehand that we should walk in them'.*

If you ever feel lonely within your four walls, worthless, forgotten about, have no name to be called upon, be further reassured that you matter to God, *'Fear not for I have redeemed you, I have called you by name, you are mine' (Isaiah 43:1).*

Just remember that you are special. God has made you special, *'which in time past were not a people, but are now a people of God: which had not obtained mercy, but now have obtained mercy' (1 Peter 2:10).* Be encouraged.

Missionary M Fraser

International Cheese Day

THURSDAY 28th

...the LORD shall sell Sisera into the hand of a woman... - Judges 4:9

DEBORAH & JAEL: GOD'S INSTRUMENTS – Reading: Judges 4:1-24

We have heard about the conveyor belt of sin that existed in Israel in the period of the Judges, where the nation fell into sin and idolatry. The people fell into bondage to allow them to get to a point of surrender. When the pain of the oppressor was unbearable, they cried out to God for help. They were sent a deliverer in the form of a Judge - in this instance, the Judge is Deborah, a woman and a mother in Israel. Deborah was instrumental in confirming to Barak, the leader of Israel's army, what God had commanded him to do.

She had the whole armour of God on. Breastplate of righteousness, feet shod with peace, a shield of faith, the helmet of salvation and the sword, which is the Word of God (Ephesians 6:14-17). Deborah sweetly held Barak's hand like a mother holding tightly to her child's hand. We would say Barak took a while to get up and move, however, the Word tells us in Hebrews 11-32-33 that Barak is famous for his faith. I encourage us to be faithful in our weaknesses. Barak was not the one to personally defeat Sisera the commander of Jabin's army, a woman would be the one. We see the mighty hand of God disable all the flash chariots. I muse to myself that there is nothing too hard for God.

Sisera fled on foot and came upon Jael, the wife of Heber, and asked her to hide him. Although Deborah had been pivotal in supporting and encouraging Barak, Jael was the woman God used for His glory to bring about victory. We must always remember God is sovereign and uses who He chooses.

We see God uses Jael, a 'nobody'. This woman was skilled in tent building! Sisera was glad to see a friendly face (Jael) as the Kenites were at peace. But while Sisera slept, Jael used a hammer to drive a tent peg into his temple, pinned him to the ground, and he was dead. Our God used her treachery to accomplish His purpose. Whatever God says, must come to pass to bring about deliverance for His people. We learn it is not only about defeating sin, we must not rest until sin is dead (Romans 6:10-12).

Missionary Audrey Simpson

*FRIDAY 29th

...his mother's name was Athaliah, the daughter of Omri king of Israel – 2 Kings 8:26

ATHALIAH – WHO WAS SHE? – Reading: 2 Kings 8:25-29

Athaliah means *'Jehovah is strong or has afflicted'.* She was married to Jehoram who was the son of Ahab and Jezebel. Athaliah is rarely mentioned in the Bible, probably because of the severity of her wickedness and love of idolatry.

Ahab and Jezebel did evil in the sight of God and what we see here is a transferring of evil spirits from generation to generation. They were worshippers of Baal; their hearts were polluted with the spirits of whoredom and witchcraft. But there came a time of judgment when many from the household of Ahab, including Ahaziah, were killed during the reign of King Jehu (1 Kings 19:16-17 & 2 Kings 9).

Athaliah was not a legitimate ruler, but used her power as Ahaziah's mother to commission the death of all male children from the house of Judah. The enemy comes to kill steal and destroy, and the ultimate plan was to destroy the lineage from which the Messiah would be born. However, Athaliah's sister Jehosheba (another woman rarely mentioned), took Ahaziah's baby, Joash, and hid him in the temple of the Lord for six years, and in the seventh year he was anointed king. He was hidden for purpose and when his existence was made known, although Joash also did evil in the eyes of the Lord, his life maintained the preservation of the royal seed of Judah which Athaliah had tried to wipe out.

Joash's early years of life in hiding is like a seed that is planted in the ground. That seed is hidden for a long period of time. Once germinated the root emerges first, followed by the shoot that contains leaves and stems. Sometimes we fail to realise that storms within our lives happen to fulfil purpose. Many are hidden for great purpose and their time of revealing their gifting will soon be made known.

Consider a tree, when a storm comes branches are broken off, but since it is the roots that keep the tree alive it remains standing. Trees have an amazing ability to recover from the damage of a storm and this is an analogy of what happened to Judah.

Athaliah's character did not require much mentioning. What's revealed in the Scriptures is that, regardless of any spiritual attack, God is still in control. God's plan can never be aborted - Athaliah had to learn this the hard way.

Rachel Lewin

Good Friday

SATURDAY 30th

But Jehoshabeath...took Joash...and hid him...2 Chronicles 22:11

THE GREATER CAUSE – Reading: 2 Kings 11:1-3; 2 Chronicles 22:10-12; Psalm 27:5

Here is a biblical woman we rarely hear of; yet this princess' name carried her purpose: *'Jehoshabeath'* means *'Yahweh is Oath'*. This is indeed of great significance to her act; one of a far greater cause.

Jehoshabeath's rescue mission was an act of God. Hiding Joash, her baby brother (whose name means *'given by the Lord'*), in the house of God from among the slain was more than bravery on her part. Full coverage or not, she was walking in her destiny, being true to the meaning of her rarely mentioned name.

Think of a snippet of the backdrop by reading the previous chapters. Despite the hostility and more likely death than life, Princess Jehoshabeath took a high risk to save the future generation in that, Joash became the next king of Judah (2 Chronicles 24:1).

God was working out His purpose through Jehoshabeath to preserve David's royal lineage from being cut off, from which our dear Christ our King would ultimately come.

Named, not named, or rarely mentioned, there are times in our lives when we have to take needed action, a testimony of being faithful and true. It can come with varying consequences but to the glory of God.

As with Jehoshabeath, there was necessary initiative and gumption. So as and when: Did you? Have you? Will you too?

Pastor Josephine Lewis

*SUNDAY 31st

...Woman, why weepest thou?... - John 20:15

EVIDENCE OF HEALING – Reading: Matthew 27:55-61; John 20:1-18

Mary Magdalene, a woman with a troubled past of being tormented by seven devils. She'd had no control over her emotions and behaviours.

Excluded from society, not fitting in with the community, living without hope, and in need of a Saviour. Upon meeting Jesus, everything changed. His power poured into her heart and banished all evil.

This Mary is the first person at the grave of Jesus after His burial. Maybe not honoured and respected by many; she may not have had a history that one would want to own or share with the world, but such was the impact of Jesus that she found herself at His burial to continue to honour the One who had given her freedom and liberty.

There are many women who carry troubled pasts - I daresay that every woman has something, if she has lived long enough, that she may not feel proud of. She may feel she's not accomplished all, she may feel torn, tormented and tortured by circumstances that felt bigger than her. But when we meet Jesus, and He comes as a rescuer to cleanse and purge us from the inside out, it brings us from a place of mess to ministry.

There is a degree of honour and respect Mary developed for Jesus that even quietly she loved Him, and publicly she honoured Him. This reminds us that humble or broken beginnings are not a place to hide away, they are platforms to honour God with our lives. The evidence of healing in Mary Magdalene was that she showed up to be a balm of soothing to someone else.

When we are healed, we strengthen, we pour in, we become a role model. Let's take lesson from Mary to be healed, and show up to minister to others.

Joy Lear-Bernard

***Easter Sunday**

Clocks go forward (BST)

COPD - LET'S BREAK IT DOWN!

COPD (Chronic Obstructive Pulmonary Disease) is an 'umbrella' term for any of a group of chronic (long-term) and progressive lung conditions, used to describe the damage to lung tissue caused by restricted airflow due to obstruction.

The obstruction in the most part tends to be caused by years of smoking, but can also be due to occupational causes such as flour deposits from working in a bakery for a long time; dust deposits when working in construction, or air pollution, e.g., due to working at a vehicle garage or outside at an airport. Genetics may also play a part in the causes of developing COPD, especially in families where close relatives also have the condition. People with Alpha-1-antitrypsin deficiency are more prone to the condition particularly if they smoke, as without this substance the lungs are left more vulnerable to damage. Other diagnoses which come under this umbrella, and cause similar symptoms, include Emphysema, Bronchiectasis, Chronic Bronchitis. There are other lung diseases which cause similar symptoms, which may follow a similar path of treatment.

INCIDENCE – COPD was the third leading cause of death worldwide 2019, and tobacco smoke accounts for over 70% of COPD cases in high income countries (World Health Organisation)

SYMPTOMS – the main and most distressing symptom of this condition is increasing shortness of breath; other symptoms include frequent coughing, production of phlegm, and difficulty taking deep breaths.

DIAGNOSIS – Usually a patient may first present to their GP with shortness of breath, feeling tired all the time, perhaps have a chesty mucous cough (thinking it may be just a smoker's cough) and perhaps frequent chest infections. The GP will take a full history of symptoms, length of time of those symptoms, smoking history, and family health history. Other health conditions need to be ruled out first by various investigations so that they can be treated, e.g., blood tests to check whether the patient is short of breath due to anaemia; an ECG to investigate the condition of the heart, a Chest X-ray to determine whether there are any other lung anomalies, and finally a lung function test called Spirometry. A chest X-ray may show signs of the disease but cannot confirm the condition, but when everything else has been ruled out then it is spirometry which will give a conclusion.

TREATMENT – the first and foremost help to slow down the progression of the disease is to stop smoking. To a 40-a-day smoker of 40 years, this is the last thing they want to hear, but smoking would have probably been the main cause of their COPD, and quitting is the main way to decrease the rate of progression. If a person works in an environment which seems to be causing increasing lung symptoms and breathing difficulties, they should consider ways to prevent or reduce the amount of exposure to, and inhalation of lung-obstructing agents, or seriously consider changing their occupation.

Other than removing the agents that cause COPD, inhaler devices may help to aid the breathing. Inhalers used in COPD are slightly differently prescribed from those used in Asthma as the causative agents and main presentations are different. Unlike in Asthma, where the first inhaler of choice is a corticosteroid inhaler to reduce inflammation, the first inhaler of choice in COPD is initially a Bronchodilator (e.g., Salbutamol) but then when symptoms become worse, the patient would benefit from a LAMA (Long Acting Muscarinic receptor Antagonist) inhaler, followed by stepping up to a LABA/LAMA (Long Acting Beta Agonist combined with the LAMA) ; if needed as the condition progresses, there may be a further step up to a LABA/LAMA/ICS (inclusion of an Inhaled Corticosteroid).

If the patient has difficulty expectorating their phlegm because it is so thick, then a medication called Carbocisteine (a mucolytic) may help to thin that phlegm so that it can more easily be expectorated off the chest. This is particularly helpful when a person has Bronchiectasis, which is characterised by the over-production of phlegm.

Antibiotics may be needed if the person has a chest infection – every untreated chest infection causes the loss of further lung function due to scarring of the lung tissue. So prompt treatment should be sought. When a person with COPD increasingly struggles with their breathing, they may be offered Pulmonary Rehabilitation. This is where classes are held for people with similar conditions where breathing is affected (this may even include Long Covid), where a Respiratory Nurse and Physiotherapist work together with the patients to help them exercise to their individual ability, and improve the methods used for easier breathing. We have to bear in mind that as much as we want patients to keep active for their health, people with COPD need as much oxygen as possible to get to their lungs for breathing, so they must not over-exert themselves otherwise the oxygen they need for breathing is diverted to their muscles to enable them to be active!

Oxygen Therapy may be required for those who have severe COPD but can only be offered if the patient fits strict criteria of severity (e.g., very low blood oxygen levels (a pulse oximeter would show this) and who do not smoke…). Weight loss may need to be addressed also because if a person is so short of breath, they may be literally too tired to eat regular meals and may need softer foods or food supplements.

Homecare assistance will help with keeping their home in decent order if they are too short of breath to carry out activities of daily living for themselves. Vaccinations, especially annual Flu, and one-off Pneumococcal (Pneumonia) should be offered because not only as people get older, but people with lung conditions, both are more prone to chest infections which they find more difficult to fight off. Sadly, there is currently no cure for COPD, but the sooner it is identified, and the sooner the treatment begins, the slower will be the progression of the disease.

Be blessed, and don't forget to access your GP or Health Professional for advice, and if diagnosed, remember to keep in touch AT LEAST for your annual review.

REFERENCES:

www.nhs.uk;

www.who.int

www.asthmaandlung.org.uk

Nurse Elaine Richards 2023

april
In the Psalms

*MONDAY 1st

The LORD is my shepherd; I shall not want – Psalm 23:1

THE GOOD SHEPHERD – Reading: Psalm 23:1-6

What a blessing to read and BELIEVE the words of this verse! Jesus is our Lord and Saviour; the psalmist David compared Him to a shepherd in the following way:

LOVE: He loved us so much that He lived, then died for us – He was sinless but suffered and gave His life so that we could live in eternity with Him

PROTECTION: Like earthly shepherds, Jesus has a vested interest in the welfare of His sheep (us). The earthly shepherd in biblical times would lay down across the opening of the sheep pen so he would be aware of any intruders. God is omnipresent so knows where we are and who is trying to attack us. St John 10:10 tells us that *'...the thief cometh not, but for to steal, kill and to destroy...'.* Not only does Jesus protect us with His presence, but He has also equipped us with His armour (Eph 6:13-17)

EXAMPLE: There is a song which says, *'Jesus shall lead me night and day'*. As our Shepherd, Jesus has shown examples of living in this world not only through His life on earth as a man, but has also given us His Word, the Word of God, to show us how to live in every circumstance we may face!

PROVISION: Psalm 23 shows us how Jesus provides ... v1 says, *'I shall not want'* – The apostle Paul reminded us in Philippians 4:19 that, *'...God shall supply all your need according to his riches in glory'*

RELATIONSHIP – Just as a shepherd knows every sheep in his flock, Jesus knows each one of us that are His – we know His voice and we are known of Him. We're in good hands!

Sis Elaine

****Bank Holiday***

TUESDAY 2nd

...that I may dwell in the house of the LORD all the days of my life...- Psalm 27:4

MY SOUL'S DESIRE – Reading: Psalm 27:1-6

Most of us have ambitions, a list of things that we hope to accomplish in our lifetime. We should continue to set ourselves goals as we advance in age, because dreams are not only for the very young. Caleb was eighty-five years old when he said, *'Now therefore give me this mountain...' (Joshua 14:10-15).*

So how high up on your list of, *'Lord, please may I…'* is this prayer? '*One thing have I desired of the LORD, that will I seek after, that I may dwell in the house of the LORD all the days of my life, to behold the beauty of the LORD, and to enquire in his temple' (Psalm 27:4).*

To dwell in the house of the LORD speaks of permanency. To sit down and to stay-put, in spite of...! It is a fact that some of us have remained, not because we weren't at times tempted to backslide, but we have taken the vows which we made to God so seriously that we have to hold on. At our baptism when we said, *'Thy vows be upon me O Lord until death'… 'Jesus I'll go through with thee…'*, we understood that the promises we made were forever, and more binding than the marriage vows of, *'…For better, for worse, for richer, for poorer, in sickness and in health, to love and to cherish, 'til death us do part'.*

As a child, I used to hear it said in testimony services, *'Keep your seat in Zion!'*. This was not referring to a favourite chair in the sanctuary, but meant let nothing move you. Satan will try all kinds of tactics to push you off your seat and leave it empty, but like Jephthah in Judges 11:35, tell him and anyone else who needs to know, *'I have opened my mouth unto the LORD, and I cannot go back'!*

JEJ

WEDNESDAY 3rd

Examine me, O LORD, and prove me; try my reins and my heart – Psalm 26:2

EXAMINE ME – Reading: Psalm 26:1-7

A test can be a great revealer; it exposes what we know and what we don't know.

It forces us to acknowledge the things about ourselves that we so desperately try to hide, as well as highlighting some positive character traits that we did not realise we had. Whatever form the test takes, whether it is an exam, testing a product, or dealing with the trials of life, we know that it will often bring us to the point of reality.

The word *'examine'* in Hebrew is *'Bachan'* which means, *'put to the test'*. Throughout our lives we have experienced challenges and tests in many ways that have shaped us to be (to some degree) what we are today.

When David asked God to, *'Examine me'*, what was he asking the Lord to do?

In Psalm 26, verses 1–7, David spoke about his love and commitment to the things of God, and strongly voiced his integrity. But this was not enough. There was a cry from the depth of his heart to be more like his Heavenly Father. This could only come about through God looking within David's heart; exposing and removing what did not glorify Him.

So, God, examine me! Look within every crevice of my heart. Let every closed door be opened. Let your light shine in every dark space. Let everything in me that does not glorify you be exposed until you are completely formed in me.

Deveen Smith

THURSDAY 4th

He maketh me to lie down in green pastures – Psalm 23:2

PLANS – Reading: Psalm 23:1-6

The well-read Psalm 23:2 sees David likening his relationship with God to a shepherd tending to his sheep. (God) makes me to lie down in green pastures. This suggests a time of rest and nourishing at God's bidding. Right where we are He provides us this complete peace. Have you ever felt the sweet rest of God when you most needed it?

God grants us spaces in our lives when we simply and safely rest in Him. Not with self-reliance but trust. Our resting is made secure by two things. One is that we trust that we are in a place of no lack - that all supplies for our needs are right there at the ready: green, wholesome and available. The needs of our weary hearts, e.g., finances, our understanding, our spiritual wellbeing, or need for wisdom, whatever has brought us to a need for rest, is met in the wholesome greenness of God's presence where there is ZERO insufficiency!

The second thing preludes this sweet access to the storehouse of God. It is found in verse one. It says, *'The LORD is my shepherd'*. Imagine this intentional statement as a walk of faith towards the storehouses of God. A statement of confidence as we simply lie down. It is a defining declaration that, *'He shepherds me. I am His sheep. I rely on Him'.*

Sheep do not always want to follow, they often have to be shepherded with rods and staffs, urged from behind as they make clumsy judgments in their quest for pastures. Notice only the first verse focuses on *'I'*. Once this decision of will is made, it is followed by the shepherd's leading - once we give up leading ourselves! As we approach God's presence, let's see Him as our Shepherd and relinquish our independence. This guides us to the rest we can only ever find in Him. That is, the place of no lack and green pastures.

Joy Lear-Bernard

*FRIDAY 5th

...they got not the land in possession by their own sword...Psalm 44:3

THE RIGHT HEART-POSTURE – Reading: Psalm 44:1-26

Psalm 44 reveals the writer's agonising plea for deliverance; but how beautiful these few verses are that show the heart-posture of the writer.

Let's look into at the 3rd and conclusive verse, *'For they got not the land in possession by their own sword, neither did their own arm save them: but thy right hand, and thine arm, and the light of thy countenance, because thou hadst a favour unto them'.*

What a wonderful approach of acknowledgment unto the LORD: *'You did it!'*. It is very insightful as there are always challenges of every kind to face that sometimes seem like high mountains. However, taking the writer's approach helps us to see the great God of the mountain instead.

It is good to draw on testimonies of victory and remember to credit God, like David did in 1 Samuel 17:37; *'...The LORD that delivered me out of the paw of the lion, and out of the paw of the bear, He will deliver me out of the hand of this Philistine...'.*

Such an attitude shows the right heart-posture, i.e.: *'You have done it before and you can do it again'*. New covenant believers in Christ, have this favourable assurance that deliverance is always sure in the LORD.

Pastor Josephine Lewis

Walk to Work Day

SATURDAY 6th

The LORD has done great things for us; whereof we are glad – Psalm 126:3

COUNT YOUR BLESSINGS – Reading: Psalm 126:1-6

In our day-to-day lives, the Lord has done, and is still doing, so much for us that we often forget the blessings. There's a song by Johnson Oatman (1897) that says:

'Count your blessings, name them one by one
Count your blessings, see what God hath done
Count your blessings, name them one by one
And it will surprise you what the Lord has done.'

In the early days of my marriage, when my boys were babies, the Lord had given dreams to our leaders that we were to be transplanted into ministry. In the middle of a recession, when homes were not selling, we sold our home and moved into a new area. Oh, finances were so tight the situation became unbearable!

I remember receiving a letter from our electricity company giving a date that the electricity would be cut off due to non-payment of our bill. My youngest son had developed severe asthma and there was no way he could be in a cold house. On the day of the 'cut-off', before going to work, I prayed and left a note on the front door, pleading with whoever came not to turn off the electricity. At work, I asked for urgent annual leave and rushed home. The note was still on the door; I waited and waited and waited - no one came. The electricity had not been, and was not, cut off. We didn't hear from the electricity company again and guess what? The Lord made a way for the bill to be paid – what a God!

This is only one of my many great blessings from the Lord. Join me today in giving God thanks for all our blessings and the blessings to come.

Lady Pam Lewin

*SUNDAY 7th

Then they cried unto the LORD in their trouble, and he delivered them…Psalm 107:6

THEN THEY CRIED – Reading: Psalm 107:1-28

Quite often our habit is to, by trial and error, work through our problems by ourselves. We have a tendency to depend on our own capacity or understanding, and hope for the best rather than exercising our faith.

We can relate so easily to Psalm 107 because it speaks of those who wander in the wilderness, in a solitary way, experiencing hunger and thirst. It tells us that we, as human beings, move from one land, one situation, one norm to another - often going ahead of the peace of God.

A famous book called, *'Who Moved my Cheese',* speaks about humanity and how easily we find a place to 'rest on our laurels', i.e., be satisfied with our previous achievements to the extent that we feel we need to do nothing more. We can convince ourselves that it's our own abilities that allow us to live peaceful and fulfilled lives. It is easy to lose our sense of wonder and childlike faith.

However, as is always the case, we find ourselves at a place where our very best is not good enough. Something changes and 'upsets the apple cart', and we humbly turn back to God. When we've tried everything within our power, when we have reasoned situations and put in all the effort that we can muster, many of us will know the feeling of sitting slumped with more questions and answers.

The Prodigal Son felt this way. The Rich Young Ruler felt this way. Martha in her hurried busy-ness felt this way, and we - like them - come to the end of ourselves. Then, like the Prodigal Son who came to himself, we make a decision to go back to the Father. This temptation to lean on our understanding is not uncommon. In the Garden of Eden that fleshy DNA was prevalent. In fact, God is so able to understand His creation that He appeals to us throughout time to come and reason with Him (Isaiah 1:18). God reminds us that if we draw near to Him, He will draw near to us. He lets us know that He is our refuge and our strength, a very present help in times of trouble. We find in Psalm 91 that, 'He who dwells in a secret place… shall abide under the shadow of the Almighty',… and Psalm 107 says more than once, *'THEN they cried unto the LORD in their trouble…'.* It reminds us that we all take the journey of humble acceptance back to God.

After wandering, gathering, being in solitary places, feeling lack, hunger and thirst, with nowhere to settle, with nowhere that their hearts could find peace, only then they cried unto the LORD. Deliverance and peace are forever present and available even as we wander in search of it within our own means. Our dwelling place is found in our cry when we raise our hands and say, *'Lord, I haven't the capability to do things myself'.* Imagine that our surrendered hands are the key to what we most need, God Himself.

Indeed, Lord, I am the sheep and you are the shepherd. I am the clay and you are the potter. I am the creature; you are the creator. At that point, we open wide the door for God to show

His perfect strength in our weakness. A hymn says, *'O, what needless pain we bear, all because we do not carry, everything to God in prayer'.*

We are born understanding that we have a need for our father and mother for security and for nurture; for a source far greater than ourselves. When we are born again, we take the position of a child with our Father and learn to cry to Him. Somewhere over time, we may have simply forgotten that we are to do so. Wouldn't it be a wonderful acquisition if the people of God can say, *'and firstly they cried unto the LORD in their trouble'?* If our first place of contact is the face of Jesus.

Wherever you are, whatever walk around the wilderness has caused you longing and weariness, pause in the stillness. It's time to *'then cry'*. Having tried all sources, and exhausted your best, God waits for you to simply cry to Him and then we find rest and completeness.

Joy Lear-Bernard

World Health Day

MONDAY 8th

O LORD God of my salvation, I have cried day and night before thee – Psalm 88:1

A CRY FROM THE HEART – Reading: Psalm 88:1-18

How often do we have a prayer of desperation which moves the heart to cry unto God, where floods of tears stream down our face, and the urgency to get into the throne room is quickly made known? The need to touch and commune with Jesus is all that matters. When He sees our tears, He knows our heart's condition. When we are broken before Him as the Great Potter, He is able to put us back together again.

Tears are said to be a language that only God understands. The psalmist is dealing with a cry from the heart, making his petition known to God to intervene and save him from death. This cry is made with passion and urgency and in humility. While we seek Him, we ask God not to hide His face nor turn us away from Him.

When we pray His Word and remind Him of them, He inclines His ear to our cry. Women of God, Jesus *'can be touched with the feeling of our infirmities' (Hebrews 4:15).* He has given us the mandate to, *'Seek Him while He may be found and call upon Him when He is near' (Isaiah 55:6).* We have the privilege to do this! Therefore, casting our cares upon Him is no problem. The psalmist acknowledges that God is our rescue and that in His time, His choosing, this will happen.

Sisters, no matter the circumstance nothing beats prayer, prayer beats everything; our help comes from above.

Missionary Audrey Simpson

TUESDAY 9th

I pray that the LORD will listen when you are in trouble; and that the God of Jacob will keep you safe - Psalm 20:1 (CEV)

WHEN TROUBLE COMES – Reading: Psalm 20:1-9

A wise person once said, *'Be careful what you say about others when they experience misfortune. Add a spoon of sugar, in case one day you have to eat your words'*!

David, the author of today's psalm says, '*The LORD hear thee in the day of trouble…*'. He has crafted his words in a way to allude that trouble happens to all of us, and may God hear us when that day comes.

A Day of Trouble unfortunately does not mean only 24 hours, it can last for years, depending on the test(s).

This psalm is a prayer of preparation for challenge and battle, written and prayed by David before going out to war. Psalm 20 encourages the reader to invest their trust only in God, not in *'chariots and horses'*, i.e., not in material possessions or self-help. You've heard the true saying, *'Seek a friend before you need one'*. We need to have a relationship with God before the Day of Trouble, not least because it can come upon us suddenly. It is the strength of our existing relationship with God that will allow us to stand.

Never think that XYZ could not happen to you – or those things only happen to other people! That kind of mindset means you will be unprepared for trouble, not armed for battle, ignorant of Satan's devices. Instead, pray that if XYZ happens you will not faint, and that God will in His mercy send help to you from His sanctuary.

JEJ

*WEDNESDAY 10th

It is better to live right and be poor than to be sinful and rich – Psalm 37:16 (CEV)

SPIRITUAL RICHES LAST – Reading: Psalm 37:10-16; Romans 14:10-23

It is true that there are wicked people who prosper and flourish. When we see this, we may be tempted to envy them or more still doubt God's goodness. Though despised, rejected, and opposed by the world, as grounded women of God we can trust God to take very good care of our needs according to His riches in glory.

Psalm 37:16 tells us, *'A little that a righteous man hath is better than the riches of many wicked'*. Not all Christians are poor, but if we are, our righteousness is more to be desired than the wealth of the wicked. The Bible tells us that, *'Better is a dinner of herbs where there is love, than a stalled ox and hatred therein' (Proverbs 15:17); 'For the kingdom of God is not meat and drink…' (Romans 14:17).* It is about living righteously, having peace with God, the peace of God within ourselves through the Holy Ghost, and with others.

It behoves us not to spend our lives seeking this world's goods which are temporary and will pass away. Sisters, we are not always easily satisfied and often want more, but *'godliness with contentment is great gain…'* (1 Timothy 6:6-10). Our priority should be to, *'Seek first the kingdom of God and His righteousness and all these other things will be added…'* (St Matthew 6:33). These are what are most important and will last.

Missionary M Fraser

Siblings' Day

THURSDAY 11th

Blessed is the man whom thou chastenest, O LORD... - Psalm 94:12

BLESSED IS THE MAN – Reading: Psalm 94:1-23

If we were to ask anyone whether they like being punished, they will look at us in astonishment. *'What kind of foolish question is that?'*, is likely to be our default response.

We often quote the verses of Matthew's gospel 5:10-12, that there is great reward for those blessed by affliction. Having said that, we then default into saying, *'Spare me Lord!'* because we do not want to actually experience those testing qualities.

In this psalm, we question whether or not our God is paying attention to the affairs of this world. Does He not see that the wicked are prospering in their wicked ways? Does He not hear my cry when I call upon His name? Does He not care that I am at the point of giving up, that I just can't take it anymore?

Yes, He does! He is waiting for us to acknowledge our faults and failures, and put our trust and faith in Him. We can no longer excuse ourselves while blaming the nation. There is a need for us to accept corporate responsibility and approach the throne of God in humbleness of spirit.

He then blesses us with a calmness of spirit in the midst of troubles and trials. This is the immediate benefit of learning that some punishments can result in bringing us closer to God – the God who desires only good things for us.

Pastor Londy Esdaille (Nevis)

FRIDAY 12th

God is our refuge and strength, a very present help in trouble - Psalm 46:1

A VERY PRESENT HELP – Reading: Psalm 46:1; Job 23:1-10

One of the many things that I love about God is that He's always there.

Wherever my *'there'* has been, He's been there. Even when God was silent, when I couldn't feel or see Him, in life's absolute chaos, in different types of pain and every kind of sickness and loss. I couldn't always pinpoint exactly where God was but, somehow, I knew that He was there.

Job in his distress said, *'Oh that I knew where I might find Him!' (Job 23:3)*. This sounds like Job thought that God was hard to find, being elusive, perhaps avoiding having a conversation with him to answer his list of questions concerning the calamities that had befallen him.

Job started his search for God by going forward (towards the east). He didn't find God there so changed direction and went backwards towards the west. There was still no sign of God! On the left side, i.e., towards the north where, surely, Job felt, he would connect with God, *'...where He doth work'* but still no results! Job then tried to locate God on the south, i.e., on the right side, but The Omnipresent God seemed to be missing over there too!

Job's dilemma is quite an interesting contrast to that of David's commentary in Psalm 139:7-9, '*Where shall I go from your spirit? or where shall I flee from your presence? If I take the wings of the morning, and dwell in the uttermost parts of the sea; even there shall your hand lead me, and your right hand shall hold me'*. Job couldn't find God, yet David couldn't get away from Him!

We, like Job, do experience times of anxiety and frustration when it seems like God has vanished. But since *'God is!'*, and is never 'not', we can be assured that, '*He is a very present help in trouble'*. **God is always there**!

JEJ

SATURDAY 13th

In my distress I cried unto the LORD, and he heard me – Psalm 120:1

PRAISE DESPITE TROUBLES – Reading: Psalm 120:1-7

Another term for psalms is praises.

It's no wonder for, in The Psalms, are a large portion of songs of praises; they are a collation of individual songs, a selection of praises and thanksgiving, with many other themes.

The Psalms include today's focus verse, a song of deliverance, one of the 'Songs of Degrees'. The writer is praying for deliverance from anguish by the enemy's dishonesty. Wanting just peace, but having to pursue a journey from distress and war.

It's so good to know that we have a God to cry to, the Almighty, the Ever-present Help. He is our Comforter and Friend who hears every prayer, and attends to every need. Only He can transport us out of darkness into light.

In The Psalms, we see many situations where God brings the psalmists *'out of'*, and *'into'*! God transfers from trouble to peace. Delivers from sin unto righteousness. Restores from brokenness to wholeness, and from sickness to health.

In The Psalms we get encouragement such as, *'He that dwells in the secret place of the Most High shall abide…' (Psalm 91:1).* Even Scripture recommends the psalms, to help our spiritual growth and comfort. We often pray from the psalms, *'This poor man cried, and the LORD heard him…' (Psalm 34:6).*

Altogether there's many genres to suit our conditions in The Psalms.

Sis Jx

SUNDAY 14th

Behold, how good and how pleasant it is for brethren to dwell together in unity
Psalm 133:1

UNITY FROM ABOVE – Reading: Psalm 133:1-3

As a child of God, have you ever asked yourself do we have a dysfunctional Church? When we see division, contention, unforgiveness, nepotism, cronyism, and much more - all of these are man-centred. When we are God-centred, we know the Church is the body of Christ, and it is His Church. He is supreme over all things, the completion of Him who Himself completes all things everywhere (Ephesians 1:23).

Thank God for the psalmist who exhorts us on the benefit of unity in the body of Christ. When we are tied together with each other it is, *'good and pleasant' (Psalm 133:1).* We are joined as a whole together with Christ.

As believers we represent the body of Christ, where each member has their own unique function. Similar to the natural body, our hands, fingers, eyes, ears, etc., are used to carry out the work of the ministry. We must be sensitive to each member, no matter how 'small', that member fulfils an important role in the body of Christ.

It is God's purpose and heart for His children to strive to attain unity in the body (John 17:20-23). When the people of God stand together with the same mind and heart, we are a mighty force against the adversary. Believers will enjoy a lifestyle of fellowship, working together and pressing together which is much more enjoyable. Whereas when there are cliques, division, backbiting, and conflict, this hinders the work of the ministry as this is self-centred.

Believers are mandated to build and maintain good relationships with each other. Daily the Holy Ghost teaches us to understand the importance of having a relationship with God. Therefore, unity in the body of Christ brings tremendous blessings.

Have you ever asked yourself how a child of God has unity in the body of Christ? The Word clearly describes the precious ointment upon the head that runs down upon the beard (Psalm 133:2). Wow! Holy Ghost Unity comes down from above. We may try to manipulate and coax others to unite, but true unity comes from God by the Spirit.

Women of God, let us strive to have a spirit-filled heart, and endeavour to keep the unity of the spirit through the bond of peace (Ephesians 4:1).

Missionary Audrey Simpson

MONDAY 15th

I will bless thy name for ever and ever – Psalm 145:1

A DECISION TO PRAISE – Reading: Psalm 34:1-6; 145:1-2

To extol, as described in Psalm 145:1, is to praise with enthusiasm: an outward exclamation of an inward thanksgiving and acknowledgement of God.

Interestingly, David continues in verse two with decision after decision to bless God and to make Him the focus. He doesn't stipulate a time or circumstance in which his praise will happen. He did not say for this moment, for today, or for as long as my situation allows me. No, he boldly says forever and ever. David makes a decision based on who God is, continuing in verse three to declare the greatness of God.

We are invited, implored, even commanded in Scripture to do something that our time and seasons kick against vehemently. Although we do not dismiss our situations or distresses, we make them somehow subject to a greater power, that is to say, even in our darkest hour we take on the character, the thoughts and the ways of Jesus Christ.

We can often feel like David, a man of great emotion. Like him, we endeavour in the deepest part of our being to simply make a decision that God is God. We should make no mistake though that our emotions and challenges will diminish permanently as long as we're in this human flesh, and neither should we ignore them or have to suffer pretence on how we navigate our God-given emotions. In the thick of a storm with tears and sighs, with happiness and celebration, or in sadness, *'I will bless the LORD at all times: His praise shall continually be in my mouth. My soul shall make her boast in the LORD: the humble shall hear thereof, and be glad' (Psalm 34:1-2).*

David made a decision that somehow, in spite of, he would bring the goodness of God into the balance. Even today, God wants to remind us that He cares, and that we should cast, throw, shed with vigour, all our cares onto him, because He cares for us. And as He holds you today, declare, *'I will bless you LORD at all times. Forever and ever'.*

Joy Lear-Bernard

TUESDAY 16th

One generation shall praise thy works to another... - Psalm 145:4

GENERATIONS OF PRAISE – Reading: Psalm 145:1-21

This psalm speaks of the goodness of the LORD.

It speaks of how great is our God and greatly to be praised, and His greatness is unsearchable, hallelujah! Unsearchable: hidden, unfathomable, and mysterious is God's greatness.

He is Alpha and Omega, the beginning and the end. One generation shall praise His works to another and shall declare His mighty acts.

David is encouraging us to be full of praises for all that God has done, is doing and is yet to do. Our praises should be personal and flow ceaselessly. As a family we should teach our children, and our grandchildren, through our lives and actions so that they follow in our footsteps and pass what they learn on to the next generation.

The generation before our generation inspired us, and we should seek to inspire the one behind us by declaring the fresh, new and mighty things God is doing for us. Every day from now until our last breath should carry more than a hundred praises!

I encourage everyone to start the day praising God, and continue throughout the day. Then see how those praises turn to medicine, bullets, blessings, protection, guidance, motivation, and peace, in Jesus' name. Amen!

Sis Esther Miller

*WEDNESDAY 17th

Great is the LORD, and greatly to be praised... - Psalm 48:1

GOD IS GREAT – Reading: Psalm 48:1-14

'Great is the LORD, and greatly to be praised in the city of our God, in the mountain of His Holiness. Beautiful for situation, the joy of the whole Earth, is Mount Zion, on the sides of the north, the city of the great King. God is known in her palaces for a refuge' (Psalm 48:1-3).

I remember this psalm being sung when I was a child in the church growing up. This psalm is also known as a song of the sons of Korah who were inspired to write Psalm 48. It begins with praise and joy for God, *'Great is the LORD and greatly to be praised'*. Truly our God is great; He is an excellent God.

A definition of greatness is, *'of an extent of an amount, or an intensity considerably above the normal or average'*. In verse 2, the psalmist mentions Mount Zion, i.e., Jerusalem, *'the city of the great King'*. Jerusalem is seen and situated as the centre or place of God's greatness; it is the presence of God which is at the centre of such greatness. Jerusalem will be what God has always intended, *'the joy of the whole earth'*.

I encourage everyone reading this; there is greatness in God's presence. God is great.

Missionary Maxine Barclay

International Banana Day

THURSDAY 18th

Why are you discouraged, my soul? Why are you so restless? – Psalm 42:5 (GW)

IN THE DARKEST NIGHT, GOD IS THERE WITH YOU – Reading: Psalm 42:1-11; 43:1-5

There is myth that Christians do not suffer from depression (Ref. David Jeremiah).

Depression does not pick and choose who to cast down. King David and many mighty men of God such as Job, Elijah, Heman, - to name just a few - experienced and struggled with depression. Although the Bible does not directly use the word *'depression'*, except in a few translations and verses, depression is often described as, *'cast down'*, *'despairing'*, *'mourning'*, *'troubled'*, *'terrors'*, *'darkness'* and *'billows gone over me'*.

Depression is defined as a mood disorder that causes a persistent feeling of sadness and loss of interest, which can interfere with your daily functioning (Mayo Clinic.org). There are different types of depression, e.g., Major Depressive Disorder, with symptoms and feelings of sadness, emptiness, worthlessness, guilt, hopelessness, loss of energy, loss of appetite. Depression can present itself in several ways; it can be mild or severe, short-lived, or chronic. Also, Clinical Depression can be chronic and reoccur over many years. Situational Depression is usually shorter, more intense, and mainly tied to a particular event such as a major life change, e.g., illness or trauma, the death of a loved one, divorce or the loss of a job/financial difficulties (Ref: Healthline.com).

David in many of the psalms wrote about his loneliness, heartbrokenness, mourning, being cast down, and struggles (see Psalm 42). Heman, the Ezrahite, is one of the sons of Korah. He wrote Psalm 88 which has been described as one of the darkest chapters recorded in the Scriptures. Heman cried out to God at his lowest. He wrote, *'I am forgotten, cut off from your care, you have thrown me into the darkest depths, your anger weighs me down…'.* Job, with a body full of boils and sores reported, *'I loathed my very life. Therefore, I will give free reign to my complaint, and speak out in the bitterness of my soul' (Job 10:1-2 - NIV).* Though Job maintained his integrity and his faithfulness to God, he struggled deeply mentally and emotionally through the valleys of pain.

I will now share a personal experience of Situational Depression after a Bereavement: I struggled immensely with depression after the death of my husband. I was consumed with grief, fear, and worry at my plight of being (I thought) too young to be a widow. I lost interest in mostly everything around me except of my children. I had their best interests at heart but still felt hopeless, terrified, lonely; cast down and very sad; I could not get myself together. I was also very good at masking over the pain so I could be strong for my children. I kept on telling myself that it was early days and that I would soon feel better. But I felt empty.

My GP called me in for a consultation as a matter of review. He stated that he'd expected to have seen me sooner. He diagnosed me as suffering from Situational Depression after I explained my condition, and recommended three choices of treatments, i.e., going away from the environment, counselling, or medication. I opted to go away. Whilst away, I was able to take the time to reflect, pray, and decide my next course of action. I cut short my time away as feelings of guilt started to trouble me, I felt that I had abandoned my children and had to see and be there for them. I returned home to try and manage.

Within this terrible season of loss and pain, I felt like David in his despair and emptiness, and like Heman in his darkness. But I realised that God had not abandoned me. Gradually I started to feel better. The darkness started to subside and I started to see light in my dark corners. I found healing and relief from my pain and groanings, and my faith grew stronger.

I can evaluate that as a Christian I was not immune or exempt from depression, but rediscovered my hope in the midst of my troubled and darkest of times. My faith was re-established in God. He was always there though it was difficult to acknowledge that during the period of heavy darkness which sometimes I could almost taste.

Missionary M Fraser
Dip HE.
RMN Univ Soton Dip Mental Health Studies

FRIDAY 19th

A father of the fatherless, and a judge of the widows is God – Psalm 68:5

GOD CARES & UNDERSTANDS – Reading: Psalm 68:1-12

There are many people who yearn to be part of a family, and there are those who take their families for granted, even complain about them. I've heard it said that*, 'you can choose your friends but not your families'.*

To those in need of a family, the Lord is a Father to the fatherless, a mother to the motherless, a parent to the orphan, a protector to the widows, and whatever you need Him to be, He will be.

If you have lost precious loved ones, or are on your own and lonely, God cares and understands; He will never fail to care for you. He cares for the afflicted, the oppressed and the helpless. He wants to bring you into His family so that you can experience joy, love, and peace. If you choose to remain outside of His family, then Scripture says you will, *'dwell in a dry land' (Psalm 68:6)*, which is not what God wants for you.

To those of us who know Christ, we should reflect His character by helping the fatherless, widowed, lonely, and those in need, by encouraging them into the family of God.

Rest assured that whatever your situation, God cares and understands. Let us pray today that we exhibit the same compassion and mercy as Christ always does for us.

Lady Pam Lewin

SATURDAY 20th

O my God, I trust in thee: let me not be ashamed – Psalm 25:2

JUST TRUST – Reading: Psalm 25:1-10

To trust God is a learning process, one that can only be based on a true and genuine relationship with Him.

To trust God, you will need to obey Him. Trusting God is a continued discovery and revelation of who God is. As we walk with Him, get to know Him as LORD, our trust grows and becomes stronger. Through knowing Him in our daily walk we confidently rest in our personal experiences, and the Word of God, for who He is.

The process of trusting God and confidence in Him is a life journey. It takes faith, consistency, faithfulness, discipline, sanctification, commitment to prayer, believing and obeying His Word to enable us to go through and withstand our trials. It takes faith (trust) to serve God, for without faith it's impossible to please Him. The experience of God's goodness, grace, mercy, deliverance and healing gives us the confidence to call on Him.

When going through trying times, difficult times, or a tremendous test of faith, reflecting and knowing who God is, like David we say, *'O LORD, I will lift up my soul to you'.* Why? Because we know Him to be our God, we are accepting that we are His child, so we confidently call, letting Him know that we trust Him with what we are going through. Whatever you or I face, we must believe and put our trust in Him knowing that His promises are sure.

David had been through many experiences where God had delivered him. God had done it before and David had no doubt that God would do it again. David trusted, and we can trust God too because He never changes, He is always the same and never fails.

Evangelist June Johnson

*SUNDAY 21st

Yea, let none that wait on thee be ashamed – Psalm 25:3

GOD WILL SHOW UP – Reading: Psalm 25:11-22

David stated, *'let none that wait upon thee be ashamed'.*

Many times, I too like David remind God that He has to come through for me. Why? Because God has always honoured His Word in my life.

Sometimes you have to wait, but He always comes through in the end. I have lost count of how many times I thought I wouldn't make it through but God showed up in the nick-of-time. *'I am counting on you'*, David said, *'the enemies are watching, they surround me and want to eat up my flesh, please don't let me be ashamed for boasting in you, for bragging of my confidence in you.* ***I know*** *you will come through again'.*

David recognised that without God he had no strength so he cried to God, the only one that could weaken the hand of his enemies and destroy them. We have to realise when we are facing our battles that we cannot do it on our own, we must call on the only one who is able deliver. Be persistent and travail. David trusted God and so must we. Talk to Him about our fears.

David, pleaded with God, '*Don't let me be ashamed'.* He was telling God, *'Glorify yourself in my situation, show your almighty power'.* I encourage you to take your problems to the Lord in prayer. Everything we go through we must put our trust and faith in God. God will never let the enemy have the final say, they will stumble and fall. God is the strength of our lives and in this we will be confident. We are victorious, we are overcomers.

God honours His Word above His name. Every battle will be won through Jesus Christ. Continue to call upon Him when you are in trouble. He never let David down and will never let us down.

Evangelist June Johnson

***National Tea Day**

MONDAY 22nd

In God we boast all the day long, and praise thy name for ever – Psalm 44:8

GOD IS TRUSTWORTHY – Reading: Psalm 44:1-8

In a time when they faced difficult and crushing situations, weary and defeated, and it seemed like God was far from them, the psalmists (the sons of Korah) reflected on God's past goodness. They remembered His deliverance in battle and how He overthrew the enemy. Based on history, they felt confident that God would restore.

The spiritual warfare that we face daily we do not fight in our own strength, but in the power of the Holy Ghost. We use every piece of the armour of God as outlined in Ephesians 6:11-13. Truthfully, yes, sometimes we do get weary on the journey, and even question some of the things that happen in our lives. However, we can be assured that God is faithful and can be trusted to keep His Word. He has commanded the victory for us. With His power we can put the enemy to flight and we do so by building up our spiritual muscles with fasting and prayer, thereby getting to the heart of God.

Always our focus must be on God, our own strength will fail us. And to Him always we give the glory and the praise!

Evangelist Marjorie Burgess

TUESDAY 23rd

Teach us to use wisely all the time we have – Psalm 90:12 (CEV)

TEACH ME – Reading: Psalm 90: 1-17

Lord, help us to recognise our limitations and frailty, so that we will be wise and acknowledge our mortality and transiency.

To understand and to appreciate the time that we have, and utilise our allotted time carefully, living to glorify you, just as you have given us the wisdom to know that we need a deliverer, a saviour, who we cannot live without, or die without knowing in order to inherit everlasting life. We need you Lord for salvation, also to know that you are always there to help and to guide us according to your promise, *'I will never leave you nor forsake you…' (Hebrews 13:5).*

Instruct us, for in our weakness we do foolishly! We are strong only by your Divine Power. Secure us for life, and abundant life, through your grace that we may live forever in your presence.

We are reminded that you, O LORD, *'sit on the circle of the earth. And the inhabitants are as grasshoppers' (Isaiah 40:22).* As tiny, vulnerable creatures we are in your hand. You manipulate, move and change us, and work for and through us. We are your handmaidens. You skilfully control and orchestrate our existence as you desire. We're completely at your mercy, both to will and to do according to your good pleasure. Because of your lovingkindness and tender mercies we are saved and protected, hence there's no need for us to worry or fear. You are a great, loving Father and a good and gracious King who rules justly. Your intention towards us is that we should prosper; your thoughts for us are for a good outcome.

The prayer of division 90 of The Psalms, is only one of many prayers in The Psalms which address our humanity. In The Psalms, all the ways of life are covered.

Sis Jx

WEDNESDAY 24th

It was good for me that I have been afflicted Psalm 119:71

THE VALLEY EXPERIENCES – Reading: Psalm 61:1-8

I remember listening to the testimony of a man who became so upset with the Lord because of his present situation, and it seemed as if his prayers fell on deaf ears.

After some time, he had to take his son of four months to the GP for his injections. After the first injection his son was crying uncontrollably. Although the father wanted to protect his son, he had to allow the nurse to give the remaining injections. He had no way of explaining to his son that the pain was necessary. It was then that he began to thank God for what he was going through.

There are times when God allows us to go through some experiences that are uncomfortable, to say the least! We are told that in order for muscle to develop, it has to be put through the stress of exercise. In the book of Hebrews, the writer encourages the saints by letting them know that, *'no chastening seems to be joyful; for the present, but painful; nevertheless, afterwards it yields the peaceable fruit of righteousness to those who have been trained by it' (Hebrews 12:11 - NKJV).*

There is so much we can learn from these experiences:

1. Patience – *'Wait on the Lord and be of good courage' (*Psalm 27:14)
2. Our focus must be on God alone – *'Lord my eyes are upon you' (*2 Chronicles 20:12)
3. We must use our God-given resources – *'Pray without ceasing'* (1 Thessalonians 5:17)

And so much more.

When we begin to understand and accept that God is perfecting us, we will truly join with the psalmist and say, *'It was good for me that I have been afflicted' (Psalm 119:71).*

Deveen Smith

THURSDAY 25th

Let every thing that hath breath praise the LORD. Praise ye the LORD – Psalm 150:6

WORSHIP IN EFFECT – PLEASE DO NOT DISTURB – Reading: Psalm 150:6

When breath and instruments unite to rejoice in the Lord, a reception is released for worship. His consuming fire will receive our offerings of praise. Let time be suspended in His presence. Let no stone take your place…

The sound of praise, let it ripple through the air.

The sound of praise, let the echo fill the surroundings.

Praises to God within His sanctuary, let my temple honour His majesty!

From His sanctuary, let worship overflow to soar the sound of praise in the realms, where the heavens declare the glory of God.

When the trumpet sounds, the feast to come as we await the trump of God.

Hands, arms, and feet we coordinate in honour of His worthiness, making melody through the strings that meet to vibrate sounds sweet.

With each pluck and strum of the hand making melody of praise to God.

The clashing crescendo of cymbals send vibrations, reverberates through hands.

With our vocals we release our joy containers of blessings thanks and honour from lungs opened to praise the Lord.

We worship our Royal Majesty.

He is Lord Jesus Christ.

Amen.

CDP

FRIDAY 26th

If it had not been the LORD who was on our side, now may (you) say – Psalm 124:1

THE LORD IS ON OUR SIDE – Reading: Psalm 124:1-8

It is thought that Psalm 124 was written by David after he defeated the Philistines (2 Samuel 5:17-25). He was probably mulling over events and how God had preserved his life.

During my times of reflections, my mind often takes me on a journey. Sometimes the journey is as close as yesterday, at other times it can be as far away as 20 years ago or beyond. It is good to think on the past, as long as we don't stay there.

The memories, especially the unpleasant ones, occasionally make me think of today's psalm, *'If it had not been…' (v 1-2).* The truth is that, even though we had bad or traumatic experiences, how much worse might they have ended, '*if it had not been…*'!

The KJV says: *'If it had not been the LORD who was on our side'.* LORD in capital letters refers to Jehovah, eternal and self-existent one. He who needs no help was who was on our side in battle, when the enemy came in like a flood. The LORD was on our side during unemployment, sickness, marital and family turbulence, separation, depression, false accusations, grief, poverty, scandal and shame – yes, through it all.

I can't be the only one who dreads to imagine what life would have looked like, '*If it had not been…'.* Sometimes we give credit for our survival to a good doctor, good lawyer, a counsellor or good friend, when really all glory and praise should go to the LORD who was on our side; *'…show me where **you** brought me from and where I could have been…'.*

Let's pause right now, and thank the only one that we need to have on our side. Magnify the LORD for fighting and winning on our behalf!

JEJ

SATURDAY 27th

…yet have I not seen the righteous forsaken – Psalm 37:25

UNPRECEDENTED – Reading: Psalm 37:23-31

In 2020, the world experienced a pandemic called COVID-19. We will never forget the devastating impact that the virus had on us in so many different ways; our world has not been the same since then.

During 2020, we repeatedly heard a particular word used, i.e., *'unprecedented'*, which means *'never done or known before'*, or, *'unparalleled'*, *'singular'*, *'out of the ordinary'*. News of the indiscriminate virus dominated the headlines for many months, the constant repetitive reporting instilled fear into some hearts and affected the minds of many. The blast of COVID-19 has been recorded in history books worldwide.

David in Psalm 37:25 boldly states and testifies of something which throughout his generation was unprecedented and, thank God, is still unheard of today. He said: *'I have been young, and now am old;* ***yet*** *have I not seen the righteous forsaken, nor his seed begging bread'.*

I am confident that as you read this page, you can join with David, and with me, and say that not once in your lifetime, have you ever heard of or seen the godly abandoned or left alone by God. Never!

There are no accounts of failure anywhere! God's record remains unbroken! His faithfulness still is, and will always be, unprecedented!

JEJ

SUNDAY 28th

...thou art my hope, O LORD God...- Psalm 71:5

CONFIDENCE IN GOD – Reading: Psalm 71:1-24

David petitions God in a time of vulnerability. He was not the ruddy-faced youth anymore who defeated Goliath with help of God (1 Samuel 17:50-53). Neither was he the overconfident warrior king that inadvertently numbered Israel (2 Samuel 24: 1; 1 Chronicles 21:1) incurring the anger of God.

He was still the King, more mature but not necessarily 'old' as we may suppose, but rather looking toward old age (Psalm 71:18). The enemies of King David may have misread the situation by presumption, saw his vulnerability and thought God had forsaken him (v 9-11). There are reasons to consider that this psalm was possibly written at a time of the rebellion of his son, Absalom.

Amid David's concern, he remembers the faithfulness of God to him when he was a younger man. He reflects on the years of experience that shaped him to be able to testify and confidently bless God. His memory of the goodness of God boosted his confidence. At this point he declares continuity in praise, his joy in the Lord revived his spirit.

When we reflect how far God has brought us, we can also declare like King David, He is our Lord, our hope and trust. Let us know Him.

Our life is in the Master's hand.

CDP

MONDAY 29th

He...shall doubtless come again with rejoicing, bringing his sheaves... – Psalm 126:6

THE RISK OF FAITH – Reading: Psalm 126:5-6; James 2:14-26

Disappointment can bring discouragement and with that, demotivation. When you've done your best and your plan failed, it can take much effort to try again. When we retry, although going through the process, in our minds we may well be wondering if we're wasting our time.

Fear of failure can keep us inactive as we convince ourselves that, *'it's not going to work – look at what happened last time'.* But I heard someone say once, *'Faith is a risk and needs no facts'.*

While we ponder on that powerful, thought-provoking statement, I encourage each of us to try one more time at the thing which God has spoken to us and said that it will come to pass.

The anonymous writer of today's Word, Psalm 126:6, describes the sombre, solemn mood, and I'd say even reluctant mood of the sower, *'He that goeth forth and weepeth, bearing precious seed…'.* They're sowing – giving away – losing something precious – letting something go - and they're broken whilst doing it in a place that seems to be less than fertile. Still they bring their basket of seeds and sow. They know the Law of Nature. Nature's law says that, in time, not only will you reap what you sow, but you will get back more than what you sow. Nobody knows how many apples are in one seed planted, but we know it will be more than one.

The psalmist then looks to the future and concludes by talking of the same sower; God has given joy to replace the sower's sorrow. He who was sad sowing seeds returns one day from the field with shouts of rejoicing bringing sheaves, they are no more just seeds.

Note: you will never get a sheaf, if you don't take the risk to sow a seed.

JEJ

TUESDAY 30th

God is in the midst of her; she shall not be moved: God shall help her and that right early – Psalm 46:5

I SHALL NOT BE MOVED - Reading -Mark 4:35-41

Many readers of this page will be familiar with the lesson from Mark 4:38-40, where Jesus' disciples are caught in a severe storm. The severity was such that everyone on board feared for their lives – everyone apart from Jesus! He was fast asleep.

Mark, who generally doesn't give 'minor' details, thought it necessary to record that the water was not just outside but had also filled up the ship. It's one thing to deal with a crisis that's at a distance or outside your walls, but it's a different feeling completely when the problem invades your space and there's water in your boat!

The disciples stared at Jesus in amazement as He slept peacefully while they were (they thought) at the point of death. Probably I'd have said, *'Jesus! Are you being serious, are you for real?'*. The disciples didn't quite put it that way - they woke Him up and said, *'Master, carest thou not that we perish?'*. They didn't realise that a ship could not sink with Jesus on board.

That's the angle from which the psalmists of today's focus verse, i.e., the sons of Korah, are coming. *'God is in the midst of her'* to protect where His people dwelt. *'Her'* meaning Jerusalem. *'In the midst of her',* for us means that as Spirit-filled believers, God dwells in our innermost being, it is He *'that is able to keep us from falling and to present (us) faultless before the presence of His glory with exceeding joy' (Jude:24).*

'*When all around my soul gives way…'* a songwriter said. People and things around me will crumble and fail, but I'm glad that God keeps my soul so that it does not give way. With God residing inside of me, it is well with my soul, I shall not be moved.

JEJ

INHALER TECHNIQUE - LET'S BREAK IT DOWN!

Most of us will know somebody who has an inhaler. Inhalers come in all sorts of shapes and sizes but they all have one thing in common – they are used to help manage long term respiratory conditions such as Asthma and COPD (Chronic Obstructive Pulmonary Disease). They may also occasionally be prescribed for temporary use in short term conditions such as chest infections.

Inhalers come in three basic types – DPI (dry powder inhalers), MDI (metered dose inhalers) or Respimat (mist) inhalers.

A person may be prescribed the best inhaler in the world with the most effective combination of medications to help manage their condition, but they are of NO USE if they are used incorrectly! The medication needs to reach the base of the lungs to be able to work, not being sprayed into the air, or breathed back out the nostrils.

I hope that these basic inhaler technique instructions will help, even if you say, "I've had Asthma since I was a child so I know how to use my inhaler", we all need a refresher:

DRY POWDER INHALERS – are kinder to the environment as they do not contain CFC gases; they do not require a spacer (aerochamber) to enhance their efficacy, and are often easier to use than the MDI inhalers. There are many DPI devices such as Nexthalers, Turbohalers, Accuhalers, Ellipta's and Easybreathers, to name but a few.

METERED DOSE INHALERS – (spray inhalers) have often been the inhaler of choice in the past, but as they contain CFC gases and can sometimes be difficult to use correctly, are more commonly being 'swapped' for DPI inhalers. MDIs are recommended to be used with an aerochamber (spacer) as this piece of equipment reduces incorrect technique; but it can be bulky and doesn't really quite fit into your evening purse!

RESPIMAT INHALERS – often used if patients do not have the inspiratory effort (I call this 'suckability') to inhale the other types of inhalers efficiently enough. They produce a mist which can simply be breathed in with little or no extra effort.

SO WHAT IS THE CORRECT TECHNIQUE?

Always check your inhaler is in date, and the exit hole is not blocked. Take the lid off the mouthpiece.

1. MDIs need to be shaken a few times, so that the medicine and the propellant are mixed correctly (otherwise you may get too much propellant with no medicine, or too much medicine with not enough propellant to come out of the device). DPIs and Respimat do not need to be shaken.
2. Sit upright or stand, with head slightly tilted back, as if about to sniff the air.
3. B-R-E-A-T-H-E O-U-T in order to empty your lungs and make space to receive the inhaled medication (if you don't breathe out, there's no space to receive the medication!!)
4. Put the inhaler in your mouth and seal your lips around the mouthpiece, taking care not to block any air vents.

5. Next – just after you start to INHALE, activate the inhaler device so that the direction of airflow is into your lungs. For DPIs, inhale deep and quickly; for MDIs inhale slowly and deeply; for Respimats inhale at normal breathing pace.
6. HOLD YOUR BREATH for 5-10 seconds, or as long as comfortable. This will enable the medication to reach the base of your lungs and be deposited where it is needed. Just think – if you inhale your device, and then start talking or breathing out straight away, all the medication will go into the atmosphere and not into your lungs which need it!

For Further Advice:

www.asthmaandlung.org.uk – this has a video section to show all types of inhalers and their corresponding techniques.

www.nhsggc.org.uk – NHS Glasgow has a wonderful step-by-step guide to inhaler technique. You can print out your particular inhaler so you have it to refer to as a reminder.

If in doubt, visit your local Pharmacist or GP/Practice Nurse.

Nurse Elaine Richards

2023

may
Inner Beauty

WEDNESDAY 1st

...if anyone is in Christ, the new creation has come...2 Corinthians 5:17 (NIV)

TRULY BEAUTIFUL – Reading: 2 Corinthians 5:11-21

When we decorate or 'spring clean' our homes it is then that we often realise the bad state it was in. It's also not until we replace something old and worn that we realise how bad its condition was. From the outside, the house looks the same, but when you step inside it's different, more beautiful.

Think about how good we feel when we discard our old clothes, shoes, furnishings, etc., and replace them with new ones. We feel good and our homes look good. Well, that's how the Lord feels when we replace our old self with a new self – He feels good! Our old selves were fleshy, dirty, and in need of a makeover until the day Christ found us and we left our old selves in the baptismal watery grave, rising to walk a new, clean, and beautiful life in Christ.

Scripture says in today's reading that, *'old things are passed away…'* meaning they're gone, never to return. Satan sometimes tries to bring back those old ways, but they have, or, should have been, buried in Christ.

Today, give thanks to the Lord that you are no longer the person that you used to be, but someone new and beautiful. From the outside your features are the same, but the inner-you has been transformed. The reason why the inner-you is now so beautiful is because you are walking in the joy and peace of God.

If your ways are not beautiful, try walking with Christ Jesus who will make you truly beautiful from the inside such that your inner beauty will shine through to the outside for all to see.

Lady Pam Lewin

THURSDAY 2nd

But the fruit of the Spirit is love, joy, peace, longsuffering, gentleness, goodness, faith... - Galatians 5:22-23

SOAKING IN THE CHARACTER OF CHRIST – Reading: Galatians 5:16-26

Some say the fruit of the Spirit being singular is love, and from it is developed the others named in Galatians 5:22-23, such as joy, peace, temperance, meekness... Knowing that God Himself is Love, we can be confident that the influence of His Holy Spirit on the inside of us will result in the development of His character in us as women and sisters.

Our beauty shelves, media, and TV ads, are brimming with lotions, pills, miracle creams and supplements that, should we use them continually, we're promised to emerge ageless and flawless. The idea being that what we ingest, or absorb on the inside, has a dramatic and inevitable effect. It has to work!

The Word of GOD, the Holy Spirit of God, is potent and inevitable in changing a person. Given time, the effects of His Living Word cannot help itself in giving a glow to the character of women who are called daughters of God.

It may seem a callous but much needed reality to challenge us as women in these times. It is neither the outward appearance, the gifting, articulation or affluence, or influence, that names you or I as God's child, but the abundance of the heart. It is the character marked by the Fruit of the Spirit or the works of the flesh that determines who our spiritual DNA comes from. The Fruit (evidence) of the Spirit is critically named in order for us to honestly ascertain and measure ourselves to get nearer to Him and know who He is.

Like Esther bathing in pure ointment, a soak in the Word of God is shown by our fruit.

Joy Lear-Bernard

FRIDAY 3rd

...every good tree bringeth forth good fruit... – Matthew 7:17

CHECK THE FRUIT – Reading: Luke 6:43-45

We are warned repeatedly that we are living in the end times. Sisters, we must be on our watch, we cannot be sleeping and oblivious to the fulfilment of prophecy.

We live in a world where the signs of the times are visible everywhere. The Word of God describes what to look for. One aspect that will be evident is, *'a form of godliness, but denying the power thereof: from such turn away' (2 Timothy 3:5).*

God's Word reminds us in this season to be mindful of false teachers and prophets. The description rightly attributes to wolves in sheep's clothing. They look the part outwardly, but inwardly are ravenous wolves ready to kill, steal and destroy the children of God. The Word raises the red flag and warns believers that evil company will corrupt our behaviours, which will ultimately turn us away from the truth.

Sisters, we must be observant of the fruit which is being exhibited in ourselves and in others; if this is to propel self-agenda, it is false doctrine and not the inspired Word of God.

Therefore, we must pay attention to the lifestyle of prophets/teachers and not be blinded by their eloquence! Look for righteousness, faithfulness and humility in the way that they live their lives. Always remember that when one submits to the will of God, this becomes a lifestyle. Examine what is being taught. I implore every woman to be like the Berean brethren and check the Scriptures to see if what you are hearing is so. Check whether what is being taught is man-centred which will appeal to itching ears, or Jesus Christ and Him crucified. If what is being taught is merely a form of entertainment, where there is no substance, ask God for the spirit of discernment, as the next step will be falling away from the faith.

If there is no good fruit, or no fruit of positive virtue, both are fit for the fire. The spirit of deception is rampant, but be not deceived, *'God is not mocked whatsoever a man soweth, that shall he also reap' (Galatians 6:7).*

The visible fruit is who we have become, the growth of the fruit will be seen on the day of harvest. This will either be good or bad, and will reveal the type of tree we are.

Missionary Audrey Simpson

SATURDAY 4th

...by their fruits ye shall know them – Matthew 7:20

YOU ARE KNOWN BY WHAT YOU'VE SOWN – Reading: St Matthew 7:16-20

Most plants, as they emerge from the soil, start their life with two tiny leaves known as dicotyledon. At this stage, it is difficult to determine what type of plant it is unless you were previously told. But as it grows, it slowly begins to manifest what type of plant it is. Its leaves begin to take on a different shape, a different colour and/or a specific fragrance.

Sometimes, as the plant grows and becomes a tree, we are able to identify the tree by its leaves. However, unless trained, mistakes are often made by trying to determine a tree by its leaves alone... we need to see its fruits.

We are created in the image of God. The beauty of God's creation was hidden in the seed. David tells us in Psalm 139:15, *'My substance was not hidden from thee when I was made in secret, and curiously wrought in the lowest parts of the earth'.* It is only when a seed is planted in unhealthy soil or an unfavourable environment that the true seedling is distorted; its inner beauty becomes compromised.

Let us ask God to remove every hidden thing that does not give Him glory. Sisters, God has made us beautiful. Let His beauty be seen.

Deveen Smith

*SUNDAY 5th

...your beauty should consist of your true inner self, the ageless beauty of a gentle and quiet spirit... - 1 Peter 3:4 (GNT)

INNER ORNAMENTS – Reading: 1 Peter 3:1-7

How would you define beauty? What makes a person beautiful in your opinion?

In the UK, each year billions of pounds are spent by women on cosmetics which we hope will help enhance our external beauty. We choose our skin products with care, and buy the best that we can afford. We take note of the ingredients and sometimes make a selection based on the recommendation of a friend, or we tell our sisters and friends of a product that works.

It is very important as ladies that we make time to treat and pamper ourselves, that we don't give ourselves away all week whether to our families, ministry, or career, and thereby become worn down. We should be able to look in the mirror and say, *'You're looking good, girl!',* without comparing ourselves to another woman. But what really makes us beautiful cannot be bought online or in a store, neither is it something that we pin on or add on. True beauty does not begin from the outside, it shines from within. Peter describes it as, *'the hidden part of the heart, in that which is not corruptible, even the ornament of a meek and quiet spirit, which is in the sight of God of great price' (1 Peter 3:3-4).*

Having a meek and quiet spirit does not mean that we can't voice our opinions, or stand up for ourselves. Peter is not saying that we should allow ourselves to be pushed around or bullied, neither is he saying that if you're married your husband should control you and do all of the talking. Peter is alluding to us being or becoming women of grace. When we speak, we should be mindful of what we say and how we say it. Our conduct should always be courteous and graceful, not rude and aggressive.

Most of us can think of outwardly 'beautiful' women who are only 'beautiful' when they are silent; there is nothing beautiful about their speech or temperament! So, ladies, let's not go broke or overdraw our bank accounts managing our external image! At the end of each day, as well as applying your night cream and eye gel, do some honest introspection. Take time to consider how you came across to others during the day, and re-adorn your inner-self with the fruit of the Spirit (Galatians 5:22-23).

'...beauty is something internal that can't be destroyed. Beauty expresses itself in a gentle and quiet attitude which God considers precious' (1 Peter 3:4 GW).

JEJ

***Lemonade Day**

*MONDAY 6th

...the tongue is a little member...how great a matter a little fire kindleth! James 3:5

FROM THE INSIDE OUT – Reading: Psalm 139:1-24

'Out of the abundance of the heart the mouth speaks' (Luke 6:45).

This, coupled with the power that we know resides in the words we speak, provides insight into why so much of Scripture deals with the state of the Inner Man. Conversely, the world's obsession with outward beauty brings vanity, greed, egocentrism and misattributed worth. Whilst people may focus on the outward appearance, God is primarily concerned with the state of the heart (I Samuel 16:7).

In James' epistle, he highlights the great damage that the tiny organ of the tongue can do if left unbridled. It behoves us as children of God to live in the power of a transformed mind and heart: if the root is righteous then so too will be the fruit. The psalmist prays (and we often recite) that the words of our mouth and meditations of our heart are to be acceptable to the LORD (Psalm 19:14).

Our inner beauty can only be found in conforming to the image of Christ. His meekness, temperance, kindness, self-sacrifice, and total submission to the will of the Father are the perfect example to us.

Here is the Believer's Inner Beauty regime:

1) Wash daily with the Word (Ephesians 5:26)
2) Put on salvation as a foundation (Psalm 149:4)
3) To brighten the complexion, engage in praise (Psalm 42:11)
4) Stay focused on the Lord for radiance (Psalm 34:5)
5) Use The Mirror: hear and do The Word to check condition (James 1:23-24)
6) Ensure daily renewal (2 Corinthians 4:16)
7) For lasting results have a gentle and quiet spirit (I Peter 3:3-4)

B E McKenzie

Early May Bank Holiday

TUESDAY 7th

Does a fountain send forth at the same place sweet water and bitter? - James 3:11

THERE IS NO INCONSISTENCY IN NATURE – Reading: James 3:1-12

When God saves us, he transforms our lives both inside and outside.

When we receive the Holy Ghost, we receive the nature of Christ which works through us to enable changes in our attitude and lifestyle to take place. The old man (old nature) is crucified and the lives of the meek are beautified with salvation. James 3 tells us that what comes out of the mouth indicates to the individual what nature you are living by, either by the sin nature or the new holy nature given by God.

According to Galatians 5:16, let the Holy Spirit guide our lives then we won't be doing what the sinful nature craves and desires. The sinful nature wants to do evil which is opposite of what the Holy Spirit desires. These two forces are constantly fighting against each other.

James asks these questions: *'Doth a fountain send forth at the same time sweet water and bitter? Can a fig tree, my brethren, bear olives berries? either a vine, figs?' (James 3-11-12).* Christians cannot live a holy life and an unholy life at the same time! This is contrary with the spiritual nature just as it is unnatural for the fig tree to bear olive berries, and the fountain to yield both sweet and bitter water at the same time. To remain consistent in our walk with God, it requires a committed life to the Holy Spirit and His Word.

What we say and how we say it indicates what kind of heart we have. Jesus said, *'A good man out of the good treasures of the heart bringeth forth good things and an evil man out of the evil treasure bringeth forth evil things' (Matthew 12:35).* Therefore, we must as Christians live in sync with the nature of Christ (Galatians 5:22-23).

When we possess and live these godly qualities, our lives will be beautiful – reflective of our source, Jesus Christ. A product is always consistent with its source.

Missionary M Fraser

WEDNESDAY 8th

Create in me a clean heart, O God; and renew a right spirit within me – Psalm 51:10

HEART OF THE MATTER – Reading: Psalm 51:10-19

The heart is the centre of our being. It is the seat of our thoughts, emotions and conscience.

Scripture says what comes out of a person is what pollutes them. Also, guard your heart for out of it is the issues of life. David prayed for a new heart. He had transgressed from the heart so that's what came out and led to sinful actions. In order for a complete change in behaviour, he needed a change of heart. The reason that David asked for creation of a clean heart is that beauty is from the inside, and then reflects its elegance on the outside. In other words, with a clean heart our behaviour will be pure.

When your inner being is unstained, your outer actions are upright. God desires truth on the inward parts, yet as women we tend to work more on portraying beauty on the outside in our appearance. We love to beautify what's visible, and also judge based on what is visual. We spend lots of time and money fixing up our externals, but we ought to be more concerned and make more effort to take care of the inner person.

Saints ought to concentrate on making the inside beautiful, this always reveals itself on the outside. Jesus criticised the custom of beautifying the outside of tombs - painted in white signified purity. The appearance of these *'whited'* (white-washed) sepulchres looked beautiful and clean yet, in actual fact, on the inside there was no beauty at all. Jesus likened some individuals to *'white washed sepulchres' (Matthew 23:27)*, who maintained their outer appearance only, but lacked inner purity and beauty.

'God will beautify the meek with salvation' (Psalm 149:4). Salvation allows the beauty of Jesus to be seen on the outside, from what is coming out from within.

Sis Jx

THURSDAY 9th

Let my words and meditation be acceptable in your sight, O LORD...Psalm 19:14

OUR INNER SANCTUARY – Reading: Psalm 19:1-14

We frequently recite this verse of Scripture as a benediction following prayer: *'Let the words of my mouth, and the meditation of my heart, be acceptable in thy sight, O Lord, my strength, and my redeemer' (Psalm 19:14).*

From a child, several of us have been taught this verse; it has become an anchor for so many in the seasons of life.

The psalmist wrote this as a revelation of how unique and transforming God's words are in our lives. The Word of God beautifies us from inside out, that's where real beauty starts, not from what the outside appears to look like. A place of inner beauty where stated, *'a place wherein His honour (God) dwells' (Psalm 26:8)*. The inner sanctuary, a space of reflection, a place that nourishes our spirit...it is a place where a sense of wellbeing provides solace, comfort, and strength in our daily walk with God.

Inner beauty does not refer to what we look like on the outside, it is where God's words are held, and we meditate on them in order to reach a place of acceptance (receiving of God's love) in our souls.

That is the inner beauty of our walk with God; we honour His Word, meditate, and apply them to our walk. We become fully acceptable in *'His sight'* and become a reflection of His image... in which we are created.

Minister Hedy

FRIDAY 10th

Let this mind be in you, which was also in Christ Jesus – Philippians 2:5

INNER BEAUTY THAT IS SEEN – Reading: Philippians 2:1-11

A prayer:

Let the beauty of Jesus be seen in me
All His wondrous compassion and purity
O, thou Spirit divine, all my nature refine
'til the beauty of Jesus be seen in me.

(Let the Beauty of Jesus – AWT Orsborn)

This song is our challenge for today, i.e., either the beauty of Jesus will be seen in us by others or, if it can't be seen, that our nature may be refined and transformed by the Holy Ghost until He can be seen!

Do some reflections later, and honestly assess how you got on.

JEJ

SATURDAY 11th

...let the peace of God rule in your hearts...and be ye thankful – Colossians 3:15

INNER PEACE – Reading: Colossians 3:1-17

'Peace does not dwell in outward things, but within the soul' - (Francois Fenelon)

Have you ever encountered someone who is always angry: walks angrily, speaks with an angry tone, is never happy, and is very hard to please? In fact, we try to stay away from them because they are not nice people to be around. Someone once said to me that angry people are unhappy people and have no inner peace; I believe this to be true.

We need a healthy working heart to live a healthy working life. If we allow anything other than peace to rule our hearts then we are not living in peace but fear, anger, and unhappiness.

Before the Lord left this earth, he said in John 14:27, *'Peace I leave with you, my peace I give unto you: not as the world giveth, give I unto you. Let not your heart be troubled, neither let it be afraid.'.*

If we have the peace of God then peace will reign in our hearts, and we will have peace with one another because out of our hearts are the issues of life (Proverbs 4:23).

Know Jesus, know peace.
No Jesus, no peace. (Anon)

The world continues to marvel at how we can remain calm in difficult circumstances – that's the peace of God that rules our hearts and gives us inner beauty. Let us be thankful to God today for inner peace and beauty.

Lady Pam Lewin

SUNDAY 12th

Blessed are the peacemakers: they shall be called the children of God – Matt 5:9

REAL BEAUTY – Reading: Matthew 5:1-12

On the day that we were born, all of us were beautiful inside and outside. As we grew, each of us developed our own personality.

Real beauty is who we are on the inside and includes kindness, love and compassion. Our true beauty does not depend on our physical appearance, hair style, complexion, stature nor the clothes we wear. The LORD said to Samuel, *'Look not on his countenance nor on the height of his stature, for men looketh on the outward appearance but God looketh on the heart' (1 Samuel 16:7).*

We are introduced to one of the most important Scripture verses about beauty from 1 Peter 3:3-4; it says, *'whose adorning, let it not be that outward adorning of plaiting the hair and of wearing of gold, or of putting on apparel, but let it be the hidden man of the heart in that which is not corruptible, even the ornament of a meek and gentle spirit which is in the sight of God of great price'.*

Real beauty reflects in how we behave towards others, how we react when we are hurt, ridiculed, and even when things don't go our own way. In the Beatitudes, Jesus said, *'Blessed are the peacemakers for they shall be called the children of God' (Matthew 5:9).* It is not just a phrase but a call to live in the light of Jesus every hour of the day.

Peacemakers are called the children of God because we have a new heart, one like the heart of God. Our lives have been transformed and enriched with beautiful godly qualities, i.e., the fruit of the Spirit. God beautifies the meek with salvation according to Psalm 149:4. This implies that God garnishes, embellishes and decorates our lives with His peace.

When our hearts are made spiritually beautiful, we exude the beauty of Christ. God desires to bring holy cheerfulness into the lives of the Christian, this is our beauty and a great ornament to our profession.

Missionary M Fraser

MONDAY 13th

Ye are all children of the light, and the children of the day...
1 Thessalonians 5:5

WOMEN OF THE LIGHT & OF THE DAY – Reading: 1 Thessalonians 5:1-11

Darkness and light are the opposite of the same coin. Everything that is about darkness spiritually separates us from God as He represents light or the day. We were all living in darkness which speaks of our past before the Father drew us to Him (St John 6:44).

Light naturally dispels darkness and allows us to see clearly what we are doing. The only light in this dark world is Jesus. He has given believers in Him the gift of the Holy Spirit to tabernacle within us. This enables believers to keep our light on the spiritual lampstand where others may see and know His good works (Matthew 5:14;16).

Believers in Christ who are Spirit-filled must imitate Christ, and shine the light of the Gospel of Jesus Christ brightly. In so doing others will be drawn into the kingdom of His dear Son, first by hearing the Word, and then becoming doers of the Word. I encourage each person reading this Daily Devotional to develop an appetite for the Word of God with the help of the Holy Ghost.

Paul the Apostle was encouraging the Thessalonian brethren to remember who they are in Jesus Christ. Paul exhorted them to represent Jesus Christ in their character, behaviour and attitude. Believers in this season must also know who we are in Christ. We are Children of the Light who are no longer bound by sin and death. God has given us His righteousness, cleansed and justified His children, making us clean just as if we have never sinned. Therefore, we must shine the light of Jesus Christ in this world of darkness which also enables fellowship with each other.

Like the Thessalonians, believers have nothing to fear concerning the coming Day of the Lord. If we live as people of the light, Jesus assures us we have the promise of the blessed hope, that one day soon and very soon we will live and reign with him eternally.

Missionary Audrey Simpson

TUESDAY 14th

Follow peace...and holiness, without which no man shall see the Lord – Heb.12:14

HOLINESS - TRUE BEAUTY – Reading: Hebrews 12:14-29

Holiness. Some say this word is outdated, but God has not changed, and His word cannot be re-invented.

Holiness, for the believer defined, is really a state of sanctification and purity: God's absolute beauty standard for His bride-to-be. The inward decoration He desires for His creation is to be like Him. This is His mind. God has seldom been interested in outward appearance; He has always been more concerned with the heart.

We have long pursued and invested in everything to perfect this temporary and fading external casing. Yet our hearts can be dark, deficient, and void of the beautiful character of our God. A pretty face but lacking in grace, temperance, meekness, longsuffering and charity.

Are you decorated with compassion and bowels of mercies? Are you following peace in the way you think, act, and speak? This is what matters!

Beloved, the Word of God is our mirror, and we must allow it to dress us in the way that God has pre-determined for us to be holy and without blame before Him in love.

The writer of Hebrews stresses the importance of pursuing peace with all men and holiness - following it like a GPS to a beautiful destination – our motivation being that we might see Him, the one whom our soul loveth: the Lord Jesus!

Name withheld

*WEDNESDAY 15th

...God...sanctify you wholly; and... your whole spirit and soul and body be preserved blameless... - 1 Thessalonians 5:23

THE INNER BEAUTY PRODUCT – Reading: 1 Thessalonians 5:12-28

As women, most of us tend to have many beauty products. Each product differing for each part of the body and purpose.

I will assume that many of us are aware of the golden rule that what is used on the rest of body is not used for the face. We use special cloths, cleansers, moisturisers, serums, powders etc., on our face, with the purpose of preserving our looks and skin health so our beauty shines through each day over the course of our lives.

We are reminded in today's focus verse that it's the very God of peace who *'sanctifies us wholly'*. Just as we have 'sanctified' products for a specific use, God uses His Spirit, His holiness, His peace, His love and His grace to sanctify us and set us apart unto Himself. This sanctification is not limited to just your face or a specific part of the body, but your entire being is sanctified, your whole spirit and soul and body. Our beauty products are created to help maintain and preserve our looks (apparently lol), and similarly in the spiritual sense the sanctification from the very God of peace is what preserves and keeps us blameless and faultless spirit, soul and body.

These products are called 'beauty' products specifically, as they're meant to maintain and enhance our external beauty, but the wonderful gift of the Holy Spirit, sanctification and holiness, are what truly makes our whole being beautiful. We are blessed to have true inner beauty because God lives within and shines through us.

Minister Kay Dawkins/ MinK

International Day of Families

THURSDAY 16th

Deceit is in the heart of them that imagine evil: but to the counsellors of peace is joy
Proverbs 12:20

A HEART CONDITION – Reading: Proverbs 12:17-28; Isaiah 29:13-17

Deceit (mirmah; dolos) is the intentional misleading or beguiling of another. Deceit can show in different forms, e.g., exaggeration, flattering lips, lying.

From the deception in the garden of Eden, deceit has found a route into the heart. The Lord Jesus teaches His disciples about the things that defile the heart. Deceit is listed among the evil thoughts that proceed from within (Mark 7:21-23).

The word used for '*heart*' in the Old Testament, '***lebab'*** (Hebrew), describes *the inner man; the mind, the will.* This is the same thought used when God was grieved in heart concerning the wickedness of man (Genesis 6:6). It grieved God to his eternal core.

We see the underhand effects of deceit in this world, from government to social living. Even with the invention of the polygraph or lie detector, human effort cannot root out deceit. Jeremiah described the seemingly hopeless condition of the heart in Jeremiah 17:9.

Surgeons can operate on the physical heart of a patient, but the Scriptures are referring to the heart of the mind, the seat of our decisions and emotions, the centre of our inner thought space, that only God can see. David recognised this when he wrote Psalm 139.

There is hope that grips like a grapple hook on the sure promises of God. He is the Wonderful Counsellor when we accept His power, He will be greater in us than the gravitational pull of the deception in the world. Glory to God, except our Lord Jesus had rescued us from our evil ways, the proclivity to sin using deceit would continue. But we pattern our Lord Jesus Christ by pursuing the peace of God. He is the wonderful counsellor. He is our Prince of Peace.

God is omniscient.

CDP

*FRIDAY 17th

Bless them which persecute you: bless, and curse not – Romans 12:14

THE BEAUTY OF BLESSING – Reading: Romans 12:1-21

Romans 11 is a beautiful journey of how every believer, Jew or Gentile, has access to salvation. Grasping this freedom that we should not have access to, Paul continues in Romans 12, *'therefore'*, he says, *'so knowing all that, then present your bodies as a living sacrifice holy, acceptable' (v1).*

The chapter spills with who we should now be as believers. Giving to those in need, prophesying, and using our gifts is all well-and-good but there may be a jolt! *'Bless those that persecute you, bless them and curse them not' (v14).* Is this possible, that the calling of being presented as a sacrifice means being like HIM when we are hurt and persecuted?

In our own strength this is not possible, but our guide is there in the fore of this text, *'therefore'*, i.e., because of that! *'But persecutors are wrong and lawless'.* Yes, but focus on the *'therefore'*. Remember the miracle you have been given by Jesus to be called His child. *'But who will vindicate the wrongdoing?'* Remember the *'therefore'*! Remember what He has already done for you through Christ. *'But I am the victim, in the line of the persecutor!'* Remember *'therefore'*, remember why you're doing what you should do. Jesus will fight for you. A persecutor has not yet found the peace of God and needs your prayers to bless them where they already feel cursed. Every blessing we pray with a sincere heart brings us closer to becoming more like HIM.

'I beseech you therefore brethren by the mercies of God that you present yourselves…'. A part of our sacrifice to a holy God is to bless just as Jesus has blessed us.

Joy Lear-Bernard

***World Hypertension Day**

SATURDAY 18th

…the LORD seeth not as man seeth…the LORD looketh on the heart -1 Samuel 16:7

THE IMAGE OF THE HEART – Reading: 1 Samuel 16:1-13

As our natural heart, an organ from which flows blood, is our lifeline, likewise from the 'spiritual' heart, streams our sentiments and intentions. However, the heart can indicate one of two pictures, or a mixture of both.

Proverbs 4:23 states, *'Keep thy heart with all diligence; for out of it are the issues of life'.* So, one can have a heart from which spews ugliness or beauty. A beautiful heart is a **PURE** heart.

From the heart of the redeemed, should flow God's love, which is His benchmark for eternal life, through His unlimited mercy and grace. Our daily walk displays outer beauty and inner beauty, the latter being the true beauty to which God pays attention.

In our key Bible verse, 1 Samuel 16:7, two characters' images of the heart are seen:

1) The heart of King Saul – TRAGEDY. Characterised by being influenced by the people; failure after failure and turning back from following after God. **In the eyes of people, he was perfect for a king**.

2) The heart of King David – SUCCESS. Characterised by worshipping God; successions of God's favours; repenting and following God. **In the eyes of God, David - a humble shepherd boy - insignificant, least likely candidate. BUT the perfect choice in the eyes of God**!

God is not impressed (although not against them) with our accolades, financial status and intellect, but He surely looks into the heart and sees its condition.

Let us humble ourselves for God to draw near to us.

Minister Carmel White

*SUNDAY 19th

Be not overcome of evil, but overcome evil with good – Romans 12:21

DON'T RETALIATE – Reading: Romans 12:17-21

These verses warn us as believers not to repay evil to someone who has done evil to us. We are admonished to instead pay them back with kindness and love. This can only happen if we are truly the children of God because it is very hard to do in our own strength.

This is inner beauty, when we behave as children of God. We were sinners and God forgave us. He set us free to also teach the world what He has done for us. By following Romans 12:20-21, God will take over our battles and deal with our adversaries; that's the heaping of hot coals on their heads!

Today I am praying for God to wash our hearts so that we can show we have the inner beauty that only He can give. God has deposited this beauty within every Spirt-filled believer. It can shine through to others who have hurt us and expect us to hurt them back. We surprise them, and rather we show love by forgiving them and loving them in Jesus Christ's name.

Sis Esther Miller

Pentecost Sunday

MONDAY 20th

A soft answer turneth away wrath, but grievous words stir up anger – Proverbs 15:1

SEARCH ME – Reading: Proverbs 15:1-14

'Out of the abundance of the heart the mouth speaks' (Matthew 12:34).

If the heart is good then good things will come out, therefore it stands to reason that if the heart is bad then only bad things can come from it. Grievous words come from a grievous place from which contempt breeds contempt. The condition of the inner self radiates to the outer self whereby the good treasures of the heart are always seen in words and deeds.

Hence, inner beauty is active in the way we live, the love we show, the patience, kindness and consideration shown in how we treat others. The peace and joy we portray are all inner beauty given by the Lord.

Recently a work colleague said to me, *'There's always an aura of niceness surrounding you'*. Before I could take any credit, I got a quick rebuke from the Holy Spirit, *'Thats not you, that's the Holy Ghost!'*.

God requires for us to live from the inside out, in purity and sincerity of heart. Only He can change us inwardly for an outward manifestation. Good treasures on the inside also consist of compassion, mercy and truth. Maintain self-control so that, even in the heat of the moment, you remain gracious and able to speak kindly under pressure.

We must allow the beauty of Jesus, and all His nature, to be seen in us.

Sis Jx

TUESDAY 21st

As ye would that (others) should do to you, do ye also to them likewise
Luke 6:31

DO LOVE – Reading: Luke 6:27-36

Looking at how important it is for human beings to live in love, Jesus gave a summary of the whole of Scriptures in two commandments about love:

'Love God with all your heart, with all your soul and with all thy mind and with all thy strength and the second is love thy neighbour as thyself' (Mark 12:30-31). This love is more than a kind feeling, but a love of great sacrificial concern for the welfare of others. This love is rooted in Christ it, *'beareth all things, endureth all things, hopeth all things' (1 Corinthians 13:7).* Treating others in the same way as you would like to be treated is a Christian principle and is godly love; God's love never fails.

We are to think about what we need and use that thought as a basis for meeting the needs of others, even our enemies. Jesus illustrates this love more fully in the parable of The Good Samaritan (Luke 10:25-37). Take up the position given by Jesus to not just avoid harming others, but to actively work for their positive good.

Fully prepared, as Christian women we are to go about ministering to a hurting world, loving them as we love ourselves. It is the overflow of God in us.

Dear Heavenly Father, I pray that my life may beam out your light and reflect your love and compassion. Help me to apply the Golden Rule in my life, of doing unto others as I would have them do unto me. Give me grace to love others with a Christlike heart so that I can be obedient to your great commandment, then my living will not be in vain. When I am like you, Jesus, you alone will receive the glory you so deserve.

Missionary M Fraser

WEDNESDAY 22nd

If you love each other, everyone will know that you are my disciples
John 13:35 (CEV)

LOVE DESPITE DIFFERENCES – Reading: John 13: 1-9, 31-38

There are several ways by which we can identify where people are from, or to whom they are related. An accent or dialect can reveal which part of the UK or abroad that you live. Perhaps you have a striking facial resemblance of another family member, or a behavioural trait peculiar to a particular family which, without your saying a word, causes you to be known.

Jesus makes a thought-provoking statement to His disciples in John 13:35. He says that they will be known as disciples of His by the love which they demonstrate to one another. Earlier in John 13, Jesus displays the heart of a servant by washing His disciples' feet. In humility, the God-man takes a basin of water, girds Himself with a towel, stoops down and completes the process. He does what only lowly servants of the house do, hence Peter's surprise and indignation, *'(Lord), you will never wash my feet…' (v 8).*

This month we're looking at Inner Beauty. Jesus, His taking on the role of a servant, showing outwardly who He was inwardly, did not detract from who He was as Son of God. John, who writes from an elevated divine and spiritual perspective, and flavours much of his writings with the subject of 'Love', thought it necessary to record this message from one of the final conversations which Jesus had with the disciples as part of their training.

Jesus intentionally selected (yes, even Judas Iscariot) a team of twelve men with different temperaments - some who were always in the headlines and others whom we struggle to remember their names. Yet He did not instruct them to try and change one another, but said, *'love each other'*. He was saying that if you can love one another as colleagues and fellow-workers, despite each other's difference of personality, irritating ways and bad habits, yet patiently and lovingly tolerate for the common cause of getting Kingdom Work done, it won't be difficult for the saved and unsaved to know from whom you received your training. For the Trainer, Me, Jesus Christ, I had to do the same!

JEJ

THURSDAY 23rd

(Rebekah) said, I will draw water for thy camels also, until they have done drinking
Genesis 24:19

FIRST IMPRESSIONS – Reading: Genesis 24:1-46

There's a saying which I heard many years ago which sometimes comes back to my mind, *'You never get a second chance to create a first impression'*. It's true. The opinion of you may change, but the first impression has already been made.

If we were to always operate with a mindset that, sometimes unknowingly, we are giving a first impression, I wonder what changes we would make to our attitude? For instance, an 'ordinary' woman walks into your office whom you've never seen before. You glance up at her, then carry on with what you're doing without saying, *'Good morning!'*. Later you learn that the woman who you ignored was the wife of your boss. The same woman walks in again tomorrow, and because you now know who she is, you say a bright, ***'Good morning!'***. She's already formed her first impression of you.

Rebekah unwittingly had one chance to create a destiny-related good impression, a first impression, an only impression. Abraham's servant, Eliezer, asked God for a sure sign to know when he had seen the woman who he should bring back with him to be Isaac's wife (Genesis 24:10-14). Eliezer could not base his decision just on an external vision of beauty. The wife-to-be had to be willing to give him water and also offer to get water for his/Abraham's **ten** camels. Do you know how many gallons one camel drinks? There were no taps in Rebekah's house, she had to go back and forth in the heat of the day to the local well to fill **buckets**, I mean **buckets,** for each of those camels to drink and be satisfied (Lord have mercy!). That was a wise sign Eliezer asked for. He knew that not many women (including the one writing this page and you reading it!) would be prepared to do all of that, not for a stranger and his camels! Eliezer therefore knew that any woman prepared to minister in that way was worthy to be Abraham's daughter-in-law. He wasn't going to do a repeat visit to see how Rebekah might behave the second time around.

Ladies, how many opportunities do we miss because we can be poor at making good first impressions? *'But I didn't know it was a first impression'*. That's the point. *'But I didn't know that I was being observed'*. That's the point. As Spirt-filled women of God, let's learn to live in 'first-impression' mode, i.e., our best is our minimum!

JEJ

FRIDAY 24th

Pleasant words are as an honeycomb, sweet to the soul...Proverbs 16:24

THERE'S SO MUCH MORE TO YOU – Reading: Proverbs 16:22-28

Take a moment to consider all of the things which we cannot see with the natural eye - those things which so clearly reflect the beauty which is beyond the surface but reveal that which is so deep within.

The essence of who we are - our kindness, strength, gentleness - are found not in our 'looks' but in our words. Our words and attitude so vividly reflect our heart and soul.

Today, let us add some honey, some comfort, some sweetness, into the lives of those around us!

Let's leave those whom we encounter feeling a little stronger inside and out, or with a smile from a simple conversation had with us.

I recently met an 86-year-old church sister, still serving with strength of mind as an usher in her home church. My few short conversations with her will remain with me for some time. Even as I write, thinking of her makes me want to smile - what a blessing she was and is!

Can you be that person today? Remember that a few simple words of kindness and love will reflect the essence of who you are, and can make all the difference to a person's day.

Christine Knight

SATURDAY 25th

Thy word have I hid in my heart, that I might not sin against thee – Psalm 119:11

REALLY BEAUTIFUL WOMEN – Reading: Psalm 119:9-16

As I consider the theme of Inner Beauty, I can't help but reflect on some lovely individuals whom I know. Not all of them are Christians but they are a joy to be around, are of a high moral standard, and would never deliberately hurt anybody. I'm sure that you know people like that too.

However, since it is *'not of works'* (Ephesians 2:8-9), nobody can be as beautiful as they should be without the indwelling of the Holy Spirit (Romans 8:29) and living by God's Word. It is the Holy Spirit that brings about true transformation (regeneration) and, when allowed, keeps our conscience alive far beyond just good morals which is all that rules the beautiful person described in my first paragraph. They still have the innate Adamic (sin) nature.

The Word in my heart is like living with a Divine GPS. It speaks out when I need direction or have taken a wrong turn in life, and flags when I've said or done something wrong. It keeps on speaking until I repent and am back on the right course. Our lives are contrary and our behaviour is out of order in the absence of God's Word. We can't be clean in the sight of God without its application (Psalm 119:9).

As women, most of us love to buy fresh and sweet-smelling bath and shower gels, hand and body lotions, eau de parfum sprays. We are even sometimes asked for the name of the fragrance that we're wearing - it is oh so tantalising! But what really stimulates the nostrils of God is holiness which is worship, *'Worship the LORD in the beauty of holiness' (1 Chronicles 16:29; Psalm 29;2; Psalm 96:9).* Worship is not just singing songs, or lying prostrate in His presence, neither is it something that we only do when we congregate in a building or on Zoom. Worship is a lifestyle. How we live reflects how much we adore (worship) God in our heart, and that rightly defines us as Beautiful Women.

JEJ

SUNDAY 26th

...forgiving one another, even as God for Christ's sake hath forgiven you
Ephesians 4:32

FORGIVENESS OF THE CROSS – Reading: Ephesians 4:17-32

One of the most challenging areas for believers to grow in is in the area of forgiveness. Sadly, many a heart has wandered from the fold after suffering hurt.

Our journey from the day we say yes to Jesus is followed by steps of growth into becoming like Him and denying our own flesh. Paul calls it *'dying daily'* and *'putting the flesh under subjection'.*

Perhaps forgiveness is so difficult because our gaze is set in the wrong direction. Paul's instruction to us is twofold: put away, (stop, abandon, dismiss and kill) malice, bitterness, anger and evil speech. However, we know that a weed cut down is not necessarily torn out. Of course, the former will spring up again if there is no process. We kill the roots of bitter weeds through acts of kindness and forgiveness!

In our own ability such as acts of kindness can be superficial at best. Ephesians 4:32 gives us the key to empower us to be able to love. Paul says, *'we forgive even as God has forgiven us' (Ephesians 4:32)*! Wrongdoing will never seem deserving of kindness or forgiveness when we fixate on the actions of another, but when we focus on the actions of Jesus towards our sinful state, forgiving is possible! It is life giving and glorifying to God as we turn hurt into gratitude to God for His forgiveness.

Let us be very honest and clear about lines and boundaries. Perhaps the struggle we have is misunderstanding reconciliation versus forgiveness. Where we hope for reconciliation through repentance and change, forgiveness has no such caveat. We are implored and empowered to forgive every man even as Christ has forgiven us, knowing that His character is growing in us daily.

Joy Lear-Bernard

*MONDAY 27th

...put off all these; anger, wrath, malice, blasphemy...Colossians 3:8

TOTAL MAKEOVER – Reading: Colossians 3:1-17

Statistics show that the beauty industry is blooming amidst (and despite) the rising cost of living.

Social media platforms and the entertainment world are constantly promoting the world's ideal image of beauty. Consequently, millions are left bewildered and feeling ugly, while others are pursuing their place on the beauty spectrum.

We can always count on Scriptures which tell us that, *'God has made everything beautiful in its time'.* So according to Ecclesiastes 3:11, beauty is attached to time with a beginning and an ending. This means that beauty is temporary (Proverbs 31:30), like the flowers which bloom in the morning but by the evening they are withered away.

Yet eternity is in man's heart. So there is that spiritual dimension, the inner man of the heart, man's spirit, that is linked to eternity. Whatever is eternal, has great weight of glory and beauty.

Colossians 3:8 reminds us that we are partakers of Christ's divine nature which is our new status, our new true self. God's knowledge gives us the right image, and to be transformed by this knowledge is a 'complete makeover'. Inner beauty is God's love, kindness, compassion, all of these functioning in the innermost part of our being.

This inner beauty shines through in love and excels time. It cannot be faded away but radiates, grows and glows into glory.

Pastor Josephine Lewis

Spring Bank Holiday

*TUESDAY 28th

Ruth said, Intreat me not to leave thee, for where you go, I will go... - Ruth 1:16

FILL THE GAP – Reading: 1 Corinthians 13:1-13

Has anyone ever said that they feel drawn to you in a platonic way which they cannot quite explain? They may say something like, *'I don't know what it is, but I feel something pleasantly different when in your company!'.*

This summarises how and why Ruth, a Gentile idol worshipper, decided to leave the country of her nativity and relocate with her mother-in-law to a place where she had never been. Ruth was drawn to Naomi by Naomi's lifestyle and commitment to Jehovah whilst sojourning in Moab. Naomi did not adopt the pagan practices of the Moabites, she remembered that she was an Israelite and abode by the Jewish laws although far from home.

I picture Ruth covertly watching and admiring Naomi, even during her time of grief – bereaved of her husband and two sons - yet Naomi held on to her faith. When Naomi wanted to sever her relationship with Ruth and return alone to Bethlehemjudah, the inner beauty of Naomi caused Ruth to say, *'I'm coming with you'.* Ruth clearly had a gap in her life, an emptiness that went beyond being a widow, now further magnified at the prospect of life without Naomi. Ruth was prepared to give up everything familiar to her as a result of the impact of Naomi's inner beauty on her life.

Ladies, our inner beauty should stand out like a beacon and touch others. Consider how you can radiate the love of God to become a channel of positive influence and blessing to someone today.

JEJ

Menstrual Hygiene Day

*WEDNESDAY 29th

Let your speech be always with grace, seasoned with salt...Colossians 4:6

WE ARE WHAT WE SPEAK – Reading: Colossians 4:1-6

Our verse today starts with the word, ***'let'***.

The Oxford Dictionary says that *'let'* means, *'to not prevent or forbid to allow'*. It's a choice - Let God reign!

We make many choices in a day: What shall I wear? How shall I style my hair? What shall I eat? What time shall I leave home? What shall I buy? Where shall I go? However, the choice to allow God (to let God) be Lord over what we say and how and when we use our tongue, is a thing of great inner beauty. How do we prepare our inner self?

A disciplined tongue is a thing of great beauty, the tongue is a little muscular organ but it is very powerful. James 3:5 says, *'Even so the tongue is a little member and boasteth great things. Behold how great a matter a little fire kindleth'*. A little organ like the tongue can cause havoc, pain and even death. We need to speak life!

Proverbs 18.21 tells us that, *'Death and life are in the power of the tongue...'*. In Psalm 141:3 the psalmist asks, *'Set a watch O LORD, before my mouth, keep the door of my lips'*.

Say little, pray much! Let the Holy Spirit speak through you!

'Let your speech be always with grace, seasoned with salt, that ye may know how ye ought to answer every man' (Colossians 4:6).

That is true inner beauty!

Beverley V Galloway

National Biscuit Day

THURSDAY 30th

A friend loveth at all times, and a brother is born for adversity – Proverbs 17:17

THE CIRCLE OF INNER BEAUTY – Reading:1 Samuel 18:1-4;19: 1-7

I was fortunate enough to overhear a conversation of a group of friends whilst at a bus stop; they were discussing another friendship group. *They asked, 'Who's in your circle? Who are the pretty ones?'.* I was rather amused by these questions and the conversation that progressed.

'Who's in your circle? And who are the pretty ones?' are valid questions to ask yourself. Can you identify who is not just in your circle, but your inner circle? Can you identify who are the *'pretty'* or truly internally beautiful ones?

A friend who is consistent in loving you through the good times, as well as times of adversity, is a friend who is in your inner circle and possesses inner beauty.

'Philia', which is Greek for the friendship kind of love, when applied consistently especially in hard times, it causes inner beauty to shine through. Secondly, when philia love is supplied and motivated by the agape love of God, it transforms a friend into a beautiful brother or sister for all seasons of life. Endeavour to be in the inner circle of someone and let your inner beauty shine through in friendship. Let brotherly and sisterly love continue.

Minister Kay Dawkins/ MinK

FRIDAY 31st

Let the word of Christ dwell in you richly in all wisdom – Colossians 3:16

THE WORD IN ME – Reading: Colossians 3:1-17

An easy way to identify that you have not been eating properly, and that your body is lacking in vital minerals and vitamins, is when you keep on getting cold after cold, virus after virus, have a dull complexion, you breakout in spots or cold sores, etc. As soon as we notice a pattern of any of these things, most of us will head to the pharmacy to buy some multivitamin tablets or a tonic. We'll also take a look at our diet and start to drink more water.

What should we do if we notice that we're becoming cranky, argumentative, short tempered, just difficult to be around (it's not always the other person's fault)? We can't keep on blaming our hormones, sometimes it's a signal that the Word is not dwelling in us richly! When the Word is within us in abundant supply, it controls our actions and reactions; we don't behave like 'a bear with a sore head'!

Many of us take supplements daily to support and give our immune system a boost. How much more should we be mindful to, at every opportunity, enhance and charge up our inner self with regular fasting, prayer, reading and applying God's Word! You will (and those who have to deal with you will) feel much better for it.

JEJ

DEPRESSION *(by Dr Eula Miller)*

For the next few minutes as you read this article, we want to share with you some information about:

- Who can become depressed?
- What is Depression?
- What are the triggers for Depression?
- What help and support is available.

Depression is one of the most prevalent mental health disorders, affecting around 1 in 6 adults over the age of sixteen in the UK. It is also associated with other mental health issues, such as anxiety, stress and loneliness.

Everyone has ups and downs. Sometimes you might feel a bit low, for lots of different reasons. People may say that they are feeling depressed when they are in fact feeling ′fed up' or feeling down, but this does not always mean that they have depression.

While some people believe that depression is trivial, or not a genuine health problem, it is a condition that affects around one in every 6 people living in the UK over the course of their lives.

It is believed that 56% of employees in the UK are experiencing symptoms of depression. Employees aged between 25-34 are the most affected group.

The difference between low mood & clinical depression

General low mood can include feelings of:

- sadness
- anxiousness
- edginess
- worry
- tiredness
- low self-esteem
- frustration
- anger

A low mood will tend to lift after a few days and can be alleviated by making some small changes to your life, such as resolving a difficult situation, talking about your problems, getting more sleep, and engaging in moderate exercise. Such strategies can usually help to improve your mood.

However, a low mood that does not respond to lifestyle changes forementioned, and persists for longer than two weeks with worsening symptoms, could be a sign of depression. The formal diagnosis of depression is usually made by your GP.

There are two broad categories of depression:

1. **Reactive Depression (more commonly known as situational depression**)
   Situational Depression usually lasts several months. It is brought on by a specific situation or event, such as:

- The loss of a job (whether it be through redundancy, retirement, or being fired)
- A traumatic injury (for instance sustained from a car accident, assault, or during combat)
- Natural disasters
- Rejection
- Financial problems
- The end of a relationship
- The death of a loved one

However, any event that an individual finds stressful can trigger situational depression. Symptoms will usually develop within 90 days of the stressful or traumatic event.

2. **Endogenous Depression**

   Endogenous Depression occurs without the presence of stress or trauma. There is no apparent external cause. Instead, it may be primarily caused by genetic and biological factors.

The manifestation of symptoms for both categories of depression are the same.

What is depression?

Symptoms of depression can include the following:

- not getting any enjoyment out of life
- becoming socially withdrawn, avoiding social settings
- continuous feelings of hopelessness, worthlessness, and guilt
- feeling tired, lacking energy and motivation
- ruminating thoughts - continuous dwelling on and overthinking situations
- unexplained pain or other physical symptoms without an apparent cause
- not being able to concentrate or remembering everyday things like reading the paper or watching television.
- Changes in appetite leading to significant weight loss or weight gain.
- Significant changes in your sleep pattern, such as trouble falling or staying asleep, or sleeping too much / too little.
- having thoughts about harming yourself. Feeling as though life is not worth living or having thoughts of suicide.

Who can become Depressed?

Depression does not discriminate!

Depression can impact people of all genders, ages, cultures, Christians, non-Christians, the rich, the poor. It is irrespective of social status.

At any one time, it is believed that one in five women and one in eight men are diagnosed with depressive illness. Studies show that around 4% of children in the UK between the ages of 5 and 16 are depressed or anxious.

Depressed men and women share many of the common signs and symptoms, however they may display and express their depression in different ways.

Depression in women

Women are nearly twice as likely as men to be diagnosed with depression. It is believed that this maybe because women are more likely than men to seek professional help and support.

Key transitional life stages such as puberty, menstruation, pregnancy, perimenopausal and menopausal women can be contributing factors for triggering depression in women. Life circumstances e.g., any significant trauma, loss, bereavement, work overload, mental and physical abuse, are also cited as causes that trigger depression in women.

Depression in men

12.5% of men in the UK are suffering from depression and anxiety. It is believed that men display depression differently, and depression among men may go under-diagnosed for a protracted period before diagnosis. Men tend to experience physical symptoms of unexplained pain, and experience feelings of anger, irritability, sleep disturbances, and loss of libido. They are also more likely to attribute depressive symptoms to 'stress' rather than being depressed.

Depression in children

Nearly 80,000 children and young people suffer from depression in the UK. Depression is thought to occur in about 4% of children and young people in the UK. It is more common in older adolescents, particularly teenage girls, but can affect children of any age. A young person with depression may experience major problems not only with how they feel, but also with how they behave. This may cause difficulties at home and at school, as well as in relationships with family and friends.

Some characteristics to watch out for in school age children who may be becoming depressed:

- aches and pains
- not wanting to play
- not wanting to see family and friends
- lacking enjoyment
- being clingy and not wanting to separate
- extreme uncharacteristic irritability

Seeking Help & Support

Whatever the cause is, if low mood persists beyond a two-week period and negative feelings do not go away, feel too much for you to cope with, or you feel you cannot carry on with your normal life, you may need to make some changes and get some extra support.

Remember, depression is both common and treatable. If you think that you are depressed, do not hesitate to seek help.

There are various treatments and support that you can access to help manage depression. Lifestyle changes play a key role in managing or recovering from depression. Making positive changes, such as getting more exercise, improving sleep, eating healthily, staying connected and engaged with others socially, can all have a significant positive impact on your mental health.

If you are diagnosed with depression, your GP should discuss all the available treatment options with you, including self-help, talking therapies, and antidepressants.

Treatments

- **Self-help** -Whether you have depression or just find yourself feeling down for a while, it could be worth trying some self-help strategies. Life changes, such as getting a regular good night's sleep, keeping to a healthy diet, and getting regular exercise, can help you feel more in control and more able to cope.

- **Talking therapies** – Counselling can help you get to understand the root causes of why you feel depressed. This is important as it will help you to cope more effectively in the future.

- **Cognitive behaviour therapy (CBT**) teaches you to challenge negative thoughts while developing a more balanced outlook on life.

- **Antidepressant medication** – If your GP prescribes you antidepressants, they will discuss the different types, and which one would suit you best. These work by boosting natural brain chemicals levels which can become imbalanced during depression. Most antidepressants take at least two weeks before you may feel any beneficial change in your mood.

In most cases of mild to moderate depression, a combination of self-help and talking therapy brings about full recovery. However, in more severe cases, the addition of prescribed anti – depressant medication may also help to alleviate symptoms.

Supportive crisis services

Emergency or crisis

- Contact your GP via phone or dial 111 – NHS Direct
- Go to the nearest Accident & Emergency hospital department
- Call 999 and ask for an ambulance.

Helplines

CALM (campaign against living miserably) - 0800 585858 **-** provide confidential services 5pm – midnight 7 days a week.

Samaritans: 0161 236 8000 (local call charges apply) or 116 123 (free to call). Open 24 hours a day. They offer confidential emotional support.

Saneline: 0300 304 7000. Open 4.30pm – 10.30pm every day. They provide emotional support and information.

The take home message

If you recognise that you are or someone you care for is experiencing low mood or may be depressed encourage:

- Openness to talk about what is happening in a non-judgemental way. What is shown to greatly help is having someone to listen and share your feelings with.
- Stay connected - a conversation, a call, a text, a visit can help others, and you, feel less isolated.
- Encourage them to seek further support if the feelings persist and are worsening

beyond a 2-week period

Further reading

Cole, B.P. and Davidson, M.M., (2019). Exploring men's perceptions about male depression. Psychology of Men & Masculinities, 20(4), p.459.

NICE quality standard 2013: Depression in children and young people www.nice.org.uk/guidance/index. 14284

Pindar, J. (2022) Depression Statistics UK: 2022: Depression Statistics UK | 2022 Data | Champion Health Accessed 30.07.2022.

Salk, R.H., Hyde, J.S. and Abramson, L.Y., (2017). Gender differences in depression in representative national samples: Meta-analyses of diagnoses and symptoms. *Psychological bulletin*, *143*(8), p.783.

Seidler, Z.E., Rice, S.M., Oliffe, J.L., Fogarty, A.S. and Dhillon, H.M., (2018). Men in and out of treatment for depression: Strategies for improved engagement. *Australian Psychologist*, *53*(5), pp.405-415.

Wong, K.C. and Parker, C., 2018. Depression in children and young people: identification and management. Clin Pharm, 10(4).

Graham, P. and Midgley, N., 2020. *So Young, So Sad, So Listen: A Parents' Guide to Depression in Children and Young People*. RCPsych Publications.

Lindsey, M.A., Banks, A., Cota, C.F., Lawrence Scott, M. and Joe, S., 2018. A review of treatments for young Black males experiencing depression. *Research on social work practice*, *28*(3), pp.320-329.

Stoll, N., Yalipende, Y., Byrom, N.C., Hatch, S.L. and Lempp, H., 2022. Mental health and mental well-being of Black students at UK universities: A review and thematic synthesis. *BMJ open*, *12*(2), p.e050720.

Bailey, N.V. and Tribe, R., 2021. A qualitative study to explore the help-seeking views relating to depression among older Black Caribbean adults living in the UK. *International Review of Psychiatry*, *33*(1-2), pp.113-118.

Thapar, A., Eyre, O., Patel, V. and Brent, D., 2022. Depression in young people. *The Lancet.*

Nguyen, L.H., Anyane-Yeboa, A., Klaser, K., Merino, J., Drew, D.A., Ma, W., Mehta, R.S., Kim, D.Y., Warner, E.T., Joshi, A.D. and Graham, M.S., 2022. The mental health burden of racial and ethnic minorities during the COVID-19 pandemic. *Plos one*, *17*(8), p.e0271661.

June
Trust God

SATURDAY 1st

...the vessel...was marred in the hand of the potter: so he made it again...
Jeremiah 18:4

BEAUTY IN BROKENNESS – Reading: Jeremiah 18:1-6

*'**B**eauty is in the eye of the beholder'* Margaret Wolfe Hungerford, 1878.

God is always seeking to make us more like Him, revealing to us the importance of being in total submission to Him. His is the eye that beholds us. He is the Potter, and we are the clay. Miracles take place on the Potter's wheel, but seldom do we sign up for our time on the wheel because of reasons such as pride or fear. We must trust that with God, it doesn't matter how many broken pieces you think your life may be in, God can perform a work on you on His wheel.

David understood something that is crucial to our relationship with God. He knew that he could not make himself righteous. Isaiah 64:6 says that, ***"all our righteousnesses are as filthy rags'***. Think about the parable of The Prodigal Son. Could it be that the son's older brother awarded himself for his own righteousness, and as such could not find compassion when his brother returned? Pride always lacks compassion and awards itself. Notice that when David's secret sins were outlined, he didn't ask God to change his desires or habits, he asked God to give him a clean heart! He asked for a right spirit! Why? Because a right spirit does not only deal with a symptom but pulls out the root of sin and will always bring us to our knees. A right spirit makes us want what God wants, like what God likes, and hate what God hates!

Brokenness can mean many things. It can imply messiness and imperfection, heartbreak, weakness, grief or despair. But brokenness before the Lord, through the eyes of God is to be crushed, and broken in spirit over sin. God can bring beauty out of all of the above. The process can be painful because we often want our own way, but God does what He will to shape us into His likeness.

Sisters, it's time to put away our own confidence and live in the confidence of God. Yield to His process - it may feel uncomfortable, messy and painful - but He who formed us is more than able to bring beauty out of brokenness.

Latoya Foster

SUNDAY 2nd

With all your heart you must trust the LORD and not your own judgment
Proverbs 3:5 (CEV)

ALL OF ME – Reading: Proverbs 3:5-6; Philippian 4:6-8

Proverbs 3:5 is probably one of the most famous of the biblical proverbs.

As we explore June's theme of *Trust God*, I am wondering how much do I really trust Him? Is there a part of me that I'm still holding back in reserve? Reserve for what, I am not sure!

We are exhorted to, *'Trust in the LORD with all (our) heart'*, but if we are doing that, why do we worry so much?

I think living in a state of fret and worry shows that we have not yet given God all of our heart, and this causes a deficiency in the relationship between us and Him. The part held back is what creates the problem.

True trust means that we have confidence in God even when we don't get the answers we want. At times this may mean having to reverse our way of thinking. Every prayer is answered. When I reflect upon my childhood (and even as an adult), some of the loudest answers from my parents to my requests were when they remained silent!

JEJ

MONDAY 3rd

You will keep perfectly peaceful the one whose mind remains focused on you
Isaiah 26:3 (ISV)

CONFIDENCE IN GOD – Reading: Isaiah 26:1-9

How many times have we been confronted with situations like sickness, destitution, bereavement, or things like viruses or addictions, and begin to worry about how we will overcome such obstacles? How often have we tried to resolve the problems ourselves and fail, or ask God why me? Sometimes it seems like we're losing our mind trying to figure out what's going on.

We often observe the behaviours of others and question why they're always smiling and continue to worship God in the midst of traumatic life experiences. The reason they're able to do this is because they confidently trust that God will take care of them (Psalm 112:7-8).

In comparison, I'll use an analogy of most birds who seek shelter in a storm whilst eagles fly above the clouds. Eagles are strong and courageous, and they use the current to soar higher. We need to learn to be like eagles and use the storms in our lives to our advantage and fly higher!

I understand that sometimes we just can't see a way out of a difficult circumstance, just like the Jews when they were in between the Egyptians and the Red Sea. But oppression and afflictions are for our learning. God's thoughts stretch beyond human comprehension, so when those dark times come, our heart and mind must be focused on God because He will show up in our situation and keep us in perfect peace.

God promised never to leave nor forsake us, and His Word will never return unto him void (Isaiah 55:5,11; Hebrews 13:5). Trust Him.

Rachel Lewin

TUESDAY 4th

What time I am afraid, I will trust thee – Psalm 56:3

LORD, MY EYES ARE UPON YOU – Reading: Psalm 56:1-11

What do you do, when you have prayed earnestly about a situation and instead of it becoming better, it gets worse? What do you when you have done all that you know how to do but there is no deliverance, no peace, and you are struggling to maintain your joy?

'Trust in the LORD with all thine heart; lean not unto thine own understanding. In all thy ways acknowledge him, and he shall direct thy paths' (Proverbs 3:5-6). To say, *'Lord, I will trust you completely even when I am in a fearful situation',* is the easiest thing to say, but more challenging to demonstrate!

In 2 Chronicles 20, when Jehoshaphat, King of Judah, was told that more than two nations were coming to fight against Judah, he was afraid. In his prayer he stated, *'... for we have no might against this great company that cometh against us; neither know we what to do:* ***but our eyes are upon thee'*** (2 Chronicles 20:12). You can almost hear him say, *'Lord, I am about to encounter a situation that I have never experienced before, help me to take my eyes off what I see and place it on you!'.*

So, Lord, I will not allow myself to become captivated by fear when you told me in your Word that the battle is not mine…it belongs to you (2 Chron 20:15). I will stand still, exercise faith, and wait on my deliverance (Exodus 14:13). And Lord, even when it does not come when I am expecting it, I will not bow to fear, because all my trust is in you.

Deveen Smith

*WEDNESDAY 5th

***...what things soever ye desire when ye pray, believe that ye will receive them...* Mark 11:24**

GOD DOESN'T MAKE FALSE PROMISES – Reading: Mark 11:20-26

Jesus spoke the words of today's key verse to His disciples to help them to understand the importance of having faith in the prayers they prayed.

A person who believes when they pray, asking in God's will, can be confident that whatsoever they prayed for it will be granted unto them. We must believe that the words of God are true, that He cannot lie. God does not make false promises and so we can trust Him wholeheartedly to do exactly as He says, *'He shall call upon me and I will answer him, I will be with him in trouble. I will deliver him and honour him' (Psalm 91:15)*. It doesn't matter how heavy our burdens are, God will surely help us.

I'd like to share a personal experience of trusting God: I prayed and asked the Lord to help me to buy a house I had seen and liked. I prayed specifically for a certain number of rooms as I had a plan in mind. I went to the estate agent about the property. One day, whilst thinking and praying about the house, I was taken there in my mind and stood beyond the gate. From there I saw two senior ladies. One of them said these words, *'I heard that you are interested in buying this house. I admire your courage and your ambition, the house is yours, go for it'.* The other lady also said something similar and added, *'you are the only one who is not going to chop it up and turn it into flats!'.*

Two days later, the agent phoned me. He began by saying, *'I have got good news for you! The lady who is selling the house said she wants you to have the house; you are the only one who is not going to chop it up to turn into flats. They are reducing the price by £15,000 to make it more affordable for you. They said to tell you to go for the property - it's yours'!* I raised my hands and said, *'Thank you, Jesus, you have answered my prayers'.*

It behoves us as Christian women to trust God and prove Him. God does not make false promises!

Missionary M Fraser

***Global Running Day**

*THURSDAY 6th

...Jesus doesn't change – yesterday, today, tomorrow, he's always totally himself
Hebrews 13:8 (MSG)

UNCHANGEABLE – Reading: Hebrews 13:1-25

Hebrews 13:8 uses a very interesting phrase. The writer says, *'Jesus Christ the same yesterday, and today, and forever'.*

His very presence commands the calm of the tumultuous sea. His name spans all time and all space. Salvation that He wrought was brought before the foundation of the world (Revelation 13:8).

John celebrated with deep contemplation and humility, the presence of Jesus on the earth. Mary bent low her whole life plans and said, *'be it unto me, as you said' (Luke 1:38)*, and throughout the ages, the name and presence and power of Jesus Christ has been time and again saluted by humankind, by nature, and even by demons!

Jesus ultimately, and He alone, brings a peace when His presence comes into play. And because there is no limit, and no exhausting of His peace, the writer is able to say with confidence that He is the same yesterday, and today and not just tomorrow, but forever.

Do you know that this means there is not a time, a situation, a dark corner, an unfathomable circumstance, where Jesus is changeable, where He cannot be trusted or is unreliable? There's not a moment where He bows out of the battle. His victory is the same in any situation. Whatever shows up, He shows up as Himself and towers over it as Jesus - salvation, hope, governance and authority. Everything that He is and can do has not diminished one bit over time. Consider how this relates to you, His child! That all of Jesus meets all of our needs.

Say this prayer of triumph every day, *'Jesus the same yesterday, and forever, but especially I thank you that you are the same today. You cannot fail'.*

Joy Lear-Bernard

****Carers Week begins***

*FRIDAY 7th

...be strong and of a good courage; be not afraid, neither be dismayed – Joshua 1:9

I AM WITH YOU – Reading: Joshua 1: 1-9

Three times in chapter one of the book of Joshua, the LORD tells Joshua to be strong; be of good courage; be not afraid; and be not dismayed. These are all qualities of a good warrior.

We are warriors in spiritual warfare and need the same encouragement as Joshua. He had a huge mission in front of him to lead the children of Israel into the promised land. Our task is to make it into Beulah land. The road will be tough, with lots of challenges and battles to fight, but the Lord is encouraging us to:

Be strong: In the context of the Scripture, strong means to sustain attack, not easily taken; to be able to withstand force. *'...be strong in the Lord and in the power of his might.'* (Ephesians 6:10).

Be of good courage: Courage is our strength of mind when faced with danger; it talks about boldness. Hebrews 13:6 says, *'...we may boldly say, The Lord is my helper, and I will not fear what man shall do unto me'* because, *'...God hath not given us the spirit of fear ...'* (2 Timothy 1:7).

Be not dismayed: Do not be discouraged or sad because, *'Ye shall not need to fight in this battle: set yourselves, stand ye still, and see the salvation of the LORD with you ... fear not, nor be dismayed; ...for the LORD will be with you' (2 Chronicles 20:17).*

Whatever we've been asked to do, trust God, because we have the assurance that He will be with us wherever we go.

Lady Pam Lewin

Fish & Chips Day

SATURDAY 8th

Blessed is the (one) that trusteth in the LORD – Jeremiah 17:7

THE ACID TEST – Reading: Jeremiah 17:1-10

God tests our faith and takes us through the refiner's fire. He takes out all that is of human origin and leaves that which has been divinely inspired.

Can we continue to trust God when we call out to Him in our broken state, but it seems He has distanced Himself from us? Our relationship, and His unshakable love for us, gives us peace in troubled times. In times of challenge the Holy Spirit comes alongside us and gives us the strength to meditate upon God's Word, His works, His mercies, and His blessings.

We must have something to say to God in prayer concerning our personal lives. Prayer is the opening of our hearts to Him as to a friend whom one can trust. Not that it is necessary to make known to Him who we are, but in order for us to receive Him. Prayer doesn't bring God down to us, but brings us up to God. We cast our cares upon Him because we are assured that He cares for us, and that our petitions will be heard and answered.

The story is told of a mother whose daughter was ill. She phoned the GP and explained that she was not able to take her daughter to the Surgery because it was closed. The GP recommended medication from the pharmacy as a temporary medicine for the child.

The mother rushed to the pharmacy to get her daughter's medicine. At the parking block she parked her car. However, in her haste she automatically locked the car with the keys inside the car. The mother phoned her daughter to tell her that she would be delayed because her car keys were locked inside the car.

Her daughter told her to get a clothes hanger from the pharmacy, and to put the wire into the side of the car window and pull it, the window would open. She saw this done on the TV.

The mother did as her daughter said, but nothing happened. In desperation she stood at the parking block and prayed, *'Father, please send me help, I need the car window open'.*
She still had the hanger in her hand when suddenly she saw a rough looking young man walking towards her; she thought that he was homeless:

'Hello', the young man saluted her, *'what's wrong?'*
The mother told him that she had accidentally locked her car keys in her car.
'Okay', he said, *'give me the hanger'.*
He put the wire of the hanger into the side car window, and it opened.
The mother gave him a big hug, *'Thank you, you are a good man'*, she said.
'No, I am not a good man. I have just been released from prison', the man replied, and with that said, he walked away.

The mother bowed her head, and prayed, *'Thank God for sending me a professional'.*

The moral of the story is; we can trust God to answer our prayers. He does not always answer in ways that we expect, but according to how He determines it.

Dr Una Davis

SUNDAY 9th

So shall my word be that goeth forth out of my mouth: it shall not return unto me void... - Isaiah 55:11

YOU WILL NOT FAIL ME – Reading: Isaiah 55:6-13

You will not fail me
In what you said you would do
You've given me your Word
And it will not return void unto you

You will not fail me
Even though circumstances
May make me wonder why

You will not fail me
For you've said you'll
Always answer when I cry.

Sister Jennifer Henry

MONDAY 10th

In God I have put my trust; I will not fear what flesh can do unto me – Psalm 56:4

GOD'S GOT YOUR BACK – Reading: Psalm 56:1-13

Trusting in God is to have absolute confidence in the Lord Jesus Christ who is omniscient, omnipotent and omnipresent.

Jesus is God manifested in flesh. He knows everything that we are going through, He has the power to protect us and deliver us, and is with us at all times. We have full assurance that God is able to do what He said He will do. Who better to trust in than our God who cannot fail and who always keeps His word?

Friends, family, and even colleagues don't always defend us when we need support the most, and so we feel let down. But Jesus is our defence mechanism.

If we trust in God, we will never be disappointed (Isaiah 41:10-13). In Psalm 56, David talks about being tormented and oppressed by his enemies, but he was determined to put his trust and faith in God. God had David's back when his enemies came against him. Do you remember when King Saul tried to kill David with a javelin? God blocked it! David said, *'I will not fear what flesh can do unto me' (Psalm 56:4)*. The hard experiences that we go through help us to learn to trust God, they build our faith, and draw us closer to Him. So, trust Him; *'God's got your back'!*

Min. Genevieve Dinnall

TUESDAY 11th

Now the God of hope fill you with all joy and peace – Romans 15:13

TRUST IN GOD – Reading: Romans 15:7-13

We are living in the last days, and things are getting harder.

We are in a financial crisis and more and more people are facing homelessness. Young families are suffering due to food being so expensive. It would be so easy to give up, but it is for us to have hope in God. Many people today do not have any hope in their marriages, jobs, finances, and even their children, etc. But as God's people we have hope. You ask the question, *'How do we abound in hope?'* God is our only hope, there is no other hope in the world today; all of our hope is in God.

The path of hope fully assures us that we are right with God. The Holy Spirit will help us have all joy and peace if we place our faith exclusively in God. Do not be discouraged in our hearts and minds. Jesus said, 'I am the Way, the Truth, and the Life' *(John 14:6)*.

Let us look up, for our redemption draweth nigh!

Missionary Maxine Barclay

WEDNESDAY 12th

But ask in faith, nothing wavering…James 1:6

UNWAVERING – Reading: James 1: 2-18

God requires His children to trust Him. Trusting God is more than just to believe that He is. Rather, trust is to have confidence, assurance, reliance, faith, dependence, and to serve the Living God in obedience.

There are varying degrees of trust, depending on the relationship with whomever faith is entrusted. The saints of God, however, ought to have credulous trust in God which is trust that easily believes, readily accepts, and is quick to commit to the things of God. A childlike trust, almost to the point of being gullible with God. Simple faith that gladly, willingly and effortlessly receives God, His Word, will and purpose, desiring to please and acknowledge Him in everything.

James explains that the trust we must have in God cannot be hesitant, doubtful, uncertain or weak, it must be blind faith, i.e., complete trust without fear, doubt or scepticism. Any kind of wavering has no virtue and therefore cannot achieve anything from God. Peter's faith wavered when he stopped trusting; fear entered into his heart as he gazed at the surrounding situation.

Unbelief is from an evil heart, according to Hebrews 3:12, rewarded only with condemnation which will prevent us from entering into His rest. The scenario in Psalm 10:4 describes the actions of someone who lacks dependency on God. The Scripture called '*wicked*', because God is not in his thoughts, only pride and confidence in themselves which fails to seek or trust in the Lord. Double-mindedness is a lukewarm spiritual condition; that person cannot receive anything of the Lord.

Nevertheless, we will trust in the Lord our God. Obeying Him is the only way for sweet fellowship divine, so fulfilling and worthwhile. Trust God, He makes everything alright. Trust God entirely, not depending on your own understanding. It's a blessing to trust and obey.

Sis Jx

THURSDAY 13th

When you cross deep rivers, I will be with you...Isaiah 43:2 (CEV)

YOU CAN COUNT ON JESUS – Reading: Isaiah 43:1-13

*'When thou passeth through the waters, I will be with thee;
and through the rivers, they shall not overflow thee:
When thou walkest through the fire and shalt not be burned;
neither shall the flame kindle upon thee' (Isaiah 43:2).*

*When the pressures of life
Really get you down
And it seems like there's no help around
You feel as if it's only you
Having trial after trial as you're pressing through.*

*Your tunnel gets longer
And so does your night
You don't seem to have the strength
For your foes to fight.*

*Cry out to Jesus, for He cares for you!
He's patiently waiting to see you through
So hold on my sister, my brother, hold on,
Trust in Jesus, for He's the one
You can surely count on!*

Name withheld

FRIDAY 14th

...I will go in unto the king...and if I perish, I perish – Esther 4:16

YOU DON'T HAVE TO SEE TO BELIEVE – Reading: Esther 4:1-17

Queen Esther in the book of Esther was a Jewish heroine.

Haman, one of the King's chamberlains, was behind a plot to have all Jews exterminated. He hated them. Mordecai was the cousin of Esther; he had adopted her following the death of her parents. Mordecai sent a plea to Esther regarding the dire situation the Jews were in as a result of the decree sent out to have them killed. He wanted Esther to go and speak with the King, to plead on their behalf. She responded to her cousin that she could not go to see her husband unless she was invited (Esther 4:11), plus he had not called for her in the past thirty days.

Mordecai replied, *'think not with thyself that thou shalt escape in the King's house, more than all the Jews. For if thou altogether holdest thy peace at this time, then shall there enlargement and deliverance arise to the Jews from another place, but thou and thy father's house shall be destroyed' (Esther 4:13-14).*

Esther decided to act on this, knowing that her people would be killed if she did nothing. She knew that her plan was a risk to her life. Esther called on her community and maidens to fast with her for three days (Esther 4:16). She leaves her fate and future in God's hands, she lets trust in God lead the way and declares this well-known statement of commitment, *'If I perish, I perish'.*

Although the book of Esther does not mention the word, 'God', yet it clearly reveals God at work. His name is not written in the book but His hand and fingerprints are all over it. The deliverance of the Jews of Persia loudly proclaims the full presence and power of Almighty God.

Missionary M Fraser

SATURDAY 15th

For we walk by faith, not by sight - 2 Corinthians 5:7

TRUST GOD'S TRACK RECORD – Reading: 2 Corinthians 5:1-10

One of the greatest challenges we face as human beings is to believe in what cannot be experienced through our five senses: touch, sight, hearing, taste, and smell.

Well, God being the only wise God, gave us something in addition to, and better than our five human senses to engage with Him - He gave us faith! Through God's Word and our relationship with Him we begin to know and understand who He is. By faith we learn to trust Him because we see, through His Word and our relationship, the track record of God being gloriously displayed.

People make purchases based on a brand name. They believe it can be trusted because it has held a space in its industry for a very long time due to consistency, quality, value, and service. There is a level of trust and assurance in the brand based on its reputation. It is the same for us as children of God when we trust in Him. We can rely on the 'brand' and the track record of God; our God, who is consistent shepherd, saviour, comforter, and friend.

Let's use our spiritual eyesight, which is our faith, to trust God even more.

Minister Kay Dawkins/ MinK

*SUNDAY 16th

...Daniel was not hurt because he believed in his God – Daniel 6:23

TRUST GOD, HE WILL SEND AN ANGEL – Reading: Daniel 6: 1-28

Have you ever been unfairly treated? Persecuted for standing up for what is right, or felt everyone is against you?

In situations like these, we often say we're in the Lion's Den because we're under attack/being persecuted from every angle, and it seems there's nowhere to run. We go to one corner and there's a 'lion'; we run to another corner and there's another lion. Everywhere we turn there's a lion, all because we stood up for what was/is right and now we're being unfairly treated.

Here, our faith in God is tested to the limit. Daniel knew prayer was the key. Despite the petition only to pray to King Darius, Daniel trusted in God and, knowing the risk, still prayed regardless! As a consequence, he was put into the lion's den.

Daniel came out of the den unharmed, in his right mind, vindicated by God, and was able to say, *'My God sent His angel and shut the lions' mouths, so that they have not hurt me, because I was found innocent before Him; and also, O King, I have done no wrong before you' (Daniel 6:22 – NKJV).*

When life puts you in a 'lion's den', pray and trust God; He will send an angel to shut the mouths of your enemies. You will come forth unharmed because you believe in God. He will not only shut their mouths, but He will provide retribution to your enemies. Just trust God, He will never fail.

Lady Pam Lewin

Father's Day

MONDAY 17th

...whoso putteth his trust in the LORD shall be safe – Proverbs 29:25

KEEP ME SAFE – Reading: Isaiah 25: 1-4; 59:19

As a small child I can remember being at home with my family during thunderstorms. If the storm came during the day, outside would usually become very dark before I heard a crack of lightning, followed by loud bangs of thunder. That would be on repeat for a while – a crack of lightning, then another crack, then a bang of thunder, then the rain would start to come down in torrents.

However, I can't say that I ever felt afraid because, as the youngest child, I was never left on my own. As long as my family didn't look scared, I was happy and sure there was nothing to worry about. I do also recall, that after the commotion of a thunderstorm came a specific 'sound' of peace to signal that the storm was over.

Ladies, in our lives, we've had some bangs of thunder, haven't we! And what about those cracks of lightning which came so quickly – when our lives changed in a flash by one event – swift and without warning – followed by being soaked in the torrential rain of dealing with the aftermath! The reality of finding out that your husband was having an affair, a surprise unwelcome health diagnosis, a sudden death, a miscarriage, a betrayal, a violation, an unexpected loss of a job...

We at those times, even at our weakest, put our trust in the LORD, curl up into His bosom and cry in Him; we let Him rock us in His arms and know that we are still safe:

'til the storm passes over, 'til the thunder sounds no more
'til the clouds roll forever from the sky
Hold me fast! Let me stand in the hollow of thine hand
Keep me safe, 'til the storm passes by.
(Unknown)

JEJ

TUESDAY 18th

Let your (way of life) be without covetousness: and be content with such things as ye have – Hebrews 13:5

BE CONTENT – Reading: Hebrews 13:1-5

The word covetousness is the opposite of contentment. Covetousness refers to our greed and desire to attain more. Many people in our world aspire to be covetous although this can be mistakenly considered as ambitious. The word covetousness was applied to believers in the Hebrew Church, and the same is said of some believers in the Church today.

Contentment is having that deep settled peace on the inside, which has no connection to the material things we possess. As a child of God, we are encouraged to let go of all of our painful experiences, and let God deal with them.

God grants all believers His grace through faith. We are assured by the Word of God that it does not matter what circumstance we are dealing with, only His Grace is sufficient to keep us. In our darkest hour, when our backs are up against the wall, He is right there with us.

Women of God, let us encourage ourselves in the Lord and know His will for our lives. Therefore, we must seek Him first and everything else God will give to us according to His will. When we are outside of the will of God, we feed our flesh by running after all the bling-bling of this world.

When we are faced with an array of difficulties and hardships, we must stand on Christ the solid rock. Whatever situation we find ourselves, God gives us the strength to go through and we come out the other side with a testimony, this is why we must learn to be content. When we are happy with our lot, there is no feeling of anxiety or jealousy and we do not have the craving for anything else.

As a believer in Christ, we inherit a priceless gift, God's love, which enables the child of God to love ourselves and others.

Missionary Audrey Simpson

WEDNESDAY 19th

...this is the confidence that we have in him, that if we ask any thing according to his will, he heareth us – 1 John 5:14

KOINONIA – Reading: 1 John 5:1-21

These days are uncertain times, when every child of God must examine themselves to determine if they are in the faith. Fundamental laws of society are unravelling as the world debates humanity and develops artificial intelligence. The world is attempting to remove any godly influence. But our Lord Jesus Christ had said; *'the gates of hell shall not prevail'* (Matthew 16:18).

The letter of 1 John was written around the times AD 80 and 95, to address false teachings. It's supposed that the correspondence was from Ephesus to churches in the Asia Minor area i.e., modern day Turkey.

False doctrine had broken out causing conflicts and doubt. The saints were weakened in faith and began to break fellowship with one another. Some had backslidden, influenced by a type of gnostic teaching, i.e., a belief that all matter was evil and only the spirit was good. They believed that Jesus was not the Christ because flesh was evil. They falsely taught that Jesus did not have a physical body and thereby denied the faith, the central message of salvation in the Lord Jesus Christ.

Although the author's name is not mentioned in the first letter, it's been attributed to John the Apostle. As a senior in the Gospel and the last eyewitness of Jesus Christ, he encouraged the saints to keep the faith and emphasised fellowship with fellow-brethren through the love of God, despite the problems they faced (1 John 3:23-24; 1 John 4:1-6).

We trust God knowing that through fellowship with Him we have confidence that He hears us. Our relationship with our Father enables us to, *'come boldly to the throne of grace'* as written in Hebrews 4:16, all problems pale into insignificance when we soak up His holy presence.

It's by communion in His presence with the joy of the Lord, that we are built up in faith, reading His Word to become more like Him.

Hallelujah!

CDP

THURSDAY 20th

The LORD is my strength...my heart trusteth in him... – Psalm 28:7

GOD BANISHES FEAR – Reading: Psalm 28:1-9

It can be daunting living in a society where there are such emotions as are described in Psalm 28, i.e., feelings of anger and fury. Anxiety is at an all-time high because of the uncertainties that face us each day.

The mischief and destruction that happens with these untamed emotions which are without compassion or temperance have countries, institutions, and communities feeling their hearts failing them for fear. Angry bosses, road rage, mistrust of law enforcement, governments and politics in disarray - how do we find peace in the tornado of calamity? We hear daily how this unbridled anger causes so much chaos and pain in our world. And with all this comes fear.

How many times have you heard it said that once upon a time we could leave our front doors open and walk safely on the streets? If we still can, we dare not. The sense of protection, of safety lost even in this alarming world causes us to cling more closely to the only true and ultimate place of trust, the one we have in Christ Jesus. Psalm 28 appeals to our trusting in God to banish fear. It dissolves the anxieties that come with this world.

It is said that it's impossible to fear and hold faith simultaneously. In the moments that we concentrate on the situation of impending calamity, our hearts are often emptied of faith. Likewise, in the moments that we cling to God and trust, we're filled with safety and protection. Faith abases those feelings and pangs of fear, even momentarily, but to dwell in God's peace and in His favour means that we have access to true safety.

The writer encourages us to continually lean into a place of safety in God. Not to trust in chariots or gold, not to trust in our own abilities our achievements, or even financial security. Ultimately, the deepest place worthy of trust is finally found in the presence of God and when we trust Him, fear has to flee. Fear, anxiousness, threat and worry are like bullies that shrink when Jesus comes into our hearts and His perfect love casts out all fear.

Today, remembering this hymn, I encourage you to, *'Be not dismayed whate'er betide. God will take care of you'*.

Joy Lear-Bernard

FRIDAY 21st

So shall they fear the name of the LORD...when the enemy shall come in like a flood, the Spirit of the LORD shall lift up a standard against him – Isaiah 59:19

TRUST THE TRIPLE COMBO OF YOUR GOD! - Reading: Isaiah 59:1-21

What a blessing it is to be able to be at ease when the enemy assails us in life. It's one thing to be confident and have full trust in Him just simply because He is God, but when we consider the multifaceted nature of God, we realise that God's name, His glory and His Spirit fights for us. So relax, God's got this!

It is often noted in Scripture that people feared other nations because of the reputation they had based on the name of a warrior king, champion, or army. Just the mention of that name would send a shudder down the spine.

Have you ever looked at a beautiful scene, the wonders of nature, or a grand building and been left awestruck? Its splendour, and wonder causes you to say, '**wowww!**' almost involuntarily.

Have you ever experienced a move of God so great that you've been swept off your feet or carried away to a heavenly realm, where the breath of God seems so close you almost think the winds of Pentecost are blowing again?

Well imagine the triple combination of the reputation, the awe or glory, and breath of God fighting for you in your battles. What an impressive defence you have, what trust you possess because the God above all gods, King above all kings, and LORD of all lords is on your side. The trust and confidence we have in our LORD Jesus Christ as believers cannot be rivalled or equal to any other god, because our God doesn't need to pull out all the stops, use every weapon, or use the full force of who He is to fight against the enemy. In this case His name, His glory, and the breath of His Spirit does the job. Trust the triple combo (combination) of your God!

Minister Kay Dawkins/ MinK

SATURDAY 22nd

God is not a man, that he should lie... - Numbers 23:19

GOD'S PROMISES ARE SURE – Reading: Numbers 23:13-26

God cannot lie.

Whatever God has promised us has already happened in His mind and divine will. We pray, fast and wait for its manifestation.

We make promises to each other, sometimes not knowing how we will fulfil what we've said. Sometimes we don't have the means to keep the promise made - we promise and then go away to make a plan to bring it to pass. Occasionally we have to admit that we can't keep our word and then retract what was said.

That's not how God works for, *'He honours His Word above His name' (Psalm 138:2).* God knows how to allow you to meet who you need to meet, how to arrange for you to have a specific conversation with a particular person, He knows how to get you to be at a particular place for a particular time, even if it's for as short as five minutes! *'...has He said, and shall He not do it? Or has He spoken, and shall He not make it good? Behold, I have received commandment to bless: and He hath blessed; and I cannot reverse it' (Numbers 23:19-20).*

The life of a true believer is not made up of good luck, bad luck, or chance. Every detail is wisely orchestrated by the LORD and will prove that He cannot lie.

JEJ

SUNDAY 23rd

Jesus was led up of the Spirit into the wilderness to be tempted of the devil
Matthew 4:1

GOD KNOWS BEST – Reading: Matthew 4:1-11

Most of us have heard the saying that, *'God does not make mistakes'*. However, there may have been times in our lives when we wondered if this was indeed true. We asked God why He had allowed certain things to happen or not to happen to us, even though we exercised our faith. Maybe the following poem, written by Helen Steiner Rice, will help us to understand some of our *'whys'*:

Our Father knows what's best for us
So why should we complain
We always want the sunshine
But He knows there must be rain.
We love the sound of laughter
And the merriment of cheer
But our hearts would lose their tenderness
If we never shed a tear.
Our Father tests us often
With suffering and with sorrow
He tests us, not to punish us
But to help us meet tomorrow.
For growing trees are strengthened
When they withstand the storm
And the sharp cut of a chisel
Gives the marble grace and form.
God never hurts us needlessly
And He never wastes our pain
For every loss He send to us
Is followed by rich gain.
And when we count the blessings
That God has so freely sent
We will find no cause for murmuring
And no time to lament.
For our Father loves His children
And to Him all things are plain
So He never sends us pleasure
When the soul's deep need is pain.
So whenever we are troubled
And when everything goes wrong
It is just God working in us
To make our spirit strong.
Name withheld

MONDAY 24th

Trust ye not in a friend, put ye not confidence in a guide – Micah 7:5

BE CAREFUL WHO YOU TRUST – Reading: Psalm 55:1-16

The prophet Micah gives good counsel when he cautions, *'Trust ye not in a friend…'.*

Of course Micah is not saying that we shouldn't have close relationships with those whom we consider to be trustworthy individuals. However, there will be people reading this page who have experienced the pain of betrayal by a friend, family member, or church brethren. Disloyalty is a wound that only God can heal, it can feel like it will bleed forever. You may have confided in that person things which you have never discussed with anybody else, and they later laid it out in the open for all to see.

David had one of these awful experiences. We can easily sense his mood of hurt, dismay, and even embarrassment, as we read Psalm 55:12-14 (GW), *'If someone who had hated me had attacked me, then I could hide from him. But it is you, my equal, my best friend, one I knew so well! We used to talk to each other in complete confidence and walk into God's house with the festival crowds'.*

Jesus also encountered betrayal by his disciple, Judas, who betrayed Him for money. Jesus said, *'Judas, betrayest thou the Son of man with a kiss?' (Luke 22:48).*

Ladies, we all at some stage in our lives need someone on which we can offload sensitive information, as well as to God in prayer. When such times come, ask God to show you the right person, or to lead the right person to you. It may not be who you consider to be your 'best friend' but if the Holy Spirit within you bears witness that they are **truly** God-sent, it's safe to talk.

JEJ

TUESDAY 25th

God is faithful… – 1 Corinthians 1:9

DIVINE FAITHFULNESS – Reading: 1 Corinthians 1:4-9

The faithfulness of God means that God is unchanging in His nature, is true to His Word, has promised salvation to His people and will keep His promises forever (Ref: Samuel Saldivar).

It could be argued that if we as Christians cannot trust what God says in the Bible, then we have no valid reason to believe. If God does not keep to His Word, then our salvation is weak and meaningless, and our hope is void. But if God does carry out His Word, does what He says He will do, then our faith and eternal future are secure.

God always does exactly what He has promised. We've seen so many of God's faithful promises fulfilled in both the Old and New Testament, and in our lives too. He is so faithful that anyone who seeks Him can find Him. He cannot break His Word because that is contrary to the nature of God, we know that God cannot lie (Numbers 23:19).

There are economic crises, famines, wars, challenges and struggles, but God will surely see us through.

Missionary M Fraser

WEDNESDAY 26th

...God is the strength of my heart, and my portion for ever – Psalm 73:26

MY EVERLASTING PORTION – Reading: Psalm 73:1-28

Today's psalm was written by Asaph, one of the temple worship leaders. He reflects on not so good times, whilst also considering the faithfulness of God. His psalm begins with a bold testimony, *'Truly God is good to Israel…' (Psalm 73:1).* All of us reading this could prefix any lamentation that we may have with, *'Truly God is good…'!*

Asaph is by now not one of the younger members of the worship team – he says in verse 26, *'My flesh and my heart faileth'* or *'my body and my mind may become weak'*. But in spite of the outward man perishing, God continued to be Asaph's strength and a constant friend.

He had seen many come and go from the temple during his time of ministry. The only one who stayed consistently faithful was God, Asaph described Him as being his portion forever. We too should be glad and thank God that when we lose people, by whatever cause, He still remains:

Thou my everlasting portion
More than friend or life to me
All along my pilgrim journey
Saviour, let me walk with Thee.

Chorus
Close to Thee, close to Thee
Close to Thee, close to Thee
All along my pilgrim journey
Saviour, let me walk with Thee.

Not for ease or worldly pleasure
Not for fame my prayer shall be
Gladly will I toil and suffer
Only let me walk with Thee.

Lead me through the vale of shadows
Bear me o'er life's fitful sea
Then the gate of life eternal
May I enter, Lord, with Thee.
(Close to Thee – FJ Crosby)

JEJ

THURSDAY 27th

…your labour is not in vain in the Lord – 1 Corinthians 15:58

WHAT'S YOUR CONCLUSION? – Reading: 1 Corinthians 15:51-58

Apostle Paul wrote to the brethren at Corinth in order to correct a dangerous error which had crept in among the believers. What was it? That there was no resurrection of the dead!

This opposition was against a foundational doctrine, detrimental to the hope of experiencing their full Salvation, *'For if the dead rise not, then is not Christ raised and if Christ be not raised, your faith is vain; ye are yet in your sins' (verses 16-17).*

We can trust God's Word as all Scriptures are God-inspired or God-breathed, which guarantees us that what the Scripture says is true. Paul's strong comforting encouragement, and doctrinal correction, addressed the mind of the church at Corinth as to settle them.

As it was then so it is now; challenges of every kind. So get settled in the truth and conclude with your *'therefore'.* Trust God; decide to stand still and He will release within you divine endurance, that staying-power to outlast all the attacks.

'Therefore, my beloved brethren, be ye steadfast, unmoveable, always abounding in the work of the Lord, forasmuch as ye know that your labour is not in vain in the Lord' (1 Corinthians 15:58).

Pastor Josephine Lewis

FRIDAY 28th

...be thou faithful unto death, and I will give you a crown of life – Revelation2:10

FAITHFUL DURING SUFFERING – Reading: Revelation 2:8-11

The Church of Smyrna is among the Seven Churches to whom a letter was sent in the book of the Unveiling of Jesus Christ (Revelation).

The Church in Smyrna, on the outside, was suffering tremendous persecution and poverty inflicted on them by compulsory worship of Caesar. All Christians were compelled once a year to burn incense on an altar to Caesar, after which a certificate was issued confirming their religious duty performed. As a believer in the true and living God, compromising was not an option back then or today.

The name Smyrna comes from the word myrrh, which refers to a sweet-smelling perfume which was used in embalming dead bodies.

Jesus informed the Church of Smyrna that He is the first and the last, which speaks of His eternal character (Isaiah 48:12). He also died and came back to life. Jesus, who is all-knowing, saw the harsh persecution and poverty they were going through. They knew abject poverty, they were robbed and sacked from earning their daily bread and others were thrown into prison for a while.

Despite all the things they were enduring, Jesus carried them through these horrendous times of persecution. It is no different for believers today, whatever our circumstances, it is only Jesus who can carry us through. We are children of God, heirs and joint heirs with Jesus. This is a condition that believers in Christ must understand, we must suffer with Him to be glorified with Him.

Suffering, my sisters, is but a light affliction for a moment; the God of all comfort is with us every step of the way. The Word of God goes before and surrounds us. When we build our relationship, and walk by faith and stand on His Word, we will always remember in our moments of light affliction that, *'He will never leave us or forsake us' (Hebrews13:5).*

Our natural body will be destroyed, however, there is hope in the Crucified One, death is not the end of life. Jesus died, was buried, and then resurrected from the dead. Believers too will also be resurrected from the dead and put on our glorified bodies. This hope enabled believers in the Church of Smyrna to keep a heavenly perspective, and also fortifies and drives believers in this season to hold on to this same hope.

Missionary Audrey Simpson

SATURDAY 29th

God is able to do exceeding abundantly above all that we ask or think – Eph. 3:20

WHAT DO YOU NEED? – Reading: Ephesians 3:14-21

If I volunteered to take you out shopping today, or to do it all online, and I promised to pay for absolutely everything **you need**, would you believe me? Would you really put everything, no matter how expensive, into your basket and just meet me at the checkout? Would you order for delivery all of those items too large to carry home in a car? If not, why?

At a guess, I'd imagine that you would be hesitant to fill up your basket and go back and get another one, and another one, until absolutely everything needed had been collected. There would be different reasons for only complying in part but the main one (I think) would be lack of trust. You may have decided that I might not be able to afford payment for everything that you need, although I was fully conscious and sober when I made the offer. You may consider my genuine offer as only a nice thought.

We sometimes bring this same mindset into our relationship with God, e.g., *'I would claim that thing, but what if God wasn't serious when He said that I can have it? It's so big! How will it happen?'*. God, through His servant Paul the apostle, wants to put us straight about something: *'Now glory to God, who by His mighty power at work within us* ***is able to do far more*** *than we would ever dare to ask or even dream of – infinitely beyond our highest prayers, desires, thoughts, or hopes…' (Ephesians 3: 20 TLB).*

I'll end by saying that God can do 'it', He can manage 'it', He can arrange 'it'!

JEJ

'But my God shall supply all your need according to His riches in glory by Christ Jesus' (Philippians 4:19).

SUNDAY 30th

Is any thing too hard for the LORD? Genesis 18:14

ANOTHER LEVEL OF FAITH – Reading: Genesis 18:1-19

Faith in God is absolute trust and confidence in Him. We believe and receive His promises even when we see no change.

Our frustration with God's pace of answering our prayers is sometimes coming from the fact the we live in time, whereas God is in eternity. There are no clocks or calendars in eternity, those are only needed where time governs.

In today's lesson where Sarah and Abraham are the main characters, the reason why they laughed at news that they would become parents, was because of time, i.e., based on time, Abraham would be one hundred and his wife ninety when Isaac was born (Genesis 17:16-17). None of this was fresh news to God, or even relevant. In the sphere of time, Sarah had passed through the menopause (Genesis 18:11), but in the will of God she was still fertile. Here lay their conflict with faith.

My mom used to say to me, *'Everybody's pot doesn't boil at the same time'*. All of our purpose does not have to come to pass when we are what we consider to be young, even if the purpose of others is obvious and completed early. Fulfilment of purpose doesn't have to happen either as soon as the Word or vision has been given. In your younger years, you may not be mature enough to manage what God has planned for you without destroying yourself and others (1 Corinthians 13:11). He therefore puts the promise on hold while He sands-you-down, matures you, develops you to receive it when you have almost given up or perhaps forgotten or dismissed the idea. Nonetheless, you are finally ready.

Is there something which you think is too hard for the LORD, something that God has released you to do now, and your only point of resistance or refusal is your date of birth? I've seen God use events, even in my life, to slow me down for His purpose – to walk behind Him rather than in front.

Another level of faith is not just for instant results, but to keep on believing the same promise **for years** that it will one day surely come to pass.

JEJ

STREPTOCOCCUS A (STREP A) INFECTIONS

STREP A

Strep A is a common type of bacteria. Most strep A infections are mild and easily treated, but some are more serious.

Symptoms of a strep A infection

Common symptoms of strep A include:

- flu-like symptoms, such as a high temperature, swollen glands or an aching body
- sore throat (strep throat or tonsillitis)
- a rash that feels rough, like sandpaper (scarlet fever)
- scabs and sores (impetigo)
- pain and swelling (cellulitis)
- severe muscle aches
- nausea and vomiting

Strep A infections are more common in children, but adults can also sometimes get them. Most strep A infections are not serious and can be treated with antibiotics. But rarely, the infection can cause serious problems. This is called invasive group A strep (iGAS). Recently there has been an increase in the number of invasive group A strep illnesses reported. It is a serious illness. Adults and children can die from it.

What to do if your child is unwell

It can be difficult to tell when a child is seriously ill, but the main thing is to trust your instincts. You know better than anyone else what your child is usually like, so you'll know when something is seriously wrong. If your child does not seem to be seriously ill, you can usually look after them at home. They should feel better in a few days. If they're uncomfortable, you can give them children's paracetamol.

Check the leaflet to make sure the medicine is suitable for your child and to see how much to give them. A pharmacist can give you advice about how to ease your child's symptoms, and whether you need to see a doctor.

If unsure how unwell your child is, request an appointment for your child to be seen.

Treatments for a strep A infection

Most strep A infections can be easily treated with antibiotics.
If you or your child has a strep A infection, you should stay away from nursery, school or work for 24 hours after you start taking antibiotics. This will help stop the infection spreading to other people. Serious strep A infections (invasive group A strep, iGAS) need to be treated in hospital with antibiotics.

How you get strep A infections

Strep A infections are spread by close contact with an infected person. They can be passed on through coughs and sneezes or from a wound. In some people, the bacteria live in the body without causing symptoms or making them feel unwell. But they can still pass the bacteria on to others.

Things that might make you more at risk of strep A infections include:

- a weakened immune system
- open sores or wounds
- some viral infections, such as a cold or flu

How to avoid getting infections

Infections like strep A can easily be spread to other people. To reduce the chance of catching or spreading an infection:

- avoid close contact with someone you know is infected
- wash your hands often with soap and water
- cover your mouth and nose with a tissue when you cough or sneeze
- bin used tissues as quickly as possible

If in doubt about yourself or a child, call your GP Surgery and request a same-day (urgent) appointment, or dial 111 for advice, or go to the Emergency Department if you are very worried and you feel that urgent care is needed.

Always follow your instincts.

Ref: http://www.nhs.uk

Author: Dr Jo Brooks FRCPCH
Consultant Paediatrician

july

More than Conquerors

MONDAY 1st

The one who loves us gives us an overwhelming victory in all difficulties
Romans 8:37 (GW)

THE WIND IN MY FACE – Reading: Romans 8:33-37

As I was walking up the slight hill
I felt the wind in my face
It was so warming
And so reassuring
So calming on that day.

I did not notice the slight hill
That I would climb
For I was basking in the wind
And God's glorious sunshine.

The slight breeze
Blew all of life's cobwebs away
The effort it took
As I walked in my stride
Was not too hard in any way.

That wind lifted me up
I could feel God's power
It made me feel so alive
It was a wind from my Creator
A wind, blown in from Him
He allowed me to see His actions.

It reminded me of Pentecost
When the Holy Ghost fell
Oh what a day
The brethren and all who were there had as well.

There were cloven tongues like as of fire
Languages - so many spoken
The disciples and who were present
Could never be the same again.

As I felt the slight breeze
I am reminded that there is a mighty

Presence deeply anchored within me
It's the awesome power of the Holy Ghost
That comes from the Father
He promised to give us, His children
It's a life-giving power
That changes a sinner
It can make them a spiritual giant
He changes into a completely new man.

The Holy Spirit
Can do the same in you and me
If we let go of our former selves
And trust and abide in Him
Then He will lead and change us
So we can live a conquering life for Him.

Sister Jennifer Henry

TUESDAY 2nd

And take the helmet of salvation, and the sword of the spirit, which is the word of God

Ephesians 6:17

USE YOUR SPIRITUAL WEAPONS – Reading: Ephesians 6:17; 2 Corinthians 10:1-6

More than a conqueror means that, as women of God, we are able to confidently overcome and take control of adverse conditions with Christ in our vessel, and if we know who we are in Him.

We must put on the helmet of salvation, and study the Word of God which is the sword of the Spirit to arm ourselves. We fight, not in the natural, but we take up our spiritual tools. The helmet of salvation protects the head - our mind, thoughts, feelings, emotions, and coping mechanisms. The sword arms us with the Word - within God's army we use the Word to speak, to decree a thing and defeat Satan and his host.

Women of God, walk through your homes, workplaces, anywhere where you encounter evil forces, and use that sword to tear down, remove, to bind and loose, to recover, because we are more than conquerors through Christ Jesus.

Evg. Angelina Cox

WEDNESDAY 3rd

Greater is he that is in you, than he that is in the world – 1 John 4:4

THROUGH GOD'S EYES – Reading: 1 John 4:1-6

How we see ourselves can have much to do with how we are seen and treated by others. If we are making a request whilst quivering and wringing our hands together, it is probable that someone else who asks confidently for the same thing will get it and move along.

My mom told me a story of a man who wanted to borrow his neighbour's donkey. He was of a nervous disposition so skirted around the issue instead of saying why he had come to visit. Mid-conversation, another man walked up and said, *'I've come to borrow your donkey – I'll bring it back when I'm finished'*. He quickly loosed the donkey and said goodbye. The first man said to the owner, *'Guess what? I also came to ask if I can borrow your donkey!'*.

I know that at times we are faced with challenges that seem like mountains. We look at our circumstance from different angles and it looks impossible from whichever position viewed. It could be a job interview for a role for which you are not fully qualified. You had the faith to put your name forward, but not enough to believe that you can get through the interview. You start to tell yourself that the other applicants are better than you, and question yourself why you even bothered to come. You talk yourself out of the confidence you had until you are left weak with fear.

When the twelve spies went to search Canaan, the majority felt that the enemy was greater than them. They reported that **they saw themselves** as grasshoppers (Numbers 13:33). It's a fact that we cannot rise above our thoughts and how we esteem ourselves.

If you woke up today feeling that you're insignificant and worthless, please start your day again! You're greater than a grasshopper for you have been *'created in the image of God' (Genesis 1:27),* and God said *'it was very good' (v31)*. Also, His Spirit is dwelling in you, you are therefore more than a conqueror through Jesus Christ.

JEJ

THURSDAY 4th

...I have overcome the world...John 16:33

KEEP ON BELIEVING YOU'RE MORE THAN A CONQUEROR – Reading: John 16:23-33

Many times we're afflicted, but all is not lost
Deny yourself and take up your cross
You're partaking in Christ's sufferings
To be jewels bright gems for His crown.

Don't go back to the world where Jesus brought you from
Press toward Jesus's Kingdom
There are mansions prepared for you and for me
Because of Calvary.

This road is not easy, as you will find
But to enter God's Kingdom as gold you'll be tried
So take example of God's only Son
Not my will, but Thy will be done.

To now lose our faith, we cannot afford
We'll receive added strength soon, if we trust in the LORD
We'll exchange this old cross, for a crown purer than gold
If in patience, we possess our souls.

Maxine Blair

FRIDAY 5th

...If God be for us, who can be against us? – Romans 8:31

PLEASE GOD FIRST – Reading:1 Kings 17:8-16

I am learning to relax in God's approval. I'm also learning to embrace what He thinks about me and accept His affirmation above anybody else's.

We can miss fulfilling our ministry and purpose by being bound by the opinion of others. We become ineffective by cutting corners trying to get people to like us, and thereby displease God. We must prove that, *'When (our) ways please the LORD, he maketh even (our) enemies to be at peace with (us)' (Proverbs 16:7)* – that's a guarantee.

I wonder how much more palatable we'd be to the tastebuds of God, and impactful we would be daily, if we served in the Kingdom to please God first? Note that God gives 100% support and backup to those whom He has called, we are never working for Him alone. Any opponent coming against us is bound to fail because the God of armies is with us (Psalm 46:11).

When God is for us, even when it looks like we've lost we have won because, *'... we know that all things work together for good to them that love God, to them who are the called according to his purpose' (Romans 8:28).*

JEJ

SATURDAY 6th

The LORD said...why do you keep calling out to me for help? Tell the Israelites to move forward – Exodus 14:15

GOD HAS SPOKEN – Reading: Exodus 14:13-31

Have you been tentatively dipping your toe, for a few years now, into God's will for the next stage of your life? He may have shown you what to do but you're fearful, or reluctant, or both.

What that ends up looking like is praying a repetitive prayer asking God for another sign to prove it's His will, or praying again with the hope that God will change His mind.

Whilst I do believe in asking God to confirm His will, and that's biblical (2 Corinthians 13:1), I do also think that sometimes we can use prayer to *'kick the can down the road'*. That means, to delay doing what we don't want to do, i.e., stalling for time.

In today's focus verse, Moses is standing at the Red Sea with Pharaoh and his army in close pursuit. I feel and understand their panic as they stand between a rock and a hard place – if Pharaoh catches up with them, he will kill them or bring them back to Egypt as slaves under worse conditions than previously. The alternative is a huge sea in front of them in which they will surely drown.

Moses, what are you going to do? Dear Reader, what are you going to do? Turn back, stand still, or go forward? Moses tries to calm the people's panic, he says, *'Stand still and see the salvation of the LORD...' (Exodus 14:13)*. However, God's response to Moses is not to *'stand still'*, God tells him, *'Go forward'*. He asks Moses, *'Why are you crying out to me?'*.

What is your Red Sea that needs to be conquered? You've been pondering on whatever it is for long enough; praying about it again and again while standing still and not going forward into your God-planned destiny. When God has clearly spoken, He does not need to speak again. Is God asking you, *'Why are you crying out to me?'*

JEJ

*SUNDAY 7th

I can do all things through Christ who gives me strength – Philippians 4:13 (NIV)

GOD GIVES STRENGTH – Reading: Philippians 4:10-20

In life you will go through some things that seem too hard to bear. At times you will feel like giving up but God sees and feels your pain. As soon as you turn to God and surrender yourself unto Him, He will rescue you!

This short story is of the time I became desperate to receive the Holy Ghost, but encountered a few setbacks as I got closer to God. The month of September 2019 was a significant month and year for me. It was in this month that I gave my life to the Lord. I was excited and anticipated receiving the infilling of the Holy Ghost. But it was not long after we were hit by COVID-19 globally which meant we had to stay home. My focus had changed and because we weren't going to church the urgency for receiving the Holy Ghost had become less important.

After COVID-19, upon our return to church, there was a drive and focus from our leaders about being ready and having the Holy Ghost. This drive, urgency, and the dreams I started to have, made me realise the importance of getting the Holy Ghost. I became very interested in how others would become consumed with this supernatural power. Before I had received the Holy Ghost, I had gotten to a very dark place mentally; I had cried many tears but God gave me the strength to carry on as He was a comfort in these times of distress. Soon I became desperate to receive the Holy Ghost, but was left discouraged each time that I tarried. I even developed the mindset that I would never receive it, but that was Satan telling me lies.

Many days I would be very hesitant to go up to the altar, afraid that I would leave discouraged. The enemy would constantly say to me, *'You'll never get it! Everyone will see you fail'; 'God doesn't love you, why would He give you the Holy Ghost'.* Unfortunately, I believed these lies back then but God knew that I was more than a conqueror and saw my future.

On the day that I was filled, I was tired mentally as the enemy knew I was getting closer and closer to my breakthrough, so it became a struggle mentally as my mind was filled with doubt, fear and worry. But as I went to church that day, and listened to the Word, it broke me and I felt led to go to the altar. There in the moment of me reaching out to God, and beginning to praise and worship Him, my mind started to fill with doubt saying, *'You're going to go home disappointed and discouraged'.* But by this point, God gave me strength and I rebuked those thoughts saying, *'No! no! Today I WILL receive the Holy Ghost, I will not let the enemy take this away from me!'.* I began to worship God again and that was when the Holy Ghost washed over me, I was consumed and felt this supernatural power that I could not control!

God sees your tears and hears your cry, and He will deliver you out of your situation. Anything is possible when it comes to God, just know that God will give you strength, especially in a time of desperation.

Name withheld
World Chocolate Day

MONDAY 8th

...be strong in the Lord, and in the power of his might – Ephesians 6:10

ON THE VICT'RY SIDE – Reading: Ephesians 6:10-18

As Christians we are constantly facing spiritual conflict with Satan and a host of evil spirits; Matthew 4:10 confirms this.

These powers of darkness are spiritual forces of evil and they energise the ungodly, oppose the will of God, and continuously attack believers of this age.

Therefore, we as Christians should be battle-ready as advised in Ephesians 6:11, *'Put on the whole armour of God that you may be able to stand against the wiles of the devil'.* In the evil day, despite any arrows that the enemy sends, we know that we are never alone!

We are more than conquerors through Christ who strengthens us. The battle is not ours but Christ's. We must be holy, faithful, truthful, obedient, and love, then victory is ours in Jesus Christ's name. Hallelujah!

Sis Esther Miller

TUESDAY 9th

Above all taking the shield of faith…to quench all the fiery darts… - Ephesians 6:16

HOW TO BE MORE THAN A CONQUEROR – Reading: Joshua 6:1-20

Recently, the LORD spoke to me and said, *'Jo, don't just GO through it. GROW through it'.*

God was referring to the situation that I was going through. To GROW through challenging times means to become greater as we progress. We become progressively greater because *'we walk by faith, and not by sight'* (2 Corinthians 5:7): that's the only way to GROW through any situation.

'DON'T JUST GO THROUGH IT, GROW THROUGH IT!'

Your situation is not to break you. God sent it, and allowed it, in order to MAKE you!

A conqueror overcomes the situation, and that's it. Becoming *'more than a conqueror'* allows you not only to overcome the current fight, but all the future fights to come.

You are more than a conqueror because God is not just preparing you to conquer your now, but also to conquer your future! You are more than a conqueror because you don't just go through it, you GROW through it.

Min Jo Earle

WEDNESDAY 10th

Put on all the armour that God supplies. In this way you can take a stand against the devil's strategies – Ephesians 6:11 (GW)

CLOTHED FOR VICTORY – Reading: Ephesians 6:10-16

To live a victorious life, we must first recognise the source of our strength - the Lord Jesus and His mighty power. It's not our own strength that sustains us, but rather it is the supernatural strength we receive when we rely upon God. In our own strength we are vulnerable and weak, but when we draw from the limitless reservoir of God's power, we become invincible.

The key to victory is found in Ephesians 6:10-11: *'Put on the full armour of God'*. Just as a soldier equips themself with armour to protect against the enemy's attacks, we too must be spiritually dressed for the battles we have to face, sometimes without warning. The armour of God is not made of metal or leather; it is a spiritual armour, and its efficiency supersedes all other kinds of defence.

The spiritual armour:
The Belt of Truth: Truth anchors us in a world filled with lies. Embrace God's truth through His Word and it will protect you from the deceit of the enemy.

The Breastplate of Righteousness: guards your heart against the accusations and guilt that the enemy tries to place on you.

The Shoes of Peace: As you walk in God's peace, you stand firm and surefooted, even in the midst of life's storms.

The Shield of Faith: Faith is your defence against the enemy's fiery darts of doubt and fear.

The Helmet of Salvation: Protect your mind with the assurance of your salvation in Christ, guarding against thoughts that would lead you astray.

The Sword of the Spirit: The Word of God is your defence. Use it to combat the lies of the enemy and to speak truth into your circumstances.

Sis. Nadine Johnson

THURSDAY 11th

...thanks be to God, which giveth us the victory through our Lord Jesus Christ
1 Corinthians 15:57

HE WILL MAKE A WAY – Reading: Isaiah 54:1-17; 1 Corinthians 15:57-58

What a blessing to know that, whatever situation we find ourselves in, we can be victorious simply because we have God on our side! There are many examples in the Bible of victories won through trusting in God and working for the Lord – read about Esther, Moses, Gideon, David - to name but a few.

Every victory we have is gained because of the grace of God, not by our own might or power, but by HIM. Let's give God thanks for being our Saviour – His salvation cannot be compared to any human help or support. HE has given us the victory, HE has brought us out of tight spots, HE has made a way when we thought there was no way, HE has made possible what we thought was impossible!

There is nothing too hard for God and let us remember that, as declared in Isaiah 54:17, *'No weapon that is formed against thee shall prosper'.*

Thanking God for the victory!

Sis Elaine

FRIDAY 12th

...we must through much tribulation enter into the kingdom of God – Acts 14:22

TRAVELLING COMPANION – Reading: Acts 14:21-28

Today's focus verse may not be what we want to read first thing in the morning, or after a difficult day, *'we must through much tribulation enter into the kingdom of God'*.

When experiencing testing times, we can be comforted to know firstly that it won't always be like this, and also that we're not alone in suffering. When Jesus was here, He wept and pleaded concerning the cup of sorrow which was made for Him to drink. Notwithstanding, although His prayers were heard (Hebrews 5:7), He had to submit His will and say, *'Thy will be done' (Luke 22:42).*

In case you're not sure what is meant by *'tribulation'*, Strong's defines it as pressure (to press hard upon), affliction, anguish, trouble. Now that we are clear, just prefix all of that with *'much'*!

Sometimes when we look over our lives we can feel, or be made to feel, that it's because of some sin why so many bad things happen to us. But the opposite is often true; God allows it because He knows that we are righteous and can bear pain without cursing His name. Composer Walter Hawkins sang, *'I wouldn't put more on you, than you can bear, so if it's there it means you can bear it!'*.

We have to keep our destination in mind in order to keep on going. If we lose focus, our cross(es) will slay us; we will buckle under life's pressures and then try to justify why we gave up. Yes, we would rather that God only allowed good things to access our lives, but are sure that in times of affliction He is present, *'on the way from earth to heaven and will guide us with His eye' (Precious Promise – N Niles).*

JEJ

SATURDAY 13th

...the sufferings of this present time are not worthy to be compared with the glory which shall be revealed in us – Romans 8:18 (NKJV)

UNCONQUERABLE – Reading: Romans 8:18-25, 36-37

What does it mean to be a conqueror? Furthermore, what does suffering have to do with conquering?

Simple stated, a ***conqueror*** is one who conquers; *'It's one who wins a country in war, subdues a people, or overcomes an adversary'.* When we think of conquerors, men like Alexander the Great, Charlemagne, the Pharaohs, and Genghis Khan may come to mind. So, what is Paul talking about when he states, *'Nay, in all these things* **we** *are* ***more than*** *conquerors through him that loved us' (Romans 8:37 KJV).*

'More than' speaks to *'greater than'*, or *'exceeding'* (the norm or expected). Invariably, Paul is saying that what we have gained, and what we will gain ***in*** Christ far exceeds what any human being has ever gained in human history. In fact, while these men gained renown for a period of their lifetime, inevitably they were defeated; the conqueror was conquered.

Not so for the one that is 'in Christ Jesus'!

Being ***'more than'*** refers to those who gain a surpassing victory (who) are completely victorious; Paul is also saying the we ***'are'*** more than conquerors, in the present tense; in other words, *'we keep on winning'* no matter what!

But, we experience this victorious living base on our perspective - how we see and think about who we are, and whose we are. Through the cross and because of the resurrection, Christ is the everlasting Conqueror, never to be defeated. Therefore, in Christ, ***we*** are also undefeated. Unconquerable.

'What shall we then say to these things? If God be for us, who can be against us?' (Romans 8:31). This is why Paul can confidently say, despite personal struggles (Romans 7:22-25), we are not condemned. It is also why he is not dismayed at his current sufferings, i.e., because he has an eternal perspective, *'But if we hope for what we do not see, we eagerly wait for it with* **perseverance***' (Romans 8:25 NKJV).*

If we maintain the right perspective, there is nothing we are experiencing now, or will experience in the future, that can defeat us. Not even death, *'Who shall separate us from the love of Christ? shall tribulation, or distress, or persecution, or famine, or nakedness, or peril, or sword?* ***Nay!*** *In all these things we are more than conquerors...' (Romans 8:35, 37).*

AT (Canada)

SUNDAY 14th

These little troubles are getting us ready for an eternal glory – 2 Cor. 4:17 (CEV)

CAN I BEAR IT TO THE END? - Reading: 2 Corinthians 4:11-18

This is a question which no one can answer on our behalf. It is also the question that we struggle with ourselves, particularly when everything seems to be working against us.

It's a natural reaction for us to pamper our bodies. We avoid opposition at every cost. We loathe experiencing any type of loss. The desire for undisturbed peace is our default setting. When this does not happen, we find ourselves questioning God and expecting an answer that is acceptable to us.

Being overlooked for that promotion at work in favour of someone else who only knows how to 'make nice' with the bosses but does not have the same work ethic that we do, stings. Losing our loved ones in death without warning hurts. Being diagnosed with any type of illness causes us to howl in pain. Losing our friends through the deception of others leaves us broken.

Yet the Scripture calls these *'light afflictions'* and declares that they are but *'for a moment'*! I can recall going through all of the above and barely surviving, but I did. I questioned God and rejected the answers, but He kept me. I look back now and see His hand in every situation, but I could not see it at the time.

Could I bear it to the end? Only by scraping the bottom of the 'faith' barrel was I able to. I have learned to now say, *'Lord I believe, help thou mine unbelief'*.

Pastor Londy Esdaille (Nevis)

MONDAY 15th

There was given to me a thorn in the flesh... - 2 Corinthians 12:7

THE THORN COMES WITH GRACE - Reading: 2 Corinthians 12:1-9

There are some things that we do to protect ourselves against unforeseen circumstances. We hope that we can drive our vehicle all year without being involved in an accident but still take out insurance as a precaution. Likewise, many of the monthly premiums that we pay are not for tangible items but to prevent us struggling financially should something unpleasant occur.

We would all agree that Paul the apostle was an outstanding gift and blessing to the body of Christ having written the larger portion of the New Testament, and sharing explicit details of some of his missionary journeys detailed by Luke in the book of Acts.

In my studies, I haven't yet seen evidence that Paul was in any way veering towards being proud of his accomplishments in ministry. In fact, Paul went to great lengths to verbalise how insufficient he felt, recalling with regret his behaviour in the past towards the church. He describes himself as, *'the least of the apostles...'* (1 Corinthians 15:9). To the church in Corinth, he rebukes in his letter those who tried to elevate him for his calling. He asks, *'Was Paul crucified for you? Or were you baptised in the name of Paul?'* (1 Corinthians 1:13) *'Who then is Paul? I have planted...but God gave the increase'* (1 Corinthians 3:4-7). I'd say that Paul did a good job of actively distancing himself from taking praise that belongs only to God.

However, God knows how easy it is to slip from humility into pride. Paul was therefore given a permanent enemy, unspecified but speculated to be a medical condition related to his eyes. It is called *'a thorn in the flesh, ...',* sent to buffet Paul (pound, torment, harass) should he hear one too many, *'Well done, Paul!'* (2 Corinthians 12:7).

If you have something going on in your life which no amount of praying and fasting seems to shift, it could be a lifelong thorn sent from God as a restrainer. He will not remove it, but will instead give you sufficient grace to bear it.

JEJ

TUESDAY 16th

When I am weak, then am I strong – 2 Corinthians 12:10

WHAT IS THIS FOR? - Reading: Romans 5:3-5; 2 Corinthians 12: 9-10

Most parcels that we receive, we can easily work out what they are and what they're for. There may be instructions enclosed to help us to assemble an object if it's in pieces.

But in life, we sometimes have events that happen to us and we struggle to work out its purpose. God's intention is not always immediately obvious and He does not always answer the questions we may rightly ask. Or if He does reply, He doesn't necessarily do so in a hurry.

Yesterday's page talked of the Thorn in the Flesh given to Paul. Not something which he would want to receive or keep but, upon closer inspection, Paul realised its value. In his state of feeling weak from the effects of the thorn, he relied upon God's grace and God's strength rather than his own. Paul right there identified that he was actually strongest when he was at his weakest. For if God's strength is only activated when we surrender our own (v9), then weakness or dependency is the best place to be, *'for when I am weak, then am I strong' (v10).* Paul realised that the anointing upon his life was in some way connected to the less-than-ideal challenges he faced and overcame each day, *'…insults, distresses, persecutions, difficulties for Christ's sake'* (v10 - AMP).

Whether it's oil or wine, in Scripture both are symbolic of the anointing or the Holy Spirit and neither of them comes forth without pressing. We can thus trace life's squeezes, life's tensions and grindings, to a divine unseen purpose. God's winepress and/or oil-press brings out from us what will come out no other way.

JEJ

WEDNESDAY 17th

He giveth power to the faint; and to them that have no might he increaseth strength
Isaiah 40:29

UNCONTESTED POWER - Reading: Isaiah 40:18-31

What a wonderful thing to be able to say that I, we are more than conquerors.

It is the power of God that makes a difference in our lives. There has always been a power struggle between good and evil, right and wrong, and yet it is the power of God that gives us victory over every struggle we can face. On our own, we are insufficient and unable to combat the forces that are not of God. Through the power of the Holy Ghost, there is another level of ability that is available to the believer, a power that is uncontested and undefeated.

This is the victory we have in our walk with God no matter what we face, planned or unplanned, seen or unseen, we will gain the advantage! The more the enemy confronts us, the more power we are going to need from God. We were not made to be beneath, but we were made for above, and living above what we face is through the power of God. We can rejoice because the power within us makes us more than conquerors and even when we are faint and without much strength, the power of God, through the power of the Holy Ghost, will make us the conquerors God designed us all to be.

Women of God, every time we face something, we remind ourselves, no matter how it looks, that we are more than conquerors.

Pastor Chelly Edmund (USA)

THURSDAY 18th

But those who hope in the LORD will renew their strength – Isaiah 40:31 (NIV)

THE PURPOSEFUL WAIT - Reading: Isaiah 40:21-31

The word *'wait'* can be associated with endurance because the period of waiting is something you have to endure to see your reward.

We as humans don't spend time waiting if not necessary or without seeking gratification. When you wait on the LORD, or hope in the LORD, it's a different experience. You might pray more, read more, worship more, search for more meaning - all so that you can understand your road to victory. Wait on the Lord and He will refresh and energise your weak and weary heart for the race you are running. He will strengthen and empower your faint, lost and disheartened spirit as you walk the straight and narrow path.

When you wait on the LORD it is likened to a soaring eagle, a captivating sight, yet hazardous for its prey. Do you understand that to *'mount up on wings as eagles'* means to mark your territory? It sends a warning to the enemy that he cannot touch nor defeat you because the source of your strength is beyond his jurisdiction to manipulate. When God sees your patience, faith, and determination to make Him a part of your situation, know that He has already found the solution to your problem. Continue to trust in the great, big, wonderful God that you serve and wait for Him to deliver you.

Let us pray:
Lord, thank you for fighting for us. Thank you that you see it fit for our only participation in the battle is to completely depend on you to win the victory. We trust you to intervene on our behalf as we wait. In Jesus' name. Amen.

Laylah Walker

FRIDAY 19th

...even when we don't know what to do, we never give up – 2 Corinthians 4:8 (CEV)

GOD, OUR HOPE IN DIFFICULT TIMES - Reading: 2 Corinthians 4:1-10

The Christian journey is not an easy one.

When we study God's Word, we read of challenges faced by the early Christians and children of God. The way they overcame serves as a source of encouragement to us when we too face difficult times.

I came across this quote, *'though we may seem to be at the end of our rope, we are never at the end of our hope'*. Praise God! We serve a God who has promised to be with us to the very end. He is not a 'pop-up' God who disappears and reappears like a Jack-in-the-box! He is a faithful God who starts the journey with us and stays the course. We sometimes become unfaithful but He is God, unchanging.

'We are pressed by trouble on every side but we are not crushed' (2 Corinthians 4:8a NLT). Our knees may buckle under the pressure, but the trouble will not be more than we can bear. God is with us. Often it is right there on our knees that we cry out to God and find the strength to carry on.

'We are perplexed but not driven to despair' (2 Corinthians 4:8b NLT). God has promised to, *'keep in perfect peace whose mind is stayed on him' (Isaiah 26:3).* Our hope is in God and He will never let us down. In tough times we are to praise Him and keep holding to His unchanging hand. We hold on to hope because we serve the Victorious One. Through Him we are overcomers, more than conquerors, and victors by the blood of the Lamb.

Sister Barbara Hendrickson (Nevis)

SATURDAY 20th

...this is the victory that overcomes...even our faith – 1 John 5:4

MATURING FAITH – Reading: 1 John 5:1-6

Have you ever admired a butterfly, or at least wondered at the change in its character from a caterpillar?

During the chrysalis stage, the soft and skin-like shell hangs on to branches until it gradually hardens and is transformed into a butterfly.

I recall my own life chrysalis moments: feelings of despair as I looked at my mouldy kitchen roof, the house falling apart, debt rising, relations failing, and God's Word reminded me, *'He that is faithful in that which is least, is faithful also in much' (Luke 16:10).*

Drowning in my circumstances the journey was long, lonely and laborious, but I had faith believing, trusting, pushing, overcoming, daily maturing through the circumstance, seeing a light - often just a pin-prick - but holding on.

Just as the caterpillar hangs in the cocoon, I mature through my struggles. Today I choose to hang on in faith, as God upholds me with His right hand.

Yes, as a child of God, born into His family, I am overcoming struggles. I push through the hard times emerging daily, flying free through faith in what God says about me, not bound by my circumstances but maturing in faith.

Sister Dorcas (nee Simmonds)

*SUNDAY 21st

...for without me ye can do nothing – John 15:5

STAY CONNECTED – Reading: John 15:1-8

In teaching His disciples, Jesus illustrated the relationship with the vine and the branches, and the process the branches will experience, also the dependence and the need to stay connected.

To abide is to remain or stay. Therefore, for us to maintain a close and intimate relationship with Jesus, we must stay connected or remain in Him. If we do not stay connected, we cannot draw from Him what we need to sustain us, and to be productive in His kingdom and in our community. Fruit bearing is inevitable when we abide in Jesus. The fruit of the Spirit comes only out of an abiding relationship with Him, and the fruit will show our character as outlined in Galatians 5:22-23.

There is work to be done in the Kingdom and we cannot do this in our own strength; for this we must remain in Christ Jesus. As we spend time with Him, in His Word, He reveals more of Himself, and show us things about ourselves which we did not know. There can be no hiding away, it will come to light at some point, whether we are connected to The Vine or not. When we abide in Him, the result is that He will abide in us. He is the source of everything that we need.

Evangelist Marjorie Burgess

World Ice Cream Day

MONDAY 22nd

For I know the plans I have for you, declares the LORD…to give you a future and a hope – Jeremiah 29:11 (ESV)

YOUR FUTURE IN GOD IS HOPEFUL – Reading: Jeremiah 29:1-14

According to a YMCA publication on the challenges facing young people, an estimated 1.25 million children and young people are diagnosed with a mental health issue, the equivalent to one in eight young people. Mental health issues affect their confidence, performance at school and their future prospects of employment. Without support, mental health issues can lead to attempted suicide, addictions, and self-harm.

There is still a stigma in society associated with mental health issues, preventing those suffering from speaking out and seeking help and therefore suffering in silence. Support from the NHS is limited due to an inability to meet the increasing demands.

Two issues affecting young people are body image anxieties, due to the constant focus and attention on social media and advertising. Secondly, isolation and loneliness due to spending a lot of time on the internet and not leaving their bedroom or house, leading to a lack of physical connection with friends and family.

The influences of the world on a young person's view of themselves contradicts God's view. The thoughts that God has towards them are good. The Word says that God loves us with an everlasting love. We are the apple of His eye, symbolic of what is fond and precious. We are fearfully and wonderfully made; distinguished, and uniquely designed to give reverence to God.

It is God's voice that makes the difference, and when He speaks, He settles the troubled mind. God's expectation is that our young people, and all of us, have a future full of hope.

Name withheld

TUESDAY 23rd

The LORD your God is going with you. He will fight for you…and give you victory
Deuteronomy 20:4 (GW)

THE APPOINTMENT – Reading: 1 Samuel 17: 33-51

Most of us maintain a diary of some sort to keep track of forthcoming events. On our *'At a glance'* page, there are usually at least a few appointments during the year that we wish we could cancel.

It could be an appointment for another cervical smear or mammogram because the first one was not conclusive. It could be a meeting with HR about pending redundancies at your workplace. Maybe it's an appointment at the school which your child attends and you have to address a sensitive issue. Perhaps, in these difficult financial times, you have fallen behind with payment of your rent or mortgage and you're being threatened with eviction. Are you due in court today on trial or to give evidence for something which you feel that you cannot share?

If you're thinking, *'I wish that I had someone to come with me and speak on my behalf'*, read the following verse a few times and allow it to be absorbed into your spirit, *'For the LORD your God is he that* ***goeth with you****, to fight for you against your enemies, to save you' (Deuteronomy 20:4).*

Remember that David picked up five stones to prepare his defence against Goliath (1 Samuel 17:40, 50), but he only needed one. You too only need one stone, He's a Rock actually, and He's promised in today's Word that He's going to be at your appointment with you!

JEJ

*WEDNESDAY 24th

God will with the temptation also make a way of escape – 2 Corinthians 10:13

A FIXED OUTCOME – Reading: 1 Corinthians 10:1-13

In our recent Convocation one of the preachers encouraged us by sharing these words, *'The struggle is real, but the fight is fixed…'*.

Reflecting on these words, their truth demonstrates the fact that, *'we are more than conquerors'* (Romans 8:37). The Apostle Paul in his writings to the church in Corinth supports *'the fix'* further as shown in 1 Corinthians 10:13:

'There hath no temptation taken you but such as is common to man: but God is faithful, who will not suffer you to be tempted above that ye are able; but will with the temptation also make a way to escape, that ye may be able to bear it'.

God's faithfulness to His children takes the 'sting' out of the fight. He produces a way for us to be able to bear our struggles and not become overwhelmed.

Not only will God make a way of escape but also, He provides the strength to handle the very thing that produces the struggle. God allows us to bear it (coming through it) making us more than conquerors!

Let us be consistent in learning to identify the struggles; petition God, and with thanksgiving allow Him to fight and win our battles.

Minister Hedy

Cousins Day

THURSDAY 25th

Knowing this, that the trying of your faith worketh patience - James 1:3

FAITH + PATIENCE = PROMISE – Reading: James 1:1-18

Here in today's reading we see how faith has to go on trial to birth patience in order for us to come to maturity. However, the work of patience comes slowly and must be allowed to work in us.

We are encouraged in Hebrews 6:12 to be *'followers of them who through faith and patience obtained the promise'.* Abraham and Sarah had to wait many years for them to receive the promise that was prophesied to them in Genesis 18:14.

Beloved, don't get lost in the circumstances of what you are going through. Look for what God may be doing in your life. Sometimes you may not know but it requires faith to trust Him, '*We walk by faith and not by sight'* (2 Corinthians 5:7).

I'm encouraged by this Scripture as I wait for my own healing. I have confidence that in the waiting it's bringing forth patience and maturity in my life. This confidence in His faithfulness brings a joy knowing that He is working to perfection.

Sisters, you are favoured by the Lord with victory and you are pregnant with His promises. Yes, at times your dreams may look impossible, and may take a long time in coming. Nevertheless, in God's perfect time, you are going to give birth to your promise, just like Sarah did. God's Word is flawless. So, trust and take pleasure in Him. He will keep your mind in perfect peace as you do so.

Shantelle Smith

*FRIDAY 26th

If we confess our sins, he is faithful and just to forgive us...1 John 1:9

THE CATALYST OF CONFESSION – Reading: 1 John 1:1-10

There isn't anyone reading this page who doesn't like to feel clean. I enjoy my morning and evening refreshing routines which include cleaning my face. I like thoroughly massaging in the cleansing agent and then wiping it off with cotton wool, and the nice fresh feeling that follows after the grime on my face is gone.

Confession should also be part of our daily cleansing; it deals with our heart which cannot be seen. Sometimes our heart is left for months and years in a filthy state because we won't admit that we have done wrong, or are trying to hide our sin.

Achan knew that he had hidden *'the accursed thing'* (Joshua 7:11) in his tent, and members of his family must have been aware too - they were not living in a mansion where things can be easily hidden, they were all in a tent and would have seen a mound of items in it which was not theirs.

If Achan had willingly admitted his sin, his life – and the life of his family – could have been spared. But he kept silent, pretending that he didn't know the cause for Israel losing the battle at Ai which should have been an easy victory. All Achan had to say, just like the Prodigal Son said in the far country, was, *'I have sinned' (Luke 15:21)*. But by the time Achan confessed, *'I have sinned'* (Joshua 7:20), the penalty was already fixed (v15).

Does it help to know that God wants to forgive us even more than we want to be forgiven? He hates the separation between us and Him caused when we transgress. Yes, though sin has consequences, let's not lose the message of God's love and Him calling us back into relationship. According to John, the catalyst for God's forgiveness and our being clean again, lies with us. It is our confession, of course followed by true repentance.

JEJ

Aunts & Uncles Day

SATURDAY 27th

Fear them not…there shall not a man of them stand before thee – Joshua 10:8

WE HAVE THE VICTORY – Reading: Joshua 10:1-15

When God does anything, He does it well. He does not start what He cannot finish. Just be patient.

Sometimes our prayers are answered in stages although we would of course prefer them to be answered completely at once.

You might be dealing with more than one trial right now, or maybe just one but it involves many foes plotting to bring you down. Sometimes people rise up against you for no apparent reason - they just don't like you. David in Psalm 69:4 wrote, *'They that hate me without a cause are more than the hairs of mine head…'.*

Our focus verse today gives assurance, *'And the LORD said unto Joshua, Fear them not: for I have delivered them into thine hand; there shall not a man of them stand before thee' (Joshua 10:8).*

Satan tries to intimidate us with numbers, and wants to frighten us with who it is that is working against us. This could be at work, in our family, in the church, or elsewhere. But hear what a songwriter said, *'Tell me who can stand before us when we go in Jesus' name! Jesus! Jesus! Precious Jesus! We have the victory!'.*

JEJ

SUNDAY 28th

...so stand fast in the Lord, my dearly beloved – Philippians 4:1

ENDURANCE IN TIMES OF AFFLICTION - Reading: Philippians 4:1-4

It is often in times of great hardship and affliction that our belief is tested and tried. It is in those trying times we really see where our faith resides. Is it in ourselves, achievements, people, positions, entitlements or in God? James 1:3-4 tells us that the trying of our faith worketh patience, and we ought to allow patience to have its perfect work in us. It takes a certain kind of fortitude and perseverance to stand, withstand, and overcome the ongoing trials needed to build our spiritual muscles of faith and trust in God.

This race that we are running is not for the swift nor is it for the strong, but it is for those who can endure to the end. The word *'endurance'* means the ability to go through an unpleasant or difficult process or situation without giving way. Only God can give us the strength needed to remain faithful in the face of opposition and adversity.

In the book of Philippians, the Apostle Paul expresses his love and affection for the Philippian brethren encouraging them to stand fast in the Lord, and not to be discouraged or dismayed by their circumstances. The afflictions that they were enduring were momentary and produced the kind of people that would reflect Him, not just in words but in deeds. These people were going through a metamorphosis, a makeover, a transformation. Each experience handled correctly was bringing to the forefront a people that were being transformed into the very image of Christ.

It is our attitude of gratitude, endurance and praise that will produce the right mindset, and where we will truly experience the peace that passeth all understanding to endure in times of affliction.

Name withheld

MONDAY 29th

With God we shall do valiantly, it is he who will tread down our foes – Psalm 108:13

TRANSCENDING CONQUERORS – Reading: Psalm 108:1-13

In the exultant words of Psalm 108:13, a profound truth emerges: with God by our side, we transcend mere conquerors; it is His might, not ours, that vanquishes our adversaries. But what does it mean to be a conqueror, and why aspire to be *'more'* than that?

A conqueror, like the valiant King David, secures victories on the battlefield, asserting dominion over foes and overcoming challenges through strength, strategy, and unwavering determination. Yet, to ascend to the status of *'more than a conqueror'* is to acknowledge the inherent limitations of our own abilities, while embracing the divine empowerment granted to us through our faith in Christ.

David himself understood this profound concept deeply; he recognised that true victory remained elusive without divine intervention. In our daily lives, we encounter diverse battles, from personal trials to formidable external adversaries. These struggles, as articulated in 1 John 2:16, encompass the lust of the flesh, the lust of the eyes, and the pride of life. Moreover, our ultimate adversary, Satan, looms large on the battlefield of our souls.

To be *'more than conquerors'* signifies a humble acceptance of our limitations, coupled with unwavering trust in Jesus. Just as David relied upon God to secure triumph over his enemies, we too must lean on divine strength to conquer the spiritual foes that cross our paths. With God as our ally, we don't merely survive—we thrive as empowered, victorious beings, transcending the ordinary to become more than conquerors.

Evangelist Dr Carol Ighofose

*TUESDAY 30th

So that we may boldly say, The Lord is my helper – Hebrews 13:6

HELP IS ON THE WAY – Reading: Ruth 2:1-23

Have you ever experienced someone withdrawing their help, or offer of help, just when you needed it most? All of your plans were centred around the help that you were expecting would come, but you were left wondering what to do.

It's at these times that we prove God to be an on-time God. He sends just what we need, sometimes from an unlikely source.

Remember when Ruth was gleaning in the field of Boaz, as the owner, Boaz instructed the reapers to drop some *'handfuls of purpose' (Ruth 2:16).* The workers were not allowed to return and pick up any stray grains – those were left for whoever came behind them and the poor (Leviticus 23:22).

I can just imagine Ruth picking up those grains of blessing, not knowing why there were so many. She was a stranger, a foreigner, not a Jew, yet God granted this Gentile Moabitish woman favour in the field. She came from a nation which began from an incestuous relationship between Lot and his eldest daughter (Genesis 19:35-37). A nation who worshipped false gods, the Moabites were also known for sexual immorality. But God discounted her background and divinely showered Ruth with all the help that she needed as a reward for her tender care of her mother-in-law, for her dedication and sacrifice giving up her familiar life in Moab to go with Naomi into the unknown (Ruth 2:11).

When you have a committed relationship with God, don't you worry. When one door closes, it's only for another to be opened. Don't fret. The Lord is your helper! **Say it boldly**.

'Abide with me, fast falls the eventide
The darkness deepens, Lord with me abide
When other helpers fail and comforts flee
Help of the helpless, O, abide with me'
(Abide with Me - HF Lyte)

JEJ

International Day of Friendship

WEDNESDAY 31st

Be sober, be vigilant... - 1 Peter 5:8

KEEP YOUR ARMOUR ON – Reading: 1 Peter 5:8-14

Complacency is something which every Christian must guard against. It's easy to become complacent and not even realise it. In this state of relaxation and contentment, and even oblivion, is where we are often caught off guard by the enemy. It's the perfect time for him to set a trap and we'll walk right into it.

An attack may happen after God has used you mightily as His vessel in ministry, in whatever capacity He chose. It may occur after being engaged in a powerful week of Revival services or a Convocation. It may be after a long gap in between trials. For King David, his complacency set in at the time of year when all kings went to battle but instead of leading Israel on the battlefield, he stayed home. Long-story-short, this particular act of complacency resulted in the murder of Uriah, i.e., Bathsheba's husband, and the birth of Bathsheba and David's first child from their adulterous affair (2 Samuel 11:1-27). Ladies, how many pages could be written in our journals about what we did, or what almost befell us, when we switched off our conscience and went into complacency mode?

Peter urges us, *'Be sober, be vigilant; because your adversary the devil, as a roaring lion walketh about seeking whom he may devour' (1 Peter 5:8)*. Satan does not discriminate. He is not respectful of your age, title or background. He takes no annual leave, he works night and day, and every bank holiday and weekend! So, to be more than a conqueror, put on the whole armour of God. Live in it. Sleep in it. Go to work and to church in it. Do not dare to take it off!

JEJ

LOW BLOOD PRESSURE

Low blood pressure is probably a better challenge to have than a high blood pressure, because it's less likely to put a strain on major organs such as the heart or kidneys.

Having said that, the symptoms of low blood pressure can be very dangerous leading to light-headedness, dizziness, or even fainting. At least this alerts you to the fact that there is a problem, unlike with high blood pressure, where there may be no symptoms at all, and therefore nothing to point to the fact that there is an underlying problem.

Causes of low blood pressure include:

- It may run in your family. If so, you may be aware of this, so do tell your doctor
- Some people naturally have a low pulse rate and low blood pressure, especially if they are very fit (do regular sport). If you are very fit and exercise very regularly and to a high intensity, do mention this to your doctor
- Some medications have a low blood pressure as a side effect - do mention this to your doctor with names and doses of medications that you are taking, including medicines bought over the counter
- Pregnancy
- Some medical conditions such as diabetes
- Rapid blood, or body fluid loss (diarrhoea or vomiting) - chances are you'll be unwell enough to need a visit to the Emergency Department. In this case, the treatment will be to replace any lost fluids.
- Some people develop low blood pressure as they get older. It's only a problem if the person develops symptoms (light-headedness/dizziness/fainting).

Did you know that:
Your blood pressure is made up of two numbers: the highest reading is called the systolic blood pressure. It is the highest pressure your heart reaches when it beats. The lowest reading is called the diastolic reading. This is the lowest blood pressure reached when your heart relaxes.
A normal blood pressure falls within a range but a systolic of 120 and diastolic of 80 is normal.

Low blood pressure is described as less than a systolic of 90 and less than a diastolic of 60.

It is so easy to check your blood pressure at home these days, but if there is any concern, it is best for your blood pressure to be checked by a professional. Make an appointment at your GP Surgery for this to be done.

Did you know that:
Your blood pressure can vary depending on the time of day? It gradually increases throughout the day. If your GP or Pharmacist asks you to record your blood pressure at home, they will ask you to take measurements of your blood pressure in the morning and in the evening.

What you're doing and how you're feeling can also affect blood pressure. If you're working really hard, and feeling stressed, your blood pressure will go up. Make sure that you're nice and relaxed prior to taking your blood pressure.

- If you're 40 to 74 years old, you should have your blood pressure checked at least once every 5 years as part of the NHS Health Check.
- Some GP surgeries offer annual Health Checks. Request one by speaking to the Receptionist. Mention 'NHS Health Check' mentioned on nhs.uk website.

Treatment:
Treatment of low blood pressure depends on the cause.

Ref: http://www.nhs.uk

Author:
Dr Jo Brooks FRCPCH
Consultant Paediatrician

august
In the Proverbs

*THURSDAY 1st

...hear the instruction of thy father, and forsake not the law of thy mother
Proverbs 1:8

CONTINUE IN WHAT YOU HAVE LEARNED – Reading: 2 Timothy 3:10-17

I have heard it said that we've not really heard until we do what we heard. When I thought about this, I had to agree. A parent rebuking a child will often say, *'Did you not hear what I said?'*. The child heard, but their lack of doing provoked the chastiser to suggest that the child did not hear (although they heard).

Paul, writing to his protégé, Timothy, admonishes him to, *'continue thou in the things which thou hast learned and hast been assured of, knowing of whom thou hast learned them' (2 Timothy 3:14).*

In our early years, our parents and guardians drilled different principles and disciplines into us. Every day we were taught a different lesson, and each day came with a reminder, *'Don't forget to...'* or, *'Remember that I told you to...'* or even, *'How many times do you need to be told to...'*. We have also been blessed with fathers and mothers in the gospel who shared their wisdom.

As we matured and embraced the independence that comes with age, we consciously chose which instructions to keep, and what to disregard and do another way. It is very easy as an adult to discount counsel from the past and treat as nonsense because the warnings did not always come with an explanation. But have you ever thrown away something, only to later on discover that you need it, and then have to buy the same thing again? Key words from today's focus verse are, *'Hear'* and *'forsake not'*.

We can end this page by going back to the beginning, i.e., Adam. Try to imagine what life might have been like now had Adam continued in what he had been taught by God, *'Don't eat from that tree...' (Genesis 2:16-17)*. We are still paying the consequences today because Adam did not 'hear' and 'continue'. Ladies, every time that you have labour pains, remember that the cause is that someone did a 'don't'!

JEJ

Cycle to Work Day

FRIDAY 2nd

Every wise woman buildeth her house: but the foolish plucketh it down with her hands – Proverbs 14:1

BUILD WELL – Reading: Titus 2:1-15

According to the Office of National Statistics (ONS) 2021 census, only 15% of the UK construction workforce are women. In contrast, Solomon in the book of Proverbs puts wise women at the forefront of another type of construction, i.e., building the family home. He gives these women recognition, valuing their importance in society (Proverbs 14:1).

Building the family home takes working tirelessly, willingly, cheerfully and with sincerity. The wise woman is considerate, loving, skilful, and judicious. She keeps the family in good health with clothing and nutritious food, and handles the household business dealings carefully and honestly.

She secures the home in prayer ensuring reverence and love towards God. She extends generosity and compassion to the poor and those in need. Kindness graces her lips, and intelligence and gracefulness cultivate her mind and demeanour. She illustrates a meek and quiet spirit, and the household is managed discretely and economically (Proverbs 31).

Wise women are kingdom builders, winning souls for the kingdom of God. They are not only prudent to ensure they are equipped and prepared for Jesus' return, but they train, teach, and give godly instruction to the youth, helping to build up their faith and holiness (Proverbs 3:5; 2 Timothy 1:5; Titus 2:3-5).

I. E. Diekenga wrote the hymn, *'Build it Well'*. He penned that we're building every day and as the structure begins to grow it will reveal who we really are. In the chorus he encourages us to, *'Build well ...and build it for the eyes of God'.*

Name withheld

SATURDAY 3rd

...(the person) that winneth souls is wise – Proverbs 11:30

SOMEONE HAS TO – Reading: Proverbs 11:18-31

Someone has to step in the gap
Someone has to or there will be mishap
Someone has to cry those tears
Someone has to express to God
All their and others' fears.

Someone has to step in the gap
Is it you or someone else perhaps?
Are you willing to pray for breakthrough?
Are you willing to do what you need to?

Be a Rahab, remember your family
Make the sacrifices, like Esther did
So the Jews could be free
Esther followed God
And with His help
God did the miraculous.

God will do this for me and for you.

Sister Jennifer Henry

SUNDAY 4th

A gracious woman retaineth honour and strong men retain riches – Proverbs 11:16

OBTAIN TO RETAIN – Reading: Proverbs 11:15-23

A woman may obtain honour by her ability and accomplishments, but it is graciousness that leads her to retain that honour. Unfortunately, we have numerous examples of those who had the skill, talent and connection to obtain honour, but lacked the virtue to keep it.

Joy Haney in her book, *'The Radiant Women'*, defines the following qualities of grace that are found in the woman who is able to retain honour:

Gracious – pleasing, merciful, courteous, kindly (Proverbs 16:32)
Responsible –trustworthy (Proverbs 31:11-12)
Attitude – settled way of thinking or feeling about something (Matthew 5:16)
Character - the estimate put upon a person, moral vigour or firmness as acquired through self-discipline (Proverbs 10:9)
Example - that which is to be followed or imitated (2 Corinthians 5:20)
State of mind - outlook (Philippians 2:5)
The graces are all within. The beauty that God gives starts inwardly and its radiance shines outwardly; Psalm 45:13, *'The king's daughter is all glorious within'*.

In order to be all that the graces represent, we must make our relationship with Jesus Christ our number one priority. We must endeavour to nurture our relationship with God above all else. If we neglect the things that stir up and strengthen the inner self, such as prayer and studying the Word of God, Christian virtues will not be cultivated and our character, attitude and spirit will betray us.

I read somewhere where a church service had ended, the doors were opened, and the congregation were leaving. *'Is the service finished?'* a visitor asked. *'No'* replied one of the ushers, *'it is not finished we have only heard it; we are now going out to begin to do it'!*

CP

MONDAY 5th

...in the multitude of counsellors there is safety – Proverbs 11:14

INFLUENCE – Reading: Proverbs 2:10-20; 11:14

So what is the definition of Influence?

Influence is: the ability to affect other people's behaviours, decisions, outcomes or choices.

We all have the ability to influence others:

A loud person can be influenced to be just a little bit quieter.

A timid person can be influenced to be bold.

A weak person can be influenced to become strong.

The backslider can be influenced, with a lot of love and encouragement, to return to Christ.

So the question is...

Who are you influencing today?

Diana Ellis

TUESDAY 6th

Trust in the LORD with all thine heart... - Proverbs 3:5

TRUST, ALL ASPECTS IN UNISON – Reading: 2 Kings 4:1-7

One of my grandsons has a globe toy, given to him by one of his great grandmothers. With a light touch of my finger, it spins on the sculptured axle; for a moment I am in relative control of the direction it goes, all aspects in unison.

God has the whole world in his hand, and we are all in his hand while he spins the world on its axle, albeit with a choice to remain in Him, receiving direction.

The book of proverbs, words of wisdom, promotes life and the fear of the LORD as the beginning of wisdom. The fear that respects the all-powerful God, giving Him all glory and honour.

Proverbs 3:5-6 – 'Trust in the LORD with all your heart and lean not to your own understanding. In all your ways acknowledge him, and he shall direct your path'.

We **trust** items in the post (sometimes registered) will reach their destination; we **trust** that the foods have the nutrients written on the labels, we **trust** the banking system will give us a return on our investment, and we **trust** electronic navigation systems when travelling in unfamiliar territory.

TRUST is not always easy to implement… total reliance, not doubting!

But we must learn to trust the LORD, be totally reliant on Him not doubting His direction and leading in all areas of our lives. His ways are just, His ways are perfect, and He makes our way perfect when we trust Him.

So today, let's walk hand in hand, totally reliant on the LORD, listening and trusting Him in everything we think, say and do. Knowing He is ready, able and willing to direct the way we should take.

Sister Dorcas (nee Simmonds)

WEDNESDAY 7th

I love them that love me; and those that seek me early shall find me – Proverbs 8:17

I LOVE THE LORD JESUS CHRIST – Reading: Proverbs 8:14-31

I fell in love with Jesus Christ because He showed me how to love; His love surrounds me everywhere I go.

His love is so sweet that I taste the honey every minute! His love is so great that I cannot get over it. His love is so wide I cannot get around it. His love is a sustainer so I must never detach myself from it. His love is like a never-ending hug that holds me so secure and never releases me!

His love is tender like that of the feathers of a dove. His love makes me feel secure so that I never want to let go. He is the giver of life and loved me so much that He wanted to die for me. John 15:13 tells us: *'Greater love hath no man than this, that a man lay down his life for his friends'.*

Thank you, God, for being my greatest friend.

SSP

THURSDAY 8th

A continual dropping in a very rainy day and a contentious woman are alike
Proverbs 27:15

A BEAUTIFUL EXPRESSION – Reading: Proverbs 27:12-27

Often, we are tempted to react angrily when others come at us with nasty words. But there is a beautiful expression, *'A soft answer turns away wrath' (Proverbs 15:1).*

Why beautiful? Because when children of God give a kind and soft answer it shows the love of Christ within us. It also shows that we are the children of God and as such, His peacemakers, who prefer to suffer the wrong than have the last word showing us to be right.

Someone who continuously repeats their hurt often wants to be heard and noticed. If we find ourselves in this position, let us tell Jesus everything in prayer. Tell Him with all our heart and ask Him to help us overcome.

Beloved women of the Lord Jesus Christ…we are more than conquerors. We can do all things through Christ who strengthens us!

We can do it!

Minister Maxine Blair

FRIDAY 9th

Death and life are in the power of the tongue; ... they that love it shall eat the fruit thereof - Proverbs 18:21

USE OUR WORDS WISELY – Reading: Proverbs 18:21; Colossians 4:1-6

As a child I was told on many occasions, *'Sticks and stones may break my bones, but words can never hurt me'.*

Over the years, I have seen the error in this saying. Words can indeed hurt and hurt deeply, altering the course of a person's life. Our words matter! They reveal our heart, whether we are wise or foolish.

Today remember that with words we have the opportunity to speak life; talk about the goodness of Jesus, share the message of salvation. We are called to let the world know that Jesus came, died and rose again to free us from the bondage of sin, to offer hope to a dying world. We are witnesses of Jesus - of His great love and sacrifice. Let us use our words to spread light, to speak life into our communities, in the school we attend, in the place we work, or even in the supermarket whilst doing our shopping. Let us consider our ability to leave a lasting impact on the lives of those we encounter by our words - sharing the gospel of Jesus Christ and who He is.

Let us be intentional about what we say and, share Good News, offering a word of encouragement and hope – and shine our light. Use words wisely!

Our prayer today should be: *'Let the words of my mouth and the meditation of my heart be acceptable in your sight, O LORD, my rock and my redeemer' (Psalm 19:14 - ESV).*

Christine Knight

SATURDAY 10th

Say unto wisdom, Thou art my sister, and call understanding thy kinswoman
Proverbs 7:4

SOUL SISTERS – Reading: Proverbs 7:1-27

No one is immune to temptation. The Scriptures teach that, *'there is no temptation taken you but such as is common to man…'* (1 Corinthians 10:13), but God has made a way out.

Hear what today's proverb is teaching us; I say 'us' as this passage - despite it being addressed to men - the same principle also applies to women. For both men and women, to be forewarned is to be forearmed. Hearing wisdom and heeding its instruction will save us a lot of heartache. As Precept Austin noted in one commentary, *'if wisdom is not loved, lust will be indulged'.*

Wisdom is personified as a sister that we are to embrace (Proverbs 4:6-8; 8:17; Song of Solomon 8:1). Understanding is like a close relative as Boaz was to Ruth. These Soul Sisters, i.e., Wisdom and Understanding, can take the most tempting situation and show it for what it really is – bondage!

Can you picture the close attachment we are to maintain with wisdom and understanding? It is very serious. Surrounding ourselves with these Soul Sisters, internalising their words in the heart, acting upon them, and surrounding ourselves with these 'family members' will protect us from the alluring words of the enemy, the lies and its deceptive thoughts, and show us what lies ahead.

'Blessed are they that hear the Word of God and do it' (Luke 11:27-28).

CP

SUNDAY 11th

A soft answer turns away wrath but harsh words stir up anger- Proverbs 15:1 (NIV)

THE POWER OF WORDS – Reading: Proverbs 15:1; James 3:1-12

The words which we speak have power. Our words bring life or death.

Proverbs 18:21 says*, 'Death and life are in the power of the tongue: And they that love it shall eat the fruit thereof'*. The way that we choose to use words can help to build others up, or they can tear people down.

I am a 31-year-old wife and mother of two girls aged one and two, and I still have childhood memories of harsh words hurled at me by my parents. As a result, I grew up feeling angry and rejected. It wasn't until I received the Lord Jesus Christ into my life that I was able to forgive and be set free from the negative impact of their words.

In the early years of my marriage, I would speak a certain way to my husband without thinking about the impact my words would have on him. As far as I was concerned, I was in the right. Your choice of words and tone of voice can influence how someone acts and reacts. Consequently, anger would be stirred and a cold atmosphere would permeate our home. Proverbs 15:1 says, *'A soft word turns away wrath, but a harsh word stirs up anger'*. I've since learned, and I am still learning, the power of words. I now encourage my husband in love with words that would edify. I try to focus on listening, even when I may not necessarily agree with him, as opposed to thinking about my own feelings: *'Pleasant words are as an honeycomb, sweet to the soul, and health to the bones' (Proverbs 16:24).*

Tips:
'Seek first to understand, then to be understood' (Stephen Covey). Use kind words or wait for your feelings to pass before you respond.

JPG

MONDAY 12th

...the commandment is a lamp; and the law is a light – Proverbs 6:23

SELF CONTROL – Reading: Proverbs 6:19-35

Like the Israelites of old, we stray away from God and come running back when hardship befalls us.

The reading for today admonishes us to seek after the Light of Life, and resist the lure of flattery. Each one of us appreciates when we are commended for outstanding performances, and craves positive affirmation. Yet, we mess up by letting it get to our heads and start craving the adulation. This has the potential of leading us down a dark path of destruction.

God remains our best hope, our safe hope, our only hope. He lights our path and gives commandments on the only way to survive our base desires. Our eyes see, our hearts yearn, our feet walk, our hands touch. Our entire being is involved in straying from the paths of righteousness and into paths of destruction.

Control of self is a key requirement to escaping the clutches of evil, the desires of the flesh and to follow after righteousness. We are reminded that temptation is not a sin. The sin lies in yielding to the temptation. Our hope in God protects us when we call upon His name.

Pastor Londy Esdaille (Nevis)

TUESDAY 13th

A friend is loyal, and a brother is born to help in time of need – Proverbs 17:17 (NLT)

LOYAL FRIENDSHIP – Reading: Proverbs 17:17-28

One of my friends whom I've had since my primary school days, lives miles away from me. We remain close despite ups and downs – I do not recall any unkindness. We are always there for each other, it's effortless in that we don't think twice to be loyal.

This level of friendship is the kind spoken about in Proverbs 17:17, *'A friend is loyal, and a brother is born to help in time of need' (NLT).*

Yes, our family assume their job is to help in time of need, but the consistent loyalty of a friend is rare. So, I ask myself, am I a true friend? Is my loyalty constant? Do I put conditions on my friendships, and are they conditions I can keep?

Always means, *'all times'*, *'without stopping or changing at any time'*.

Quite a challenge when we are unclear of the unknown future. However, that was the choice Ruth was prepared to take when Naomi told her to go back to her people (Ruth 1:16). Ruth replied, *'Don't ask me to leave you and turn back. Wherever you go, I will go; wherever you live, I will live. Your people will be my people, and your God will be my God' (NLT).*

This level of commitment is hard to find, and often difficult to keep, yet a standard for us all to pursue.

Heavenly Father, show me today that loyal friend I want to have.

Dorcas (nee Simmonds)

WEDNESDAY 14th

She stretcheth out her hand to the poor: yea, she reacheth forth her hands to the needy – Proverbs 31:20

HONOUR WHERE HONOUR IS DUE – Reading: James 2:1-17

The last chapter of Proverbs is believed to be the words of King Lemuel (*The New Unger's Bible Dictionary*), who portrays the qualities and characteristics of a good woman or wife (Proverbs 31:10-31). King Solomon stated that a man who finds a wife, finds a good thing, and obtains favour from Jehovah (Proverbs 18:22).

She is honoured as a woman of strength, force, power, valour, and worthiness from the Hebrew word for virtuous *'Chayil'*. She is a woman that demonstrates high moral standards, whose value cannot be compared to material riches.

She is admired for her charitable nature, illuminating her selflessness by the extension of care and compassion given to those who are depressed, afflicted, poor, destitute and in need. She reflects the compassionate heart of Jesus by ministering to her community. She does not turn her back on those in need, but instead works tirelessly administering the tender loving care of a mother.

Her work is often done in the background, and may not receive the recognition it deserves, but her actions and conduct beautify her. Her praise is in the kindness she sows in her community which grows and produces sweet aromatic fruit, yielding her the honour she is due. *'Give her the fruit of her hands, and let her own works praise her in the gates' Proverbs 31:31.*

Name withheld

THURSDAY 15th

The name of the LORD is a fortified tower: the righteous run to it, and are safe
Proverbs 18:10

KEEP YOUR EYES ON JESUS – Reading: Proverbs 18:10; Hebrews 12:1-3

To run means to move at a fast speed in a particular direction.

When athletes compete in competitions, they are advised to focus on an object or the finish line. This helps them to run faster than those who let their attention wander. Athletes also wear specific clothing to allow the body to have complete freedom of movement; any additional weight can hinder their performance. It's the same in the spiritual where in Hebrews 12:1-3 we are given guidance on how we can run with endurance. We must first get rid of all baggage that weighs us down, and every sin that distracts and prevents us from running in the way that we ought.

Sometimes we forget that low self-esteem and a lack of confidence are weight - they weigh us down and cause us to take longer to reach our destination and fulfil our purpose. That's why it's so important to keep our eyes fixed on Jesus. Remember Peter, the disciple who walked on water. When he took his eyes off Jesus and focused on the boisterous wind and waves, he became fearful and began to sink (Matthew 14:26-33).

God is our strong tower, a place of refuge, a present help in time of trouble. Run to God during times of trials, try not to focus on the problem because that's the distraction that can cause us to become fearful like Peter. When we keep our eyes on God, then our eyes are fixated on the solution which is God Himself. It's God who fights our battles and keeps us safe. Tell Him everything because there's no problem He can't solve.

As you run this race, go through the straight gate; the path is narrow, but this will lead you to everlasting life. The Bible tells us that few will find the narrow way (Matthew 7:14) but if you keep your eyes on Jesus, He will lead you and keep you from all harm.

Rachel Lewin

FRIDAY 16th

It is better to dwell in the wilderness, than with a contentious and an angry woman Proverbs 21:19

THE CONTENTIOUS WIFE - Reading: Proverbs 21:17-31

Looking at this Proverb, one can't help wondering if Solomon was speaking from experience, after all he did have 700 wives and 300 concubines! He knew what he was talking about.

We know that all Scripture is inspired by God (2 Timothy 3:16-17), so here is God-inspired marriage advice. Do not be a disagreeable, angry wife. A contentious woman is not a happy woman, and her husband would rather to live in a wilderness than hear her voice. A contentious woman can range from one who is merely annoying, to one who is impossible to live with. It is a sad state when a husband becomes a doormat *'for the sake of peace'*. The question is, is it possible for a man to live with a domineering controlling woman while at the same time *'act like a man'*? I'd leave that for a husband to answer.

Solomon knows what a gracious wife is, (Proverbs. 12:4; 18:22; 19:14; 31:10–31), but in today's Proverb, he is speaking against a contentious wife. Throughout Proverbs, it is repeated that two things will grieve a wise man: a foolish son and a contentious wife.

Disappointments, hardship and rejection could cause some women to be quite contentious, always feeling that they have to assert and prove themselves to people around them. Sadly, some would say, *'it's just my personality'*, but that is not true as a woman of God. If you are that woman who is quarrelling and constantly nagging her husband, I would encourage you to seek the Lord in prayer. Acknowledge that this is not becoming as a woman of God. 1 Peter 3:4 describes what is like an ornament before God – '*a gentle and meek spirit*'. This is a far cry and opposite from what the world says but we, sisters, go to the beat of a different drummer. Our desire is to please the Lord. The quality of a meek and quiet spirit is quite a treasure. God highly values a woman who becomes this kind of strong steady force in the home. The Lord knows how many times a wife has an opportunity to get upset about something that has happened. So when she chooses to control herself, and be a contributor of peace instead of strife, He sees this kind of woman as rare and to be valued.

CP

SATURDAY 17th

...don't reject the LORD's discipline, and don't be upset when he corrects you
Proverbs 3:11 (NLT)

FATHER'S LOVING CORRECTION – Reading: Proverbs 3:11-12; Hebrews 12:5-13

Here is a command and promise that Solomon speaks regarding correction. Nobody likes correction - some may take it as an insult, some get offended, defensive or even bitter. However, when the Lord speaks, take heed and pay close attention.

Do not allow fear of correction to move you away from the mighty hand of God. Consider it a joy that the Lord is refining you and wants you to grow.

God's aim is to keep you from evil, trouble, destruction and all pain; you don't have to be afraid or dismayed. God loves you so much that through boot-camp-like training, correction and discipline will welcome you to His heart. Discipline teaches you not to sin, not to practice unrighteousness; it points out any wrongdoing and how to endure. It truly is wonderful to understand God's way. Hebrews 12:11 (NIV) says, *'no discipline seems pleasant at the time but painful. Later on, however, it produces a harvest of righteousness and peace for those who have been trained by it'*. Correction may taste bitter, but it is sweet to the soul.

Correction is necessary. God is our Heavenly Father who loves and wants only the best for His children. Just as earthly parents discipline their offspring to keep them from harm, our Father does the same with us. Hebrews 12:6-7, *'For whom the Lord loveth He chasteneth'.* Chastisement is for our own good so that we may see His glory and promises fulfilled in our life and in the earth. If we are not chastised, then *'we are not true sons and daughters at all' Hebrews 12:8 (NIV)*.

Wait longingly, patiently to hear daily from the Lord. His Word will strengthen you to exercise the fruit of His Spirt and bring joy to the lives of many. Confidently trust in Him.

Shantelle Smith

SUNDAY 18th

Remove not the ancient landmark, which thy fathers have set – Proverbs 22:28

LET PEACE BE RESTORED – Reading: Proverbs 22:22-29

Integrity and honesty are the main focus points of many of the Proverbs.

The landmarks were usually marked stones heaped into a pillar with an engraving which indicated the boundary line between fields, districts, or nations. A person could cheat his or her neighbour by removing the ancient landmarks.

Removing such a boundary marker was a very serious offence according to the law of Moses.

Genesis 31:51-53 reads:

51) And Laban said to Jacob behold this heap, and behold this pillar, which I have cast betwixt me and thee; 52) This heap be witness and this pillar be witness that I will not pass over this heap to thee, and thou shalt not pass over this heap and this pillar for harm. 53) The God of Abraham, and the God of Nahor, the God of their father, judge betwixt us. And Jacob sware by the fear of his father Isaac.

The covenant set up here was to establish a peaceful separation between Laban and Jacob who were previously embroiled in fraud and deceit. There was now a boundary between them, neither one should cross over that line with intent to harm the other.

This was indeed a commitment to bring peace, even referring to the God of their fathers. It provided a solution to their previous hostility; this was an end to it.

As we place protective boundaries in our own lives, may we pray also for the peace of God to truly rule and govern everything that we do.

May we always walk with the love of God and His peace in our hearts.

Sister Prudence McEwan

MONDAY 19th

Who can find a virtuous woman? For her price is far above rubies – Proverbs 31:10

MARRIED OR SINGLE – BE VIRTUOUS – Reading: Proverbs 31:10; Colossians 1:1-29

Proverbs 31 is such a popular Scripture, and yet one which a lot of women often read and think, *'There is no way I can be like this woman!'*. Single ladies feel that this Scripture doesn't apply to them because the chapter refers to children and a husband. However, in the times we are living in, there are many single women with children.

Proverbs 31 is not a 'to do' list for women, neither is it a recipe for biblical womanhood, but it's one of a woman exhibiting godly characteristics, which is applicable regardless of your marital status.

Firstly, what is a virtuous woman? To be virtuous means, *'having good moral qualities and behaviour' (Online Cambridge Dictionary)*. Colossians 1:10 says, *'That ye might walk worthy of the Lord unto all pleasing, being fruitful in every good work, and increasing in the knowledge of God'*. Doesn't this apply to all of us?

We are told in Proverbs 1:2-3 (NLT) that the purpose of the proverbs is, *'…to teach people wisdom and discipline, … to help them do what is right, just and fair'*. Whether you are married or single, you need wisdom and discipline. In every area of our lives, our behaviour and character affect how we are perceived by others.

The most important thing is that a virtuous woman is a woman who fears the Lord. Her character demonstrates the love of the Lord; nothing is too hard for her. Consequently, her family loves her. You may not have children or a husband, but the love and godly characteristics you exhibit will also make you more precious than rubies.

Many of us, married or single, are already doing some/most of what this woman is doing, but what makes her different is that she does more than just work hard, she exhibits a godly character, is disciplined and wise in **all** she does.

What are these characteristics that will help us to be virtuous in our daily lives, marriages, homes, and churches, and will help others trust and speak well of us?

- Fear and love the Lord.
- Be wise - know when to speak and when to keep quiet; when to devote time to your husband/job, when to devote time to God.
- Be disciplined in all you do at all times.
- Be a loving person.
- Serve others gracefully with a willing heart.
- Don't be lazy – work in your home, in your church, in the community.
- Have good morals, be trustworthy, and be true to God.

Ladies, we can all be virtuous. Remember, we are children of the highest God and as such must exhibit His qualities to be more precious than rubies.

Lady Pam Lewin

TUESDAY 20th

Mockers resent correction, so they avoid the wise – Proverbs 15:12 (NIV)

HAVING WISDOM TO LIVE ON THE RIGHT PATH – Reading: Proverbs 15:10-14

Like many, I was a teenager who rebelled. I thought I knew better than my parents; I was right, they were wrong. Now grown up, I've learnt that they were teaching me how to live on the right path. I should have been obedient so that I could have avoided different incidents.

Proverbs 15:12 says, *'A scoffer does not love one who corrects him: Because the fool and the scoffer hate correction, they will hate (not love) the one who brings it' (Enduring Word Bible Commentary 2020).* Alike this Scripture, I was the scoffer and fool; I did not want to be corrected.

Each day we do many actions to obey, to not have to suffer dire consequences. They may be: ensuring we do not go over the speed limit whilst driving to avoid a speeding ticket, ensuring we pay our rent or mortgage to avoid eviction, or paying for goods and services to avoid being arrested.

As we go through life, we need to listen and take heed when God is talking to us. Trust and obey as He knows best. Having wisdom will enable us to not encounter a path that could lead to our destruction, from being the fool.

Chloe Rebekah

*WEDNESDAY 21st

Strength and honour are her clothing; … she openeth her mouth with wisdom; and in her tongue is the law of kindness – Proverbs 31:25-26

NO REGRETS – Reading: Proverbs 31:25-26; James 1:19-21

Have you ever looked at old pictures and thought, *'Oh no, why on earth did I wear that? What was I thinking!'*. Similarly, have you ever had a conversation *and 'put your foot in your mouth'* and thought, *'I shouldn't have said that'* or *'that came out too harsh'*? If you have, you are not alone.

We often can be concerned with what we wear and how it makes us look, but today's focus verses are showing us that the clothing of *'strength and honour'* is the best kind to wear. There's a strength of character that is from the Spirit of God and it gives strength to stand gracefully against all the odds, to endure and still smile because, *'the joy of the LORD is your strength' (Nehemiah 8:10).* With this God–given strength, you automatically are adorned with dignity and honour because how you carry yourself through trials, how you interact with others, and how you honour God in your life, becomes something most honourable in you.

Wise words filled with kindness are something to be developed, desired, admired, and achieved. Through prayer, self-reflection, and discipline, we must seek for the wisdom of God and allow wisdom to flow in our actions as well as speech. Let's train ourselves in, and be well-versed in, the law of kindness. Kindness governs how we speak and operate every day and within each interaction.

A woman who has such qualities with the Spirit of God is a wonderful and powerful combination, and a treasured necessity in our families, communities, churches, and the world. We may regret many things in life from fashion faux pas, our words, and our decisions, but you'll never regret being this kind of Proverbs 31 woman. Let that woman be you.

Minister Kay Dawkins/ MinK

***World Senior Citizens Day**

THURSDAY 22nd

…Take hold of my words and you shall live – Proverbs 4:4 (NIV)

I DARE YOU – Reading: Proverbs 4:1-27

I dare you to pray
I dare you to teach
I dare you to sing
I dare you to reach.

I dare you to stand
I dare you to call
I dare you to hold up the blood-stained banner
In the middle of your storm.

I dare you to increase
I dare you to thrive
I dare you to prosper, step out
And stand firm by His side.

I dare you to shout
And cry out His name
As Jesus Christ will fall on you
And revive you again.

Diana Ellis

FRIDAY 23rd

...blessed are those who follow God's teachings – Proverbs 29:18 (GW)

TAKE A BREAK – Reading: Proverbs 29:17-27

Have you ever had those feelings, when everything feels like a chore? A sense of drifting aimlessly? Just going from day to day and really not wanting to pray about it anymore. Why? Maybe we feel guilty or ashamed.

Jesus loves me, right? But the hallelujahs are just sounding hollow. It simply means that we need to stop, take a breath or take a break. Yes, take a break. Oh, everyone knows you are busy. The question is, who are you being busy for? We need to take this thought on board and allow it to permeate us in our very soul and being.

Jesus rested. Yes, you heard right! Jesus rested. Please read Mark 6:30-32. This means that sometimes we have to put down the hallelujahs and all the noise; find a quiet spot. ***'What?'*** I hear you say, *'I have to get the children to school, go to work, plus a million other things'*. As the words of an old Diana Ross song says, *'Stop, in the name of love'*, our *'stop'* is in the name of the I AM. The One who says, *'follow me, my peace I give you and leave with you'*. Take a minute wherever you are. Breathe and whisper in His ear, *'I have lost my way, who I am and where I fit'*.

The secret (or is it a secret?), our path is Jesus first, the Rock of our foundation and hope. He loves you.

Sandy Hemus

SATURDAY 24th

Favour is deceitful, and beauty is vain: but a woman that feareth the LORD, she shall be praised – Proverbs 31:30

GOD FEARING BEAUTY – Reading: Proverbs 31:30-31; Micah 6:7-8

The reading of today's proverb highlights the passing nature of outer beauty and the deceitful nature of charm which can be manipulative. In contrast, a woman who fears the LORD has beauty that does not pass, and favour that does not deceive. What is on the inside is of much greater value than the outward appearance.

Charm is defined by Webster's dictionary as, *'compelling attractiveness, a trait that fascinates, allures or delights'*. Charm is the power that someone possesses over another by means of attractiveness or persuasion.

I think of a situation where a beautiful young woman came into a Christian couple's life. The road to hell is paved with good intentions and, before long, this beautiful woman had charmed her way into the husband's heart and snared him. *'As a jewel of gold in a swine's snout, so is a fair woman which is without discretion' (Proverbs 11:22).* In God's eyes, a beautiful woman without discretion is not beautiful at all. The wife, clothed with strength, prayed and the grace of God saved their marriage. Those who think they stand take heed lest they fall into the trap of deception.

The woman who fears the LORD will be praised by her husband, praised by her children, and most importantly praised by the LORD. Look at what she does to gain such praise! She fears the LORD. What is the one virtue that sets her above other women? She fears the LORD. How do we fear the LORD? Fear is defined as reverence. One who truly fears the LORD has complete reverence for Him, and desires to please Him. *'The fear of the LORD is the true foundation for true wisdom, knowledge and understanding' (Proverbs 9:10).*
A woman who fears the LORD is a rare and precious thing, she is a gift of God's grace.

Physical beauty fades with time, but God-fearing beauty increases with time.

CP

SUNDAY 25th

The LORD is far from the wicked: but he heareth the prayer of the righteous
Proverbs 15:29

HOW FAR IS GOD? – Reading: Proverbs 15:25-33

That is a question that we ask on a regular basis when trouble manifests itself in our lives.

We long for the days when everything seems to be alright. Our behaviour, in times like these, takes us on a journey similar to running a marathon on a treadmill. We are exhausted at the end of it, but have not travelled an inch from our current location.

Likewise, we run around trying to fix the troublesome situations as they arise; it seems to be one after the other. We get out of one dark moment and seem to fall directly into another. Fixing one problem creates an avalanche of other problems because we see only the immediate needs affecting us.

If we give in to our baser desires, evil becomes our default position in every situation. If we put our trust in the Lord, faithful prayer becomes our default position. Trouble will still surround us, but it can never have dominion over us.

The distance between us and God is only as far as we make it. If we keep still and let God fix the problems for us, peace then becomes our ever-present shadow. The Lord hears our cry, our prayers and our petitions. In hearing, He provides deliverance as only He can.

How far is God? I submit that He is as far, or as near, as our next prayer.

Pastor Londy Esdaille (Nevis)

*MONDAY 26th

Trust in the LORD with all your heart, and do not lean on your own understanding. In all your ways acknowledge him… - Proverbs 3:5-6 (ESV)

LIFE'S JOURNEY WITH GOD – Reading: Proverbs 3:1-8

In life's non-linear journey, you're not on your own
Days tough and confusing, like waves you are thrown
Through hardships and swerves, you struggle to stand
Yet surrender not to confusion's demand.

Lean not on your thoughts, let God guide the way
Through the darkest of nights and the brightest of day
In God's hands, the landing is sure to be true
Trust Him with your heart, let faith carry you through.

When seeking the path that is righteous and clear
Let God chart your course, and keep Him near
One step amiss, and you wander astray
Stay aligned with His will, never lose your way.

Include Him in all that your hands find to do
Let His strength lift you up, make your spirit anew
Master architect, wisdom divine
God's power and grace forever entwine.

No matter how clever, how far you might see
God's wisdom surpasses all knowledge, all glee
So worry not, fear not, just stay by His side
In this turbulent journey, He'll be your guide.

With all of your heart, put trust in His name
A promise unbroken, His love stays the same
His presence remains, in cars or at home
No matter life's strains, you're never alone.

Name withheld

Summer Bank Holiday

TUESDAY 27th

Receive my instruction, and not silver; and knowledge rather than choice gold
Proverbs 8:10

THE VALUE OF GOOD INSTRUCTIONS – Reading: Genesis 2:16-17; 3:1-24

If I could go back in time, there are some instructions which I'd ignored then, I would reverse and take them. I'm sure that you would too. It is said that, *'Hindsight is a wonderful thing'*.

The writer of today's key verse emphasises the value of listening to those who know more about life than we do. So important is this that he says if given an option of taking silver rather than good instruction, forfeit the silver and take the advice. He suggests that the worth of knowledge is more than if you are financially challenged and are presented with an offer of gold.

Ignoring the voice of wisdom is like opening a box of feathers. Once it's opened, you can never re-gather them all. You now know why you were told to leave the box alone, but at what cost?

Let's go back again for the second time this month to Genesis 2:16-17; 3:1-8. Here we read the first account of what happened as a result of curiosity, and esteeming things as being greater than receiving instructions. We are still living with the consequences for the first disobedience today.

JEJ

WEDNESDAY 28th

Hope deferred maketh the heart sick: but when the desire cometh, it is a tree of life
Proverbs 13:12

DON'T LOSE HOPE – Reading: Proverbs 13: 1-13

Have you ever desperately wished for something, but held back on that hope in case it didn't happen? How sad and frustrated did it make you feel?

This verse in Proverbs tells us that putting off our hope can literally make our heart sick! Imagine missing out on our potential, or missing out on opportunities because we were afraid to just go for it. There's a saying, *'Let Go and Let God';* by trusting God in all things and leaning on Him, not on our own understanding, we CAN fulfil our hopes and dreams. Jesus said (Matthew 6:33), *'But seek ye first the kingdom of God, and his righteousness; and all these things shall be added unto you'.*

Think of the refreshing and relief when the desires of our heart are realised – a tree of life is not simply a tree, but *'of life'* – it is alive and flourishing, it is well rooted, drawing water and nutrients from a source and will bear fruit.

When we ask anything of God, in His name, He will supply our needs. We may sometimes ask for things that are good – or not so good for us – but God knows us inside out. He knows what we can manage, He knows what we cannot manage; but when we trust Him and hope IN Him, we will accept His will for us and enjoy our blessing.

Sis Elaine

THURSDAY 29th

When God approves of your life, even your enemies will end up shaking your hand
Proverbs 16:7 (MSG)

PEOPLE PLEASERS OR GOD PLEASERS – Reading: Proverbs 16:1-7

Who among us wants to have enemies? Most of us would certainly prefer not to, and in fact, the Word of God encourages us to live peaceably with all men.

However, this is not always possible. Try as we might, we cannot please all of the people all of the time. But what is more important to us as believers? Is it to please people or to please God?

God's words point us to pleasing Him. Yes, gaining God's approval is the most important thing in the world. **Always** pleasing Him is what really matters. Wanting people to like us can cause us to do things which do not befit our Christian lifestyle. The choice is clear. Seeking God's approval, and giving Him pleasure with our ways, is far more beneficial in the end - the ultimate overflow is that even our enemies will be at peace with us.

In this tumultuous world, peace is a precious commodity and though complete peace can only be found in Jesus Christ, if we can live peaceably with those around us, we have struck balance. As our ways please God, our enemies will see His miraculous work in our lives. What joy it will bring if that serves to draw them to Him and to be saved!

In my career, I often prayed for God's approval. Though it was a challenging career, I know that I made it because the Lord was with me.

Sister Barbara Hendrickson (Nevis)

FRIDAY 30th

The fining pot is for silver, and the furnace for gold: but the LORD trieth the hearts
Proverbs 17:3

RESPONDING TO TRIALS – Reading: Proverbs 17:1-9

The book of Proverbs outlines important principles and truths in which practical advice can be found. The truth embedded in today's focus verse represents a concept which is hard for many to accept. It is the concept of trials. Yes, trials are one of those things that we have to deal with, especially as Christians. And no, it does not come from Satan, it comes from God.

There is a distinction between temptation which is orchestrated by Satan, the enemy of our souls, and trials which are God-ordained. Temptations are aimed at enticing one to act in disobedience to God's will. On the other hand, situations that God allows in our lives as trials are sent to test our motivations, loyalties, character, and commitment to Him as He seeks to help us mature, grow in grace, and ultimately advance His purpose as we bring glory to Him.

Our response to temptations and trials should be different. The Scriptures admonish us to resist the devil (James 4:7) and not to yield to temptations (Romans 6:13). We should however rejoice when tried (James 1- 2-4). This response to trials is certainly not the most natural. I dare say we are more apt to resist trials and want them to end as soon as they begin.

Often, therefore, the focus when we encounter trials is not on the lesson to be learned, the blessing to be obtained, or ultimately understanding what God is doing and seeing His glory. Armed with the understanding that it is the Lord who through trials is testing our hearts (Proverbs 17:3), let us seek to respond appropriately to that which the God of love and truth is allowing in our lives. Let us rejoice!

Ask God today to give the enabling, through His Spirit, to see trials in your life for what they are; God's tool to make you more mature in Him and to experience Him at another level. In turn, ask for wisdom, strength, and a heart of thanksgiving to respond appropriately.

Embrace the spirit of rejoicing, even in trials.

Keshawna Salmon-Ferguson (Jamaica)

SATURDAY 31st

Many daughters have done virtuously, but thou excellest them all – Proverbs 31:29

YOU'RE GOOD AT SOMETHING – Reading: Matthew 25:14-30

We are all good at something, at least one thing – maybe more – we just need to identify what that thing is.

We can waste a lot of time trying to copy others and get frustrated by poor results, rather than focusing on being the best that we can be in what we do easily naturally. That's not to say that we can't support projects that do not fall within our natural skillset, but do identify what is 'you'.

Once that thing is discovered, don't be afraid to expand on it; develop it into more than what it's always been. Especially don't just think about it, but decide to put your idea into action – have a conversation with someone if you must.

I don't know how many women there are in the world today, but consider this: there's no other woman who can do what you were born to do, the way that you can do it!

We sometimes see being inactive or always being in the background as humility, *'I'm just staying in my humble little corner'* (!), and then class those who are busy trying to make a difference, sometimes by need on the frontline, as proud. See in today's main reading, a parable from Matthew 25. The lord upon his return from a long journey commended only those servants who had excelled with the talents (money) he'd given them. The servant who did nothing, who did not excel and made excuses for his non-productivity, was called *'slothful'* (v26).

Today, resolve that you will no longer be average at everything but you are going to excel at something. Simply do something better! You just don't know what will be the outcome.

JEJ

HIRSUTISM

Hirsutism means excessive bodily hair.

Hair on our heads, men's faces, under arms and in private areas of our bodies is normal once we go through puberty.

Hirsutism is where women have thick, dark hair on their face, neck, chest, tummy, lower back, buttocks or thighs. See a GP if it's a problem for you. It might be caused by a medical condition that can be treated.

Other reasons for hairiness are conditions leading to excess testosterone.

Hirsutism is linked to hormones called androgens. It can happen if the level of these hormones increases, or if your body becomes more sensitive to them. The most common cause is polycystic ovary syndrome (PCOS). This is a condition affecting the ovaries that can also cause symptoms such as acne and irregular periods. Sometimes there's no obvious cause.

Rarely, hirsutism can be caused by:

- certain medicines
- using steroids
- other hormonal conditions
- a tumour affecting your hormone levels (very rare)

If you have hirsutism, your GP may suggest:

- losing weight if you're overweight – this can help control hormone levels
- things you can do at home to remove or lighten the hair – such as shaving, waxing, plucking, hair removal creams or bleaching
- a prescription cream to slow hair growth on your face (eflornithine cream)
- taking a contraceptive pill if you've not been through the menopause yet – this can help control hormone levels

If these have not helped after six months, your GP may refer you to a specialist. They may recommend other medicines to control your hormone levels.

Longer-lasting hair removal

There are treatments that can get rid of unwanted hair for longer than the things you can do at home, but they're not usually permanent. They're also not usually available on the NHS and can be expensive.

The two main treatments are:

- electrolysis – where an electric current is used to stop your hair growing
- laser hair removal

Make sure that you research these treatments before trying them. They both have risks and the results are not the same for everyone.

Reference:
https://www.nhs.uk/conditions/hirsutism/

Dr Jo Brooks
Consultant Paediatrician

september
Don’t Give Up

SUNDAY 1st

...hope and quietly wait for the salvation of the LORD – Lam.3:26

WAIT PATIENTLY – Reading: Lamentations 3:24-26

In this passage of Lamentations, Jeremiah was reflecting on the season of affliction Israel was experiencing because of the discipline of God. Due to disobedience, the rod of His wrath led them into a dark place. They were surrounded by bitterness and woe, feeling that they were imprisoned and carrying a heavy chain.

We have all gone through the hardships of life. It may have been the loss of a loved one, the loss of a home, a car repossessed. Perhaps you may have been given a devastating diagnosis from the doctor, or you may have gone through difficulties because of your own bad choices.

But here the prophet humbled himself under the mighty hand of God, and there his hope was revived. He started to reflect on the many times God had delivered Israel and brought them through, thus rekindling his spirit of hope. David said, *'The Lord is my inheritance' (Psalm 16:5)*. Through spiritual DNA - his genetic qualities as the offspring of his Father - those traits of goodness, grace and mercy were his to possess.

We know that we can depend on our Heavenly Father as we seek Him, search for Him diligently, read His Word, pray and consecrate ourselves. His Word declares a broken spirit and a contrite heart He will not despise. Humility is an attribute that attracts God. He is good to those who know that when we are weak, then He gives His strength. Lord, teach us to wait patiently for your salvation. May we always stay in a place of expectation, as we quiet the noise of the turmoil around us.

I*saiah 40:31, 'But they that wait upon the LORD, shall renew their strength, they shall mount up with wings as eagles, they shall run and not be weary, and they shall walk and not faint'.*

As we wait on you Lord, fill us with peace as only you can.

Lady Winsome Saunders, USA

MONDAY 2nd

...for consider him that endured...lest ye be wearied and faint in your minds
Hebrews 12:3

WON'T HE DO IT? – Reading: Hebrews 12:1-13

Starting any journey without knowing the details can be very daunting. Yet all I had was a vision of being something greater than I was.

In pursuit of this vision, I came across many obstacles but with the one Word given to me by the Lord at the end 2022, to *'Focus'*, I found myself having to do just that, to remain focused regardless of the storms that rose whilst on my journey to accomplish my goal.

My student finance was delayed for months. I then failed my first assignment, which was also a miracle, as the university had a recall for all assignments. They stated that there were technical matters, and every student would be given the opportunity to re-sit without a cap, of which I passed on the second round. My first observation was inadequate and I wanted to give up and find work to avoid becoming a financial burden to others. In addition to this, my son was losing out on family time, only for me to fail?!

Yet the word kept ringing out, *'Focus'*! Everywhere I went I kept seeing the word, everyone I spoke to kept encouraging me to remain '*Focused*'.

Today, after all the many challenges, I can truly say that God has been faithful, and He helped me to now be looking to graduate as a qualified teacher with QTS.

Name withheld

TUESDAY 3rd

...cheer up! I have overcome the world – John 16:33 (GW)

TRUST GOD – Reading: John 16:17-33

God knows exactly what you need, in every point of your journey. God knows what is best for you, from the very steps you take to the decisions you make.

'Then Jesus answered and said unto her, O woman, great is thy faith: be it unto thee even as thou wilt. And her daughter was made whole from that very hour' (Matthew 15:28).

This is no fable, but an absolute truth of a Canaanite woman and her sick daughter. She displayed desperation and persistence that any woman would have for her sick child.

However, for this woman, her encounter with Jesus Christ revealed to her the importance of strengthened faith in Him. Untainted by human emotion, you find great wisdom and humility amid trouble. Jesus healed the Canaanite woman's daughter that very hour. God, a great teacher, as his intent was never to deny this woman a miracle, but to demonstrate and illustrate her faith.

In every situation God will find you; all He wants is for you to trust in Him.

'I have said these things to you, that in me you may have peace. In the world you will have tribulation. But take heart; I have overcome the world' (John 16:33 - ESV)

Name withheld

WEDNESDAY 4th

...now is come strength...for the accuser of our brethren is cast down...
Revelation 12:10

THE LITTLE VOICE! – Reading: Genesis 3:1-16; Revelation 12:10

Ladies, how many times have you been multi-tasking in a rush before leaving the house? Now that you're on your way to Wherever, a *'little voice'* says to you, *'Have you turned off the iron?'*, or, *'Have you turned off the oven?'*. You are 99.9% sure that you've done so, but that less than 1% seed of doubt quickly swells to the point that you can't think of anything else. The right thing to do would be to go back and check, to prevent a situation if the appliance has inadvertently been left on.

But here comes a similar *'little voice'* when you start to pray, *'Have you closed the window downstairs?*', or, *'Have you taken the fish out of the freezer for tomorrow's dinner?'.* Because you don't want to forget, you get up and go downstairs only to see that yes, the window is already closed, and the fish is already in the fridge half-thawed for dinner tomorrow.

You're back upstairs and now attempt to pray again. Guess what? Yes, here comes that *'little voice'* again which says, *'Do you remember how you used to curse and swear – it was **terrible**! God hasn't forgiven you!'*, or, *'Remember how you used to behave at the night clubs - it was **disgraceful!**'*, or, *'Do you remember that guy you had a two-year relationship with ten years ago, he's not saved **but** he's still single...'*, or, *'There's no way you're going to make it to heaven – **not a chance**!'.*

Does anybody know that Satan is *'the accuser of the brethren' (Revelation 12:10)*? The *'little (**destructive**) voice'* that intrudes when we want to pray and meditate, is the same voice used in Eden to Sister Eve (Genesis 3:1). When you start to pray, pray past that *'little voice'*. Put the owner and his reminders under your feet; press and pray your way through!

'How far has the LORD taken our sins from us? Farther than the distance from east to west!' (Psalm 103:12 – CEV)

JEJ

THURSDAY 5th

...we glory in tribulations...knowing that tribulation worketh patience – Romans 5:3

GIFT OF GRACE – Reading: Romans 5:1-11

Even in the most challenging and difficult times, there is hope for better things to come. Just as dawn follows the darkest part of the night, moments of light and positivity can emerge after periods of hardship and adversity.

In Romans 5, the Apostle Paul takes it further, teaching us that as believers justified by faith, we actually triumph in our sufferings! This doesn't mean that we're happy about our troubles; we certainly don't pray for them! However, they do accomplish something in our lives.

Suffering ought to make us better Christians. Remember when God asked Job some questions after Job had his afflictions? Questions such as, *'Who is this that obscures my plans without knowledge?' (Job 42:3)* Job's response is, *'Surely I spoke of things I did not understand, things too wonderful for me to know... My ears had heard of you* ***but now my eyes have seen you****'.* Job is saying, *'Lord I thought I knew you but now I see that you are good even when things aren't going my way'!*

Trusting God whilst navigating through trials and tribulations will ultimately make you <u>see</u> God, and see Him in a way you didn't see Him before. Our access by faith is the channel to this revelatory gift of grace that makes us good stewards and ambassadors for God. See 1 Peter 4:10-11:

'As every man hath received the gift, even so minister the same one to another, as good stewards of the manifold grace of God. If any man speak, let him speak as the oracles of God; if any man minister, let him do it as of the ability which God giveth...'.

Our own ability is very limited. We find a peace in God that we could not have in a state of sin and guilt. It is justification that takes away all guilt and replaces it with a grace that completely changes our posture from condemnation to one of rejoicing, and confidence that while we were still sinners, Christ died for us. What a demonstration of love! It is this love that allows us to endure the trials of life. The love of God preserves and protects us.

Sisters, giving up is not an option. You have a harvest to reap. Do not miss your harvest! Press on, and God will let you know when it's harvest time.

Latoya Foster

*FRIDAY 6th

And let us not be weary in well doing... - Galatians 6:9

YOUR REWARD IS IN DUE SEASON – Reading: Galatians 6:1-10

The National Health Service (NHS) which began on 5 July 1948 is currently in a state of crisis due to low staff retention, low staff morale and the daily risks to patient safety. In December 2022 the Royal College of Nursing (RCN) members across the UK went on strike for the first time in its history. It was the first of numerous strikes by other NHS staff, including junior doctors and ambulance personnel.

There have been widespread reports that NHS work is stressful and tiring, leading to staff burnout and a rise in mental health issues. Some staff work extra shifts on their days off to be able to pay their bills, and some utilise local foodbanks. Many feel that striking is the only way to instigate change as there are no reward for their efforts.

Sometimes in our Christian journey, we may get fatigued by the good work we do, or feel undervalued or unappreciated and want to give up. Paul encourages us through his letter to the church in Galatia, *'...let us not grow weary while doing good, for in due season we shall reap if we do not lose heart' (Galatians 6:9 NJKV).*

Our journey might be a struggle, painstaking, sorrowful, pressured, and unrewarding, but our reward is not here. Peter said that, *'...we commit our souls in well doing to a faithful creator' (1 Peter 4:19)*. Our life's good work, in God's time, shall reap its rewards in a glorious heaven if we endure to the end.

Name withheld

Read a Book Day

SATURDAY 7th

I have prayed for you...and when you have come back to me, help the others
Luke 22:32 (CEV)

ANOTHER CHANCE – Reading: Luke 22:31-38

Making a mistake is the easiest thing to make, and that's why we all make them!

Jesus forewarned Peter that he was going to make a 'mistake', i.e., that Peter was going to deny three times that he knew Jesus (John 13:38). Peter was offended at such a suggestion; he loved Jesus so much that he could never deny Him. At least that's what he thought!

Sometimes in order to correct a mistake you have to start all over again, but not always. Luke who writes about Jesus in His role of Son of Man, and the perfect man, presents Jesus to us as one who is in touch with our humanity, understanding the weaknesses with which we struggle in our flesh. Rather than telling Peter that his pending denial would be the end of his discipleship training, Jesus said, when you mess up, get up. Your brethren will still need you after you fall. You're going to learn a big lesson from this mistake but it will qualify you to strengthen and support your brethren at a greater level than before (Luke 22:32).

Years ago, I heard someone say, *'If you're going to fall, fall in The Way - at least someone will see you and pick you up!'*. It's not always people who write us off when we fail, we can be our worst critic. Reluctant to accept God's forgiveness, and the forgiveness of others, we write-off ourselves like a bad debt which cannot be recovered.

You didn't give up on me, though I failed you, you forgave me once again, again
You didn't give up on me, you revived me and then you tried me once again
You tried me once again
You didn't give up, but you tried me once again!

(You Didn't Give Up on Me - Milton Brunson & Thompson Community Singers)

JEJ

SUNDAY 8th

We are filled with hope, as we wait for the glorious return of our great God and Savior Jesus Christ – (Titus 2:13 CEV)

JESUS IS ON HIS WAY BACK – Reading: Luke 21:7-38

Everywhere we look there are signs that our Lord is on His way back for His people. Daily there is something which has happened, near or far, to remind us that we are waiting at the brink of His return.

As Jesus sat on the Mount of Olives, He tells His followers, *'And there shall be signs in the sun, and in the moon, and in the stars; and upon the earth distress of nations, with perplexity…'* (Luke 21:25-28). As children of God, we must not allow our minds to be distracted by the things of this life. We need to be sober, alert, and prepared to leave because, when Jesus comes, there will be no time to do anything but to go!

In 2023, there was a wildfire in Lahaina, Maui, Hawaii - a town was almost destroyed. The strange thing for me about this disaster was, I had visited that town eleven weeks before. I'd walked those said streets, walked along the promenade, shopped in some of the stores which are now burnt out. I had also taken shelter under the beautiful old Banyon trees that had been there for centuries. When looking at the devastation on the news, I recognised that part of the town on one side was untouched by the fire – many homes remained completely intact. It made me realise that when Christ returns, He is coming to take His people who are ready. For those who are not ready He will leave them, and, just like in Hawaii, parts of this world will be desolate, while other parts will not be affected and will remain occupied.

Our Saviour tells His disciples in Matthew 25:13-14, *'Watch therefore, for ye know neither the day or the hour wherein the Son of man cometh…'.*

SSP

MONDAY 9th

But those enduring to the end shall be saved – Matthew 24:13 (TLB)

HOLD OUT – Reading: Matthew 24:1-13

A songwriter wrote:

If I can hold out
If I can keep the faith
In God's own time
My change will come, ***it will come!***

If I can do my best
If I can pass the test
In God's own time
My change ***will come***

Hold out! Just a little while longer
These heavy burdens, they will soon pass over
Run the race! keep The Faith!
My change will come, my change ***will come***
(*In God's Own Time* – Unknown)

Our focus verse today speaks about enduring until the end, not until our cross feels too heavy to bear. Whenever I see the word *'endure'*, I think of holding out under pressure; I think of a hard labour; I think of a test of stamina; I think of continuing even when I feel like I'm about to break; I think of what is at stake if I give up.

It is sad to see so many who started their journey with Christ, giving up before the end. They thereby forfeit any chance of hearing Jesus say, *'Well done!'*. Maybe certain things happened along the way which they had not anticipated; they may have thought that following Christ would be plain sailing. But Jesus, who is our example, He too had to *'endure the cross and despise the shame…' (Hebrews 12:2).* When Jesus said, *'If any one will come after me, let him deny himself, and take up his cross daily, and follow me' (Luke 9:23),* He was not asking us to do something which He hasn't already done.

Those who would discipline ourselves to endure to the end accept that this can only be achieved if we become more intimate with Christ, closer to Him and thus more like Him, *'Looking away from all that will distract us, focusing our eyes on Jesus who is the author and perfecter of faith' (Hebrews 12:2 – AMP).*

JEJ

*TUESDAY 10th

...I have hope...Lamentations 3:21

THERE IS HOPE – Reading: Psalm 42:1-11

Jeremiah the prophet writes in Lamentations 3:21, *'This I recall to mind, therefore have I hope'.*

Can you recall to mind today some of the things that God has done for you in the past? Can you also remember a Word read or spoken which lifted your spirit when you were cast down?

In this month of September which is Suicide Prevention month, we recognise that it is usually the loss of hope that causes anyone to take their own life. But however dark your situation may be or become, there is always hope. How? It is the assurance that even if the outcome is not in your favour right now, God is always in control. That gives hope.

JEJ

World Suicide Prevention Day

WEDNESDAY 11th

...after you have suffered a while, ...strengthen and settle you – 1 Peter 5:10

HAILSTONES – Reading:1 Peter 5:1-11

The mighty hailstones are falling
From the Father's beautiful sky
They have just come suddenly
And I have to ask the reason why.

They are falling, rushing down
What's that noise? It's the mighty hailstones
Ping and ponging around
They are springing up and down
Making their joyful noise
They insist on being heard.

I look up and now the hailstones are gone
There's no evidence left of them
As I cannot hear their forceful song
There is only a wet trail, where they once were
What a wonder, so glorious
To be able to picture this miraculous scene.

It reminds that God does send the hailstones
Of life in our paths to get our attention
Then God can remove those very same hailstones
Which can leave us changed by life's trials
But I praise God for the hailstones
As they will keep us on God's righteous path.

The hailstones that hit you and me
They made us feel uncomfortable you see
It could have been sickness and pain
It could have been financial worry.

It could be loved ones who we saw suffering
It could have been problems at work too
Or loneliness, disappointment
And you are asking Jesus to take you through.

But wait! While I sat to have my drink
Before I could sit on my comfy sofa
The sun was out and with a mighty shout
And you know what? I never saw the hailstones again that day.

Sister Jennifer Henry

THURSDAY 12th

...after I am waxed old shall I have pleasure? Genesis 18:12

HOPE AFTER TRAUMA - Reading: Hebrews 4:14-16

When you're tired of crying, PRAY! When the anger keeps you up all hours of the night, PRAY! When you are broken and the pain is excruciating, PRAY! I am a living witness that God is with you and hears you. When your parents don't love you, abuse you, neglect you and abandon you, PRAY!

God is training us up to prepare us for the supernatural war happening all around us. We survived, so many have not.

The idea that God doesn't let us suffer is not biblical. Apostle Paul says, *'...we glory in tribulations...' (Romans 5:3).*

Anytime you go through something, God is building something. It is hard to see this whilst you're in the midst of suffering, but you are in good hands.

God loves you. God understands even when no one else does.

Don't give up!

Name withheld

FRIDAY 13th

…this is the sixth month with her who was called barren – Luke 1:36

REALLY? - Reading: Luke 1:5-25;57-65

Today we're looking at what could be described as an overdue blessing. Overdue not in the sense of entitlement, but that the fertility window of opportunity for Elisabeth to conceive had already closed. Unfortunately, she had moved from barrenness to menopause.

In his younger years Elisabeth's husband, Zacharias, had wanted to become a father (Luke 1:11-14). Many years later, Gabriel makes a surprising announcement to Zacharias, i.e., that his prayer had been heard. Nobody would blame Zacharias if his response had been, *'What prayer?'*. Surely that must have been an old prayer taken from a dusty archive somewhere. *'Lord, please give us a son'* is not the current prayer of a now elderly couple, *'well stricken in years'* (v7)!

Miraculously pregnant, Elisabeth is overjoyed but seems to also be a bit embarrassed by her pregnancy at her age, or perhaps she is 'high risk' because of her age – whatever the reason, she goes into hiding for five months (vs 24-25). When God performs some extraordinary things for us, we can feel very humbled at the magnitude of the favour. We are amazed to have been singled out for a kind of blessing that is way beyond the norm - I'll call it a ***'Really?'*** blessing!

John is born, and others all around hear the good news. Although their initial reaction might well have been, *'Really?'*, this is closely followed by praises to God for doing such a marvellous thing for Elisabeth, *'they rejoiced with her'* (v 58).

We can at times convince ourselves that nobody has our wellbeing at heart, we tell ourselves that nobody cares – but the opposite is true. Prayers are being sent up to God on our behalf daily, even by those whom we try to avoid. They're asking for God's best, that God will strengthen us and that our hope in Him will not fail. They are also on standby to sincerely celebrate with us our answered prayers.

JEJ

SATURDAY 14th

Compete in the good fight of faith. Grab hold of eternal life – 1 Timothy 6:12 (CEB)

HOLD FAST – Reading: 1 Timothy 6:11-21

The words of our Lord Jesus Christ, written and preached by inspiration of the Holy Ghost, are being challenged and even ridiculed by those who were once believers of the same. Contradictory voices of evil are becoming louder in high places, trying to intimidate and silence those who would oppose.

Ladies, we must individually take responsibility to hold on to what we have been taught from the beginning. Many false teachers are arising, seducing those who we thought would know better. Paul, through the Holy Ghost, saw that these times would come. In his farewell speech to the Ephesian elders, he prophesied, *'I know this, that after my departing shall grievous wolves enter in among the flock. Also of your own selves shall men arise, speaking perverse things, to draw away disciples after them. Therefore watch, and remember, that by the space of three years I ceased not to warn every one night and day with tears' (Acts 20:29-31).* Discern the sorrow and concern in Paul's tone, his alarm for the safety of the vulnerable and gullible members of God's flock.

In today's key verse, rightly Paul warns Timothy not to be passive, that he must engage in resisting the attacks against the Apostolic faith, *'Fight the good fight'* to protect and keep it; *'lay hold…',* eternal life is at stake! Firmly grip the truth which you first received from your grandmother, Lois, and your mother, Eunice.

How do we not let our hope of eternal life slip away? By studying the Word, by knowing and applying the Word. By being convinced that there is no other gospel, and concluding that even if an angel or a familiar preacher comes with a doctrine contrary to the Word of God, they are condemned (Galatians 1:8 - ISV).

JEJ

*SUNDAY 15th

Get thee up, eat and drink; for there is a sound of abundance of rain
1 Kings 18:41

A SPIRITUAL EYE TEST – Reading: 1 Kings 18:41-46

Our character is usually put to the test in times of despair when it seems as if there is no hope, nothing is happening right now, when the situation is desperate. We cannot see beyond what is happening at this moment.

In the text, there was a drought in the land for over three years. However, Elijah, the prophet, was able to look beyond the now and declare, *'…there is a sound of abundance of rain…' (1 Kings 18:41).* Seven times, he sent his servant to look to the sea, but six times the servant reported, *'there is nothing' (v 43).* But on the seventh time he saw, *'a little cloud out of the sea, like a man's hand…' (v 44).*

Perhaps today you are at your wits end with a situation over which you have been praying and trusting the Lord Jesus to come through for you, and you've said in your heart there is no change, there is nothing! I encourage you to pray again; look again, look through the eyes of the Spirit beyond the now. Your spiritual vision is being tested:

Look beyond the hopelessness
Look beyond the drought
Look beyond the world's views
Look again to Jesus, and don't give up.

Today, you will see the manifestation – Jesus is working through the small things to bring the abundance of rain in your situation. Believe for it! Don't give up.

Be encouraged by this chorus:

'Never give up, Jesus is coming
It's the darkest just before dawn
Never give up, Jesus is coming
Never give up, keep holding on.'

God bless.

A Gene H (Jamaica)

***Wife Appreciation Day**

MONDAY 16th

...leave her alone, for she is in bitter distress... – 2 Kings 4:27 (ESV)

HOW ARE YOU? – Reading: 2 Kings 4:8-37

Good morning, how are you doing?

We hear this kind of routine salutation and question almost every day. It is so easily spoken, and often in such a rush, that the person who asks is not even listening or standing still to hear the answer. Likewise, the hearer does not take the customary/automatic question seriously enough to give a full reply: *'Fine thank you'* is the standard response or, *'I'm good, thanks'*.

'Is it well with thee? Is it well with thy husband? Is it well with the child? And she answered, It is well' (2 Kings 4:26). Please note that at this point, the Shunammite woman is speaking to Gehazi, the servant of Elisha. Elisha has sent Gehazi ahead of him to find out the purpose of this woman's unscheduled visit. She chooses not to confide in Gehazi but instead gives him a standard answer to all of his questions, she says, *'Fine thank you'*, i.e., *'It is well'*.

Step in Elisha. The Shunammite has a relationship with the anointed man of God, not with his servant. Under the weight of what has happened with the sudden tragic loss of her son, she falls to the ground and takes hold of Elisha's feet. She no longer says, *'Everything is fine'* but, with the right person, starts to release her pain: *'Did I desire a son of my lord? Did I not say, Do not deceive me?'*. She was angry, hurt, and wanting to apportion blame, although she told Gehazi, *'It is well'*.

Today, let's put aside Gehazi, Elisha, and the Shunammite woman, and replace them with ourselves having an unhurried conversation with God. If God asked now, *'How are you?'* followed by: *'Is it well with your husband? Is it well with your marriage? Is it well with your children? Is it well with your family? Is it well with your neighbours? Is it well with your colleagues? Is it well at the church that you attend? Is it well with your brethren? Is it well with your faith? Is it well with your heart and mind? Is it well with our (God and you) relationship?'* – how would you answer? Would you respond as though you are talking to Gehazi, an untrustworthy servant (2 Kings 5:25-27), or like you are sharing with God who can be trusted and knows the answers?

Something to think about today before your next conversation with God is, *'How are you?'*. That's all He wants to know!

JEJ

TUESDAY 17th

I will give you a crown of life – Revelation 2:10

BE FAITHFUL UNTO DEATH – Reading: Revelation 2:8-11

God knows the intimate details of our lives. He knows our works, issues, attitudes and the intentions of our hearts.

The Lord understands the tears when we are overwhelmed through the suffering we endure, the unfair treatment from others - even those we would least expect it from. Those who cause us pain are sometimes our families, co-workers, friends - they let us down. We multi-task at the best of times and although we smile, many do not know what's really behind the smile.

But God says, *'Fear none of these things…be faithful unto death'.* Even when others are unfaithful, nonetheless, we carry on because He has given us a charge. We will one day receive a crown of life. Women of God be faithful unto death our reward is PRICELESS!

Evg Angelina Cox

WEDNESDAY 18th

I have fought the good fight, I have finished my course, I have kept the faith
2 Timothy 4:7

GRACE GIVEN TO KEEP GOING – Reading: 2 Timothy 4:1-8

In our above reading today, Paul is declaring to Timothy that he had endured to the end and finished well. In fact, he gives us a vivid account of all the challenges he faced in 2 Corinthians 11:24-31. What the Apostle Paul went through is enough to have made anyone give up! No mere human could suffer all of that without the Grace of God being with them.

So, what does this mean for you today? The message is simple: you have the Grace to keep going.

The Lord revealed this truth to me whilst studying at university. The first day in class the lecturer posed a question to every student, *'What would you put on your t-shirt as a motto?' 'Just keep going,'* I thought, *'I've just got to keep going'.* Little did I know how that *'keep going'* motto would be challenged significantly in my final year. My husband was diagnosed with cancer. I struggled to keep focused and felt like giving up during his journey to recovery. However, the Lord gave me the assurance that He did not bring me this far for me to quit. His grace and strength gave me the perseverance, and He will do the same for you as you call out to Him.

Perseverance does not go without a reward. Paul was looking forward to receiving his heavenly reward, and upon graduation I was surprised when I too received an award. No, it wasn't a crown, but a prize for, *'The student who had overcome adversity while studying'.* Many students had faced obstacles, but I was the one chosen to receive the prize! The Lord has a way of using the natural to teach us a spiritual lesson. What a God we serve!

May you complete what you are destined to do by His Grace in Jesus' name. Amen!

CP

THURSDAY 19th

For a just (person) falleth seven times, and riseth again... - Proverbs 24:16

YOU CAN'T KEEP A GOD-DRIVEN WOMAN DOWN – Reading: Proverbs 24:15-34

You cannot keep a God-driven woman down
Devil you have taken away all her money
You're constantly attacking her health too
You have your evil scheming plans
But God will stamp all over you.

You cannot keep a God-driven woman down
Even though you tried to, so many times
You have taken away her family
You even harassed her in all of her jobs
You did not want her to praise her Saviour
But for her to sob about her lost opportunities.

Devil, you cannot keep a God-driven woman down
She maybe in pain today
But it's resurrection morning tomorrow!
It's tears today
But God clears away the sorrow.

As women let us be driven by God
Not our material and emotional feelings
Let's let go of our lifestyles
That don't bring fruitful outcomes.

Let us be like this woman
Driven by God's will
Let us be driven to be true to our Creator
For He will bless us now and forever.

But devil I am telling you, you cannot
Keep a God-driven woman down
You want her to give in to you
But you've not anticipated the powerful God who she serves will overcome you!

Praise God. Praise God.

Sister Jennifer Henry

FRIDAY 20th

Let not your heart be troubled: ye believe in God, believe also in me – John 14:1

HOLD ON UNTIL OUR CHANGE COMES – Reading: John 14:1-14

Just before His redemptive work at Calvary, the Lord comforted His disciples telling them not to let their hearts be troubled. He encouraged them to believe in Him and trust His Word. Jesus assured them of the many mansions in His Father's house, and that He was going to prepare a place for them to later on be with Him.

Heaven is a prepared place for prepared believers. We take comfort in the knowledge that the promises of John 14 are for all who believe on the Word of God. Many have been experiencing the storms of life as we wait for the Lord's return. The going has been tough, *'for strait is the gate, and narrow is the way that leads to eternal life' (Matthew 7:14).* In our storms, the seas may be raging, the billows tossing high: sometimes it seems as if there is no shelter near. Our heart is troubled! Similarly with the disciples the Lord consoled them, *'Let not your heart be troubled'.* It seems the only sure medicine for a 'troubled heart' is to believe, *'believe also in me'.* We are not to give up, but to trust in the Lord Jesus who is both the maker (He allows them) and the calmer of our storms.

Let us learn from Peter on the water, and take our eyes off the waves and the wind. Just focus on Jesus Christ, *'the author and finisher of our faith; who for the joy that was set before him, endured the cross, despising the shame, and is set down at the right hand of the throne of God'* (Hebrews 12:2). *'For yet a little and he that shall come will come and will not tarry. Now the just shall live by faith…' (Hebrews 10:37-38).*

Dr Anna Crouch

SATURDAY 21st

Then said his wife unto him, Dost thou still retain thine integrity? curse God, and die
Job 2:9

JOB'S WIFE – Reading: Job 1:1-22; 2:1-10

'**C***urse God and die'* (Job 2:9)!

This is the desperate statement of a woman who has lost everything and sees no further reason to go on. Everything that was familiar and favoured had been cruelly taken away from her. She mourned the loss of her children and despaired at the suffering of her husband. *'What further cruelty could be visited upon them?'* she thought.

We are so very familiar with this outburst and speak of Job's wife's failings. We comment on all that her husband had lost, and we include her support in this list. We fail to appreciate that she too has lost all!

Let us look deep inside ourselves. Do we sometimes want to do the same? Have we sometimes felt so despairing that we are ready to give up hope? Have we ever been so broken in spirit that our entire being is as one mass of pain? If so, then we have been in the same ship! We wish this feeling on no one else.

There is comfort to be found in God; He is our strength in our time of weakness.

Be encouraged and keep hope alive. Keep on believing that this too shall pass.

Pastor Londy Esdaille (Nevis)

(I Arise! 2022)

*SUNDAY 22nd

Be patient, therefore, brethren, unto the coming of the Lord – James 5:7

THE COMING OF THE LORD DRAWETH NIGH – Reading: James 5:7-12

Be patient therefore Brethren
Until the coming of the Lord
Be with Him always
On one accord
Through trials and tribulations, circumstances and situations
Don't give up! From His cup of glory may we sup.

Let nothing in this life hinder thee
For when you were in the world
You were blind but now you have spiritual eyes to see
Oh! To our great God be the glory
For He hath done great wonders with thee.

He hath brought His people a mighty long way
Therefore may we rise up and give thanks today
Come to Him without further delay
And allow Him always to have the final say
Keep us, Lord, that we don't go astray
I pray thy Word doth minister to us today.

May we receive thy healing balm
As we get down on bended knees to pray
'We love thee, Lord', that is all one can say
May we portray thee daily in the best possible way
Giving thanks unto thee for allowing us to see another day.

My brothers and sisters may we continue on
To fight the good fight of faith, never giving up
May our love and faith in the Lord both in equal measure
Continue to grow and develop.

Be ye also patient, Brethren, stablish your hearts
For the coming of the Lord draweth nigh
He shall come like a thief in the night, therefore hold on
Hold on with all thy power and might
Never give up! For every battle the Lord hath won.

Sis Pru McEwan

World Car Free Day

MONDAY 23rd

…and there wrestled a man with him until the breaking of the day – Genesis 32:24

ALL NIGHT WRESTLING – Reading: Genesis 32:22-32

Picture Jacob alone, wrestling all night with a man to receive a special blessing before continuing his journey to meet his brother, Esau, whom he had not seen for many years.

The struggle is not a short encounter, it starts at night and doesn't end until daybreak. Physical combat, an up-close struggle, fierce grappling, laboured breathing, then this mysterious being wounds Jacob on his thigh such that it is out of joint. Surely Jacob will now withdraw. But the fight continues! Who is going to let go first?

The angel speaks; he says, *'Let me go for the day breaketh'*. This fight has gone on long enough, longer than anticipated, he needs to be somewhere else. Notwithstanding, Jacob says, *'I will not let you go, except you bless me'*. Response: *'What is your name?'.*

Jacob gives us in this lesson a vision of what, *'Don't Give Up'* looks like. Have you ever felt like you were in a mental or spiritual battle to get something that you could not do without? Everyone who you spoke with concerning the matter advised, *'Maybe you should just let it go'!* But even if you had to fight by yourself, you made up in your mind, *'I will not let it go, I'm going to keep on believing God'.*

Remember Bartimaeus who was blind, calling out, *'Jesus, Thou Son of David, have mercy on me' (Mark 10:47).* The people around Bartimaeus told him to hush, to 'let go' of the noise he was making. They could easily say that because they could see! Instead of getting quieter, Bartimaeus shouted the more, *'Jesus, Son of David…'*, until Jesus stood still (v 48-49).

Ladies, we can lay aside our elegance sometimes – wrestling and elegance don't work together **at all**. You've got to know **why** you're wrestling! You've got to know **why** you're calling! Amaze Jesus with your tenacious-self! He will marvel and ask, *'What is your name?'*!

JEJ

TUESDAY 24th

We consider those who endured to be blessed. You have heard about Job…
James 5:11

WHEN WE BELIEVE GOD: A REFLECTION ON GOD'S WORD – Reading: James 5:7-12

Abram believed in the LORD; and He counted it to him for righteousness (Genesis 15:6).

When we believe God, we are steadfast in Jesus Christ. When we believe God, we are persuaded that neither death or life, nor angels, nor principalities, nor powers, nor things present, nor things to come, nor height, nor depth, nor any other creature, shall be able to separate us from the love of God, which is in Christ Jesus our Lord (Romans 8:38-39)

When we believe God, we will hold His unchanging hand.

When we believe God, we will bless the LORD at all times and His praise shall continually being our mouth (Psalm 34:1).

When we believe God, we will wait on God (Psalm 62:1).

When we believe God, the things happening in this world around us, i.e., the wars, the hurricanes, fires, earthquakes, famine, energy crisis and so forth, will not trouble us, because we know and believe that God will supply all our needs according to His riches in glory, by Christ Jesus (Philippians 4:19).

We have no need to worry but when we do, look to God who is the author and finisher of our faith and let not our hearts be troubled, when we believe God.

Jennifer Marshall

*WEDNESDAY 25th

Elijah prayed earnestly that it might not rain: and it rained not – James 5:17

YOU CAN PRAY TOO – Reading: James 5:13-18

James the apostle takes time to tell us in chapter 5:17 that Elias (Elijah) was an ordinary man, not supernatural. He faced challenges as we do, he had bad days like everybody else. He was *'of like passions'*, meaning, *'Elijah was a person just like us' (CEB).*

I guess that James felt it necessary to frame his writing in this way for his audience to understand that the power of God is not limited to a particular kind of person. Everyone who believes has the power to pray and see results.

Yes there are those who have, for instance, the gift of healing, but we all have the power to speak over ourselves or somebody else, in Jesus' name, if the person with the gift or the elders are not there. God will hear and still perform the work.

Sometimes believers are in awe of the 'hierarchy', thinking that the ministerial staff are greater than them. But if you have the Holy Ghost, you are connected to the same source as the prophet, the healer, etc., *'For from his fullness we have all received…' (John 1:16).*

JEJ

National Fitness Day

THURSDAY 26th

For ye have need of patience, that…ye might receive the promise – Hebrews 10:36

IT WILL COME TO PASS – Reading: Hebrews 10:32-39

Though hard the trial
And rough the way
You have walked forever
Or so it seems
When you reach for the stars
With your hands outstretched
And grasped only shattered dreams
Empty nest and barrenness reside
Where once grew rich green grass
Remember, whatever befalls you
It will come to pass.

Nothing lasts forever
Winds of change will blow
Bringing rays of light and hope
Bidding darkness go
Though sometimes you may feel broken
And too hard may seem the test
Remember, as sure as night turns to day
It will come to pass.

For God's infinite wisdom
Knows the way you tread
He sees your pain and heartache
And all that lies ahead
He will not leave you helpless
Nor cancel His Word,
No matter the delay
It will come to pass.

Barbara Mason

*FRIDAY 27th

(We) are kept by the power of God... – 1 Peter 1:5

KEPT BY THE POWER OF GOD – Reading: Psalm 71:7-8; 1 Peter 1:1-5

There is nobody reading this page today who could not join with the songwriter who wrote:

So I'm here today, because God kept me
I'm alive to today, only because of His grace
He kept me, God kept me
He kept me, so I wouldn't let go.

We will never remember all of the things that God has brought us through - they're too many - our brain doesn't have the capacity to hold so much information. Neither will we ever know just how many secret or random missiles have been thrown at us in our lifetime. God allowed the arrows to go another way and miss their intended mark. David was targeted by Saul because of Saul's insecurity and jealousy. Although David had on different occasions saved the life of Saul, the love that Saul said he had for David later became bitter hatred.

God by His power is still keeping us from the javelins of our haters, some of them used to be our brethren or friends. They cannot understand why their plots and schemes have failed; it doesn't make sense. The writer of Psalm 71:7 said, *'I am as a wonder to many but thou art my strong refuge'.* So we walk in the shatterproof covering of Almighty God and let others marvel. We give God thanks, honour and praise for His keeping power.

JEJ

Macmillan Coffee Morning

SATURDAY 28th

…the trial of your faith…might be found unto praise and honour and glory…
1 Peter 1:7

PRAY THAT YOUR FAITH FAILS NOT – Reading: Luke 22:31-32; 1 Peter 1:6-7

Our Lord Jesus Christ willingly carried His cross and stayed on it for us until He accomplished atonement for our sins. To Him be all glory and honour.

The fiery trials that we experience in our daily lives make up the cross that we each carry and must not give up on. We get discouraged at times and may be mocked by others urging us to come off our cross, to lay it down and walk away. Such tests are to try our faith (1 Peter 4:12). They are *'more precious than gold that perishes, though it be tried with fire, that might be found unto praise, honour and glory at the appearing of Jesus Christ' (I Peter 1:7).*

Overcoming our trials refines and conforms us into the image of Christ. So let us, '*be sober and vigilant because our adversary the devil, walks about as a roaring lion, seeking whom he may devour; whom resist steadfast in the faith, knowing that the same afflictions are accomplished in your brothers and sisters that are in the world' (1 Peter 5:8-9).* Pray that your faith fails not.

And remember that, *'there hath no temptation taken you but such as is common to man: but God is faithful, who will not suffer you to be tempted above that ye are able; but will with the temptation also make a way to escape, that ye may be able to bear it' (1 Corinthians 10:13).*

Dr Anna Crouch

SUNDAY 29th

...the LORD said...Peace be unto thee; fear not: thou shalt not die – Judges 6:23

I ENCOURAGED MYSELF – Reading: Judges 6:1-24

Oppression of the enemy is rife; he is not playing games but is out to steal, destroy and kill us and our families, especially our children.

I looked at Gideon (Jerubabbaal) in Judges 6. So many attacks from the enemy. If God had not stepped in to release His rebellious people through Gideon, what would have happened?

The children of Israel had sinned again with idolatry, flaunting their sins in God's face. He therefore delivered them into bondage for seven years. We are going through, there's no one in Christ who is not under some kind of attack. I learned from experience that you can be waiting for several prayers to be answered - waiting on a situation to come to an end, waiting on your children to re-dedicate their lives to the Lord, waiting on your health to improve, finance, etc. Just waiting on the Lord!

Can you imagine how Gideon felt in his situation? The enemy had taken Israel's sustenance, destroyed their livelihood and crops, and took their animals. Everything was taken leaving them greatly impoverished. I'm sure that their enemies took their peace of mind - if Mental Health was a thing back then, it would have been highlighted.

What intrigued me was the angel who came with a hope of deliverance and restitution for Israel. Listen, we get into these situations where we've opened doors to sin and get encumbered and trampled upon by Satan – we let him in legally. But there is a merciful Father who loves us beyond our perception, He is there waiting to set us free.

Gideon could not understand why these things were happening, so he questioned the angel (Judges 6:13*: 'Where has Yahweh been? Where is He? We are struggling, we can't move forward'*. How do I dig myself out of this depression and low self-esteem? Where are you, Lord? It's so good to cry out to God. God sees our children as mighty men and women of valour, even though they are out there hiding from God.

Let's hold on sisters, it's a new day, a new beginning, a new dawning. Whatever you've passed through or are going through, God will use every bit of it to help another. Never give up. God gives a song in the night season and all the day long.

Margaret McPherson

*MONDAY 30th

...consider it pure joy... whenever you face trials of many kinds – James 1:2 (NIV)

TRIALS MAKE YOU STRONGER – Reading: James 1:1-18

In James 1:2, we see two ideas that do not necessarily belong together. This is not a sugar-coated message. In other words, he is letting us know that temptations, oftentimes synonymous with trials, will come. They are part and parcel of our Christian walk, for ours is not 'a walk in the park' - we are in a fight for our life!

Temptations and the way that we handle them, show us what we are made of. The Word of God says, *'if thou hast run with the footmen, and they have wearied thee then how canst thou contend with the horses?' (Jeremiah 12:5).* Our courage is forged in the fire of temptation. Just as we trust God when all is well, so too we must have the same confidence to know that God, *'...will with the temptation, also make a way to escape...' (1 Corinthians 10:13.* We can make it through if we keep holding on to Him.

We are encouraged to, *'count it all joy when we encounter these diverse temptations' (James 1:2).* Though it may seem to be a contradiction in terms, the emphasis is on what we gain when we don't give up. We need to have an, *'it came to pass'* belief - a faith that tells us that there is a hope, a better way awaiting us if we only hold on... a faith that God who is with us, will bring us out or bring us through if we don't give up. The joy we feel when we come through, should motivate and increase our confidence so that we can maintain a positive attitude, even when it seems impossible to do so. Our suffering isn't meaningless. Tough times can teach us if we are willing to learn. When we look back and see how He has been there with us, through it all, we grow in the knowledge that He indeed makes us stronger.

Sister Barbara Hendrickson (Nevis)

***World Apple Crumble Day**

october

Seasons

*TUESDAY 1st

Be still and know that I am God…Psalm 46:10

BE STILL – Reading: Psalm 46:1-11

'***W****hen everything is moving and shifting, the only way to counteract chaos is stillness. When things feel extraordinary, strive for ordinary. When the surface is wavy, dive deeper for quieter waters. (Kristin Armstrong)*

In a world that is constantly demanding so much of our time, energy, focus and attention, finding that place of escapism often seem impossible. But even Jesus Christ taught us a principle regarding rest while He was here on this earth, and would oftentimes withdraw Himself from the demands of people, conflicts, noise and distractions to be with His heavenly father. It is in those quiet moments where we really find the answers to our questions and our peace is often restored.

To capture the essence of Psalm 46, the psalmist describes the importance of making God our refuge and fortress in times of war and conflict. The word *'still'* is a translation of the Hebrew word *'rapa'* meaning *'to slacken, let down, or cease'*. When the believer really acknowledges the greatness of their God, recognises His ability to remove every Red Sea in their lives, every mountain of defeat, fear and discouragement, we will cease from all worry and anxiety.

God wants to show Himself mighty and strong in our situations, but He requires a people that are willing to surrender their will for His will so that He can be exalted in the earth. Selah.

Evangelist Paula Clarke
Bethel National Women's President

****International Hair Day***

October 2024
Theme: Seasons
Breast Cancer Awareness Month
National Domestic Abuse/Violence Awareness Month

WEDNESDAY 2nd

...At the appointed time I will return unto thee...Genesis 18:14

AT THE APPOINTED TIME – Reading: Genesis 17:15-19; 18:1-14

Season - a particular period or time characterised by a unique weather pattern. We may think of a rainy season or simply the seasons of the year. For example, spring, summer, autumn and winter. But whatever the period is in your life, know that God is in control. He has designed it, He has planned it, and He has a purpose for the unique season that you now experience.

Genesis 18:14 begins with a question, *'Is any thing too hard for the LORD?'.* Whatever season you are in, the answer will always be, *'Nothing is too hard for the LORD'.* The answer given by God is a promise. He said, *'At the appointed time I will return unto thee'.* Picture a father going to work saying, *'I will be home'* or a mother saying to her children, *'I will be back soon'.* It's a promise that will come to pass.

This verse echoed words that the Lord reassured me with when I had no food to eat, when I didn't have a job, when my future looked uncertain, when doctors told me there was nothing that they could do to save the life of my husband. In the coldest and darkest times, when I felt like I was going through autumn - the leaves drying - stripped bare in winter, I had to trust God.

Trust God, He will see you through whatever season you are in. When you experience life's hardships or the joys of life, *what will you do in your season?* The answer is clear - at the appointed time, God will restore. He is standing with His precious children. Life will come back and you will grow in your season. *What will you do in your season?* Trust God. Hold to His promise. His promise is sure. In your season a change will happen. God knows why you have to experience the different unique patterns, but He will ensure that all things will always work together for good to those who love Him and are called according to His purpose (Romans 8:28).

What will you do in each season? Love God. *What will you do in each season?* Trust God.

'Is there anything too hard for God?' No, nothing!

'At the appointed time I will return', saith the LORD.

Selina Grant

THURSDAY 3rd

...the child grew, and became strong in spirit, and was in the wilderness until the day of his public appearance to Israel – Luke 1:80 (ESV)

GIVE GOD THE GLORY – Reading: John 1:1- 8; John 3:27-36

Today's focus verse is speaking of John the Baptist, forerunner of Jesus Christ, described by John the Apostle as *'a man sent from God'* (John 1:6). It is important that we take note of that piece of information, i.e., John the Baptist was sent from God.

Sent from God but spent most of his time living in a wilderness, not dressed in finery nor eating the best of food daily, still, he was certainly *'sent'* and *'became strong in spirit'*. We admire John for his focus and commitment to his call to preach the message of repentance, despite his environment, *'I am the voice of one crying in the wilderness, make straight the way of the Lord…'.*

A message of repentance is never the easiest one to preach unless you, like John, are sent from God. See that John understood his ministry would only be a short one, preparing the hearts of the people for one coming afterwards who was greater than him. John did not point anyone to him, but directed them to Christ. He deflected all glory away from himself saying, concerning Jesus, *'He must increase, but I must decrease' (John 3:30).* Another translation says, *'He must become greater; I must become less' (NIV).*

Those in ministry, especially Word ministry, often attend courses and have an extensive personal library of study Bibles and commentaries. Whilst these are useful, the most effective and memorable training that any of us will have, is in a wilderness! It's in these uncomfortable places that we build resilience and *'become strong in spirit';* the theory of our learning comes to life. Our flesh is put under subjection, *'that the excellency of the power might be of God and not of us' (2 Corinthians 4:7);* Christ alone is exalted.

John started his ministry in a wilderness. Jesus too was led by the Spirit into a wilderness to be tested of the devil at the start of his public ministry (Matthew 4:1). As well as the indwelling Holy Spirit, it is experience gained in the desert, coupled with knowledge of the Word, that certifies and makes us more effective in ministry. And from time-to-time, lest we should attempt to take any of God's glory for ourselves, we are sent for a refresher course, and the classes are always held in a wilderness!

JEJ

FRIDAY 4th

And when the devil had ended all temptation, he departed from Him for a season
Luke 4:13

STAY ALERT – Reading: Luke 4:1-13

We see in today's verse that the devil retreated temporarily from Jesus after tempting him in every area. The enemy of our soul will always seek to come back, lying in wait until he sees an opportunity to make us stumble and fall. Be alert.

Remember sisters we are not ignorant of the devil's devices. We know he comes to steal, kill and destroy, working through the lust of the flesh, but we '*do not walk according to the flesh but according to the Spirit' (Romans 8:4).* He tempts us through the lust of the eyes, but our prayer is, '*Turn my eyes from beholding vanity, and quicken thou me in thy way (Psalm 119:37).* He may tempt us through the pride of life, but we *'humble ourselves continually before the Lord' (1 Peter 5:6 James 4:10*).

You may have successfully overcome a temptation and now you are feeling victorious, however, in overcoming one temptation we may fall prey to a different temptation. The enemy of your soul will try and return in another season to tempt you again. We always must be on guard, we are warned in 1 Peter 5:8 KJV, *'Be sober, be vigilant; because your adversary the devil as a roaring lion walketh about seeking whom he may devour'.*

Thank God for the encouraging words in Hebrew 4:15-16. We are told that because Jesus was in all points tempted as we are and as a result can sympathise with our weaknesses, therefore we can approach the throne room with boldness, knowing He will meet us with mercy and grace.

Stay alert, sisters, the devil knows his time is short!

CP

*SATURDAY 5th

The LORD shewed (Joseph) mercy, and gave him favour, in...prison – Genesis 39:21

IN PRISON ON PURPOSE – Genesis 39:1-23

One of the most challenging tests for anyone is to be living out a penalty resulting from a false accusation.

This was the misfortune of Joseph. Whilst working for Potiphar, Potiphar's wife tried to seduce Joseph into having a sexual relationship with her. It's quite likely that she had been trying to get Joseph's attention for a while before that calamitous day. You may have heard the saying of playwright, William Congreve, *'Hell hath no fury like a woman scorned' (The Mourning Bride 1697).* This aptly captures the actions of Potiphar's wife after Joseph rejected her flirtations and suggestions of committing adultery. Choking with rage, she could not even bring herself to call Joseph by his name when relaying her untrue allegation to her husband. She said, ***'The Hebrew servant****, which you have brought unto us, came in unto me to mock me' (Genesis 39:17).* Have you noticed that when one is really vexed, that's how reference is made concerning the person who has caused the vexation? They become nameless: *'the woman', 'the man', 'that pastor', 'that brother', 'that sister'*!

Potiphar put Joseph in jail. We read of no trial, only a verdict. I remember speaking with a prisoner on a Prison Ministry visit. She was crying deeply and told me she was innocent, that she had been set up to cover the true culprit. It was a heartbreaking story. The positive aspect of this story was she said that when she got out of prison, she would find a church because her grandmother had been encouraging her to give her life to the Lord for a long time.

Divine purpose is still at work in our dark seasons and in our unpreferred places. Though Joseph felt that in Potiphar's house he was in the wrong place at the wrong time, God had Joseph exactly where He wanted him for the next move. Of all the cells in that prison, Joseph was put into one already occupied by two members of Pharaoh's staff. We are positioned, even in prison, on purpose.

JEJ

****World Teachers Day***

SUNDAY 6th

Thou hast turned for me my mourning into dancing: thou hast put off my sackcloth…
Psalm 30:11

WHERE IS MY PSALM? – Reading: Psalm 30:1-12

David, a king, a warrior and worshipper of the LORD really knew how to ascribe worship to God, regardless. Whether it was great victories or tragedies, be it joy and gladness or sadness and pain; his focus on God was very intense and intentional. His conditions had never affected his worship because his heart was in the right position – beholding the goodness of God and just being in holy awe.

In this psalm, we can see where David acknowledged that God did it!

We can worship God as God, in spirit and in truth, no matter what season we find ourselves in. Why? We do not worship out of our conditions as that is not the truth about God. He is still who He is as we transition through seasons.

There is something that supersedes seasons and that is the Word of God; the Word testifies of who He is (2Timothy 4:2). Therefore, the Word which is not seasonal, will cause us to rejoice and sing in all seasons, thus overcoming conditional and seasonal worship.

We can look to God instead of our situation and respond to His call to *'come up higher'*. Then the fountains of our hearts will break forth into joyful sacred singing, finding our psalm.

Pastor Josephine Lewis

MONDAY 7th

***...there shall arise...seven years of famine; and all the plenty shall be forgotten...* Genesis 41:30**

PREPARE NOW FOR LATER – Reading: Genesis 41:1-40

Have you ever had a disturbing dream, or a strong feeling of dread, that something terrible was about to happen, but you didn't quite know what it meant? It was not clear, but you sensed that God was forewarning you of a personal climate change.

While Joseph, son of Jacob, was in prison, the Pharaoh of the time had a perplexing dream. This disturbing dream served as the catalyst for his chief butler to remember Joseph whom he had met when he too was in prison (Genesis 41:9-14). As a result, Joseph was able to interpret Pharaoh's dream. He did not withhold anything, it was important that Pharaoh heard the undiluted message, as received from God, about the forthcoming seasons.

We could say that there was good news followed by bad news, or we could say that there was good news followed by a bit of good news. Why say that? Because the God of the good times is still good and present in the bad times, *'For in the time of trouble, He shall hide me in His pavilion: in the secret of his tabernacle shall He hide me' (Psalm 27:5).* God revealed to Joseph the methods to deploy for Egypt to survive the lean years – 20% of their crops should be put away each year preceding the famine (Genesis 41:34-36). Note that the seasons of plenty and of scarcity were dealt out by God in equal measure, i.e., there were seven years of each.

What should we do then when we have a puzzling dream or a sense of foreboding that we are about to be catapulted from what was our summer season straight into a hard winter (metaphorically speaking)? Well, and even if we have no inkling, in the years of plenty pray as much as you can, study God's Word as much as you can, be at as many church services when you can and take notes during Sunday school and Bible class and delivery of the Word. Record some of the services if you can, fast as much as you can. Then, in an abrupt and shocking change of season, which could be sickness, bereavement of any type, relocation to another place where there is no Christian community, you can draw and endure from the reserves stored from your years of plenty.

JEJ

TUESDAY 8th

...where does my help come from? My help comes from the LORD...
Psalm 121:1-2 (NIV)

MY SOUL CRIES FOR GOD - Reading: Psalm 121:1-8

In Psalm 42 David's lamentation is for God's help in his condition and trouble, vs 9-10, *'I will say unto God my rock, why hast thou forgotten me? Why go I mourning because of the oppression of the enemy? As with a sword in my bones, mine enemies reproach me, while they say daily unto me, where is thy God?'.*

David remembers his faith in God and this reassures him that he should not faint, but instead hold strong because his help would come from the Lord his God. David reminds the reader how important it is to hope in God daily. He reminds us that if we are in God then our hope can never be lost.

In this desolate land that we live in, where many have turned away from God to focus on what the world tells them is the way to live, I am reminded that everything that is not of God shall pass away. So, I will only hope in God who is my refuge and strong tower in this time of storm.

Romans 15:13 says: *'Now the God of hope fill you with all joy and peace in believing, that ye may abound in hope, through the power of the Holy Ghost'.*

SSP

WEDNESDAY 9th

You tried to harm me, but God made it turn out for the best...Genesis 50:20 (CEV)

YOU DID ME A FAVOUR! – Reading: Genesis 50:1-26

Romans 8:28 is a verse which I often recite to myself (admittedly after an event has ended rather than during).

The life of Joseph was action-packed! First son of Rachel, his birth ended Rachel's season of being barren. Loved more by his father, Jacob, because he was the son of Rachel and of his old age. Hated by his brothers because of their father's favouritism, and because of Joseph's dreams. Sold by his brethren, transported to Egypt and didn't see his family and beloved father again for many years. Accused of trying to rape Potiphar's wife. Thrown into prison, forgotten in prison. Then elevated from prison to being Pharaoh's assistant. We'll pause there.

In today's lesson, Jacob is dead. His body is carried from Egypt back to Canaan for burial. Mindful of the pain that the brothers had caused Joseph, Jacob had left instructions appealing that they should ask for Joseph's forgiveness of their past wickedness. It is an emotionally charged moment as Jacob's wish is made known for reconciliation and not revenge. Guilt, true remorse and repentance spill out of the hearts of Joseph's brothers as they reflect upon the plot which through envy and hatred they'd put together.

But here comes a, *'And we know that all things work together for good…' (Romans 8:28)* moment! Joseph is also weeping when he says, *'But as for you, ye thought evil against me; but God meant it unto good, to bring to pass as it is this day, to save much people alive' (Genesis 50:17-20).*

There is always someone or a life-event that God will use as the trigger to move us into our next chapter. Without that stimulus, we would remain stagnant and comfortable and yes, outside of His divine purpose for our lives. It could be a spiteful boss, the ending of a relationship, a redundancy, the instigation of a new law. Whatever the agent, as God's plan for us unfolds but gradually, we will then look beyond the pain, inconvenience and upheaval and see like Joseph that, *'God meant it unto good'.*

JEJ

*THURSDAY 10th

For promotion cometh neither from the east, nor from the west, nor from the south...
Psalm 75:6

IF IT'S YOURS, IT'S YOURS – Reading: Psalm 75:1-10

I have heard several times that, *'if something is for you, it can't be un-for you'!*

Such a simple statement summarises Psalm 75:6-7 very well. We sometimes see colleagues chasing after positions at work using underhanded means, or brethren forcing their way forward for a position in the church, or women chasing after a man for marriage like they're running to catch the last bus, when all of these are in the hands of God.

There is always a wrong spirit in control when we plot and scheme to get what is not in the plans or thoughts which God said in Jeremiah 29:11 that he already has for us, or when we seek to fast forward what He is not yet ready to give. If you're in doubt, read the lesson of Abraham and Sarah and see how Ishmael came into being (Genesis 16), or read the lesson of Jacob and Esau and see how Jacob obtained the birthright (Genesis 25:29-34) and blessing (Genesis 27), when God had already declared who Jacob would be from when he was in his mother's womb (Genesis 25:23). Human interference with divine plans always equals **disaster** and comes with long-lasting consequences!

So, relax! We're talking about seasons, yes? When your season comes to be elevated, you won't have to mix in some deception, neither will you have to walk on or pull others down to get it! If marriage is for you, you won't need to flutter your eyelashes at that man, nor disrespect yourself and other women to get his attention. As with nature, without any agitation or stimulation, seasons come.

JEJ

***World Mental Health Day**

FRIDAY 11th

...the LORD gave and the LORD hath taken away; blessed be the name of the LORD
Job 1:21

OUT OF DEATH CAME LIFE – Reading: Job 1:1-22

From the day that we are born, we're on a journey until the day God calls us home. We are on a journey that takes us through seasons of the soul and mind; seasons of joy, seasons of heartache and seasons of loss.

Job lost everything - his wealth, health and all of his children because God allowed him to be tested in that way. But God rewarded Job with twice as much at the end of his trial than he had ever had before. You may lose your health, you may lose your wealth, your loved ones too, but through it all **don't lose your walk**! Keep praising God even when you can't understand it. God never makes a mistake.

I'd like to share this testimony and a little insight into Divine Intervention which shows how great our God is:

It was January 1961. I was one of six children, the only girl among five brothers. We were a very happy family, then tragedy struck, loss and heartbreak came. Suddenly, due to an accident, my younger brother aged 13 was killed. It's hard to imagine what our home was like. There was complete chaos, devastation, severe shock for mom and dad and us siblings. I was 18 years old at the time and attended the little Pentecostal Mission in Bilston, West Midlands, and it was there where we had the funeral service.

A few weeks afterwards, my family came to the Lord including my mom, dad and all five of my brothers. They all repented and were baptised. Out of my brother's death came a new life for them in Christ. God, through this tragedy, brought the family unto Himself and we saw then the reason why God allowed this calamity to happen. Out of death came life in Jesus.

Mom and Dad from that time onwards continued serving the Lord, and eventually came to the revelation of the Oneness of God and were re-baptised in Jesus' name. They lived for God the rest of their lives.

Last year I lost my brother suddenly. He was the last one along with myself from our family. Also, I lost my beloved husband in 2017 after 53 years together. I was broken. Job was broken. We can be broken but God knows best. I keep on praising, praying and trusting. Jesus is, and remains, my all in all.

Barbara Mason

*SATURDAY 12th

They shall still bring forth fruit in old age... - Psalm 92:14

GOD'S PEOPLE PORTRAYED AS TREES – Reading: Psalm 92: 1-15

'***T****he righteous shall flourish like the palm tree: he shall grow like a cedar in Lebanon. Those that be planted in the house of the Lord shall flourish in the courts of our God. They shall still bring forth fruit in old age; they be fat and flourishing' (Psalm 92:12-14).*

The cedar and palm trees are symbols of strength and uprightness. The cedar as protection, wisdom and strength (ref. lovemorningmoon.com). The palm tree as victory, resilience, tranquillity and peace (ref. oceanjewelrystore.com).

When we trust and obey God we are, *'like a tree planted by the rivers of water, that bringeth forth his fruit in his season; his leaf also shall not wither; and whatsoever he doeth shall prosper' (Psalm 1:3).*

God has promised that His children will be fruitful and flourish even in old age. According to research, the palm tree bears fruit up to 80 years old. Christians can never be too old to spread the good news of salvation, nor too old to bear fruit of the Spirit. They are never too old to be used mightily by God in His service. God helps us to bear much fruit, and more fruit, by pruning us spiritually (St John 15:2-8).

Ecclesiastes 3:2 says, *'There is a time to plant and a time to pluck up that which is planted'.* This indicates the different seasons in our lives that each of us must undergo. God perfects our character through trials and difficulties, seasons of pain and struggles, so that we can gain experience to enable us to support and be of comfort to others.

We can trust God also to continue to skilfully prune us so that we not just grow, but flourish in His love and care, *'That (we) might be called trees of righteousness, the planting of the LORD, that He may be glorified' (Isaiah 61:3).*

Missionary M Fraser

World Sight Day

SUNDAY 13th

...I will not be negligent to put you always in remembrance... - 2 Peter 1:12

IN REMEMBRANCE – Reading: 2 Peter 1:12-21

Memory is powerful. As we grow older, we reminisce on moments throughout our lives, we become aware that we must leave a legacy of faith for future generations.

The seasons of change usher in more rampant opposition to morals from every major institution - increased counterfeit teachings, to an imbalanced ecological and social environment. But God is true, we have access to His great and precious promises through the knowledge of Jesus Christ (1 Peter 1:4). We have a way of escape through His divine power as the creation groans (Romans 8:22-23). We have confidence that, as we pursue His knowledge, His truth will counteract every falsehood.

Simon Peter, chief apostle, one of the 'inner circle' disciples and an eyewitness of Christ. Jesus had instructed him to feed His sheep and lambs, i.e., His people (John 21:15-17). It was Peter's duty to ensure the saints were diligent in the knowledge of God, and confident of His sure promises to be partakers of the divine nature.

Change was threatening lives, violence, and torture; believers were under pressure as they experienced persecution of Roman authorities (1 Peter 1:4-7). Emperor Nero, ruler of the Roman Empire (54 A.D -68 A.D), had become intolerant of believers in Jesus Christ. He blamed them for the Great Fire of Rome 64 AD (Christians were tortured, burned like torches).

Aware of pending execution (2 Peter 1:13-14), there were matters to deal with amongst the churches. Erroneous doctrine had circulated; false ideas that questioned the full humanity of Jesus. To counteract these false teachings, Peter purposed to stir up the memory of the saints, to ground them in the faith, and reject the lie. He purposed to remind the brethren of their faith in Jesus Christ by rehearsing the truth of this glorious gospel.

In troubled times it is easy to become unstable by what life may throw, but the unchanging promises of God are sure, they are the framework *'holding up all things by the word of his power'* (Hebrews 1:3-4). Our mind is the battle ground so we pour in the Word, we stir up our memory of the precious promises of our Lord.

The key to conquering false teachings is that we are to **remember** the doctrine taught, by searching the Scriptures, and hearing the preached Word, and also check whether it is so (see the Bereans, Acts 17).

It is only the knowledge of the truth that will empower us to reject erroneous doctrine.

CDP

MONDAY 14th

It was good that I had to suffer in order to learn your laws – Psalm 119:71 (GW)

HEAT PROVES MY HEART – Reading: Psalm 119:65-72; Proverbs 17:3

I recently learned a new word, i.e., *'crucible'.* A crucible is a vessel or pot used to refine silver in intense heat. In the heat, the silver becomes liquid and any dross it contains comes to the top and is scraped off by the silversmith. The crucible is then returned into the heat but at a higher level for further impurities to rise and be taken away.

The crucible is heatproof, it is made to withstand heat at excessive temperatures and will never crack; the content is therefore protected and will not leak out. The pot keeps being put in/out of the fire until after inspection, the silversmith is at last satisfied that the silver is pure and ready for its next stage.

Do you feel like you're in a crucible? One trial after another – you're in/out of the fire – and each test is hotter than the last? Is your will melting down? Understand that God is removing the things in you that are not like Him, and is refining you in preparation for greater service.

There are things hidden in us that will never manifest in the good times, they only come to the surface in the heat and season of suffering. That is how God, our silversmith, proves our heart.

JEJ

TUESDAY 15th

And the ark rested in the seventh month, on the seventeenth day of the month
Genesis 8:4

WHAT CAN YOU SEE? – Reading: Genesis 8:1-22

We often pray for change, yet do not always acknowledge when a change of season has begun.

I've read with interest the detailed account of the time which Noah spent in the ark. Yes, it was a place of safety during the flood, but it was also a measured-space of indefinite confinement and restrictions, no doubt with several inconveniences.

The only way that Noah could tell how close he was to a new season, i.e., coming out of the ark, was to keep looking through the only window (Genesis 6:16), and documenting the changes. He would have to compare his notes of the present with the writings of what was now past.

See that Noah records when the rain started (Genesis 7:11-12), but also notes when the rain stopped (Genesis 8:1-3). He records the time when the ark floated on swollen waters (Genesis 7:17-18), but also when the ark rested (Genesis 8:4). He writes when the hills and mountains were submerged under water (Genesis 7:19-20), but at last can record the day and month in which *'the tops of the mountains were seen'* (Genesis 8:5).

We sometimes feel that prayers are not answered if the results are not immediate. However, change can be gradual. I believe that Noah thanked God for the small changes he saw through that small window although, for a 'moment', he remained boxed-in.

You don't have to wait until you're back on dry land to give God glory. Why not check your notebook and thank Him now for the provisions He's made to keep you alive, and dry, during the flood!

JEJ

(Adapted from, From Me to You – Jackie Jacobs)

WEDNESDAY 16th

To everything there is a season, and a time to every purpose under the heaven
Ecclesiastes 3:1

THE GOD FOR ALL SEASONS - Reading: Ecclesiastes 3:1-22

In the Caribbean where I reside, the concept of seasons is not as evident as in other places where Spring, Summer, Fall, and Winter, are distinct. One gets used to the hot weather all year round. A cold front bringing cooler temperatures is a thing to talk about, being a noticeable intrusion in what should be perennial Summer.

Although we would very much like it to be, life is not like the Caribbean experience. There are varying seasons. There are periods in life marked by specific conditions. We are reminded of this in today's reading. There is a time for giving birth and later that which was born will one day die. The experiences of birth and death are both realities of life. There is a time for building and another time when some things are to be torn down. The reality is that things do not remain the same, and we should not expect them to. There are great days and other days when we would rather have other experiences. Life just happens.

Sometimes life in a particular season can be more challenging than one anticipated, and can lead to unwanted thoughts and feelings. Do you for example sometimes wonder if something is wrong with you? Probably you didn't expect it to be so cold or so hot, or the winter to last that long. Death might have shaken your world, or an illness might have thrown you off balance. How well are you functioning in the season you are in today?

There is hope in knowing that we have an able guide and support in the Holy Spirit who can teach and lead us into all truth (John 16:13). Through God's power we have all that we need for life and godliness (2 Peter 1:3). This includes the resources needed to deal with the things associated with the various seasons of life.

Pray today for God's help in understanding and accepting the season you are in, and the enabling to effectively deal with the opportunities and challenges in the season.

Jesus Christ is the God for all seasons!

Keshawna Salmon-Ferguson (Jamaica)

THURSDAY 17th

A time to weep, and a time to laugh; a time to mourn, and a time to dance
Ecclesiastes 3:4

MAKE SPACE FOR TEARS - Reading: Ecclesiastes 3: 4-5; John 11:1-35

Our exuberant gatherings, our worship and music, make space for dance and laughter. I dare say we are such social beings that we have come to enjoy everyday pleasures of being in community. And blessed we are!

It is only truly in suffering, loss, or pain, that we see the space for the time to cry is noticeably less advanced and intentional.

In a season over years of multiple losses, I made certain I would give myself that permission, to use the language of tears to make space for others to do the same.

God gave us the ability to cry, He gave us the permission to grieve. Should we not only give permission, but make intentional space for tears to flow on the journey through pain to healing? Imagine our spaces being a bowl that catches every tear just as Jesus will one day do.

If we would truly want to support one another, and bear one another's burdens, and not rush through the process to superficial healing, maybe the best way is to know the season. Knowing not every door is an open door to share but we can, where we're able to, truly weep with those who weep, and mourn with those who mourn; to make space for, accept, embrace and honour the time to cry.

Tears are a language God understands well.

Joy Lear-Bernard

*FRIDAY 18th

A time to get, and a time to lose, a time to keep, and a time to cast away
Ecclesiastes 3:6

WHY DO I PRAISE HIM? Reading: Psalm 116:1-19

I praise Him because He raised me up from a young age; He was there in the midst of all the many dangers and snares I was in.

I praise Him because He is a true friend of mine. God walks with me through all of life's journeys. He has been with me on my mountain top experience, He's been with me in the depth of my valley experiences. He was there when it seemed that the life which I was in was about to gobble me up and spit me out as just waste! I am reminded in Psalm 23:4 that, *'Yea, though I walk through the valley of the shadow of death, I will fear no evil: for thou art with me; thy rod and thy staff they comfort me'.*

God was with me when there was talk of no hope, that it was almost over, and everything was about to move into the very pit of despair. He was there to snatch me from the very brink of what was a point of no return. He saved me through His tender loving care, He was so attentive that He knew just what I wanted and when I needed it. He fed me with the Word that would bring me new life and sustain my very soul which was so downcast. Again, the Word of Life came to help me though. Psalm 43.5 says, *'Why are thou cast down, O my soul? And why art thou disquieted with in me? Hope in God: for I shall yet praise Him, The help of my countenance and my God'.*

I praise Him because He is so real to me, He is my hope for today and also for tomorrow. So while I have these days living on earth, I am storing up all my treasures for heavenly gain, by praising my God for His goodness and mercies towards me. If I give Him every praise now, then I will surely be ready for that great day when I meet Him and say, *'Holy, Holy, Lord God Almighty'.*

SSP

***World Menopause Day**

SATURDAY 19th

...prepare me also a lodging: for I trust that through your prayers I shall be given unto you – Philemon:22

YOUR RELEASE WILL COME – Reading: Philemon:8-22

Paul was in prison in Rome when he wrote to Philemon.

Although he had not yet been given a date to be released from jail, he requests that Philemon starts to make preparation to receive him for a visit after he is discharged, *'But withal, prepare me also a lodging: for I trust that through your prayers I shall be given unto you' (Philemon:22).*

Sometimes our present state can feel as though it is permanent though it is only a season. Although in the UK we apportion three months each to the four seasons of the year, we do know that summer, in terms of sunshine and heat can be short, and winter can be longer than December to February. We can't start to wear less in March, just because it's meant to be warmer weather, if there's still fog and ice. Life's seasons cannot be rushed, they must run their course for them to be purposeful. However, whilst we can't predict a season's duration, we know that change will come.

I've noticed in clothing stores that they don't wait for a new season to arrive before displaying clothes for the anticipated change of climate. You can walk into a department store while there is snow falling outside, and see that they have t-shirts and shorts, flip-flops and sandals as their most prominent items being promoted for sale. That's because retailers know that the same customers who have come in wearing two scarves, boots, a hat and gloves, don't expect to dress like that all year.

What preparations can you start to make now for when your new season comes? It won't always be like this. In the time of Noah, it rained for 40 days and 40 nights but eventually the rain had to stop. So, whilst in the solitude of this season, by faith visualise your change and with that vision, start to prepare.

JEJ

SUNDAY 20th

...I have healed these waters...unto this day - 2 Kings 2:21-22

I HAVE HEALED THESE WATERS – Reading: 2 Kings 2:19-22

Where the healing waters flow,
Where the joys celestial glow,
Oh, there's peace and rest and love,
Where the healing waters flow!
(H.H. Heimer)

Jericho was pleasant, but yet it couldn't bring forth crops due to its barrenness. This was because something was wrong with its water. The waters of Jericho were healed by putting salt into a new cruse and pouring it on the source of the problem.

Many of us are pleasant, but we're not prospering because there's something not right on the inside. Maybe what's wrong on the inside is that we need to ask God for a clean renewed heart (the cruse), and go to the source to cover our problem with the anointing (salt). Once our hearts and minds have been healed, we can then be spiritually fruitful which will then impact the natural part of our lives.

If you want your winter season of barrenness to be over, and your summer season of fruitfulness to begin, try praying the words of this verse of song written by James E. Orr after a revival in 1936 in New Zealand at which the Holy Spirit moved greatly following public confessions. The words can also be found in Psalm 139:23-24:

'Search me, O God, and know my heart today
Try me, O Savior, know my thoughts, I pray
See if there be some wicked way in me
Cleanse me from every sin, and set me free.'

There was healing for Jericho and there's healing for you today. Just ask God to search you and show you the source of the problem that's hindering you and causing spiritual barrenness. When God shows you the source, allow Him to heal you, His way.

Lady Pam Lewin

MONDAY 21st

Destroy this temple, and in three days I will raise it up – John 2:19

TOTAL WRITE-OFF – Reading: John 2:13-25

The term 'write-off' is used in the car industry where a vehicle assessor has determined that a car has either received significant damage that it's unsafe to go back on the road, or the car is beyond economic repair.

Jesus said in John 2:19, *'Destroy this temple, and in three days I will raise it up'.* The temple had become a place of corruption and abuse that Jesus called it *'a den of thieves'* (Luke 19:46). It had become like a marketplace engulfed in worldliness rather than a place that was peaceful and revered God.

Jesus did not tolerate what was happening and his action demonstrated Psalm 69:9, *'the zeal of thine house hath eaten me up'*, which was not appreciated by His opposers. This led to the fulfilment of Daniel's prophesy that the Messiah would be cut off and the people of the prince shall come and destroy the city and the sanctuary (Daniel 9:26).

Jesus' death, burial and resurrection pointed to a new and better temple, a spiritual house where God would reside within his people. It took forty-six years to rebuild Solomon's temple, but because of the Jews' rejection and crucifixion of Jesus, the glory of God was lost forever rendering it worthless.

Just like a write-off for a badly damaged or worthless car, it was time to write-off the temple and bring forth the institution of a new and living way. A temple not made with hands but a building of God, eternal in the heavens (2 Corinthians 5:1).

Name withheld

TUESDAY 22nd

...(she) came behind him, and touched the hem of his garment – Matthew 9:20

AND IT CAME TO PASS – Reading: Matthew 9:20-26

As surely are the seasons change from dry to wet, from summer to winter, from autumn to spring, so the days of our lives change with our personal seasons of sickness and health.

Sicknesses come into our lives without invitation. They sneak in, or stalk in, and take control of our every action. Each decision taken revolves around it. We are affected, our families are affected, our communities are affected. In fact, the more influential we are in our daily lives, the more people are affected when sickness invades our body.

The story recorded in this passage is focused on the end of the sickness. It was a time of change. A time which was highly anticipated without knowing when the season would come to an end. While the sickness may have been a very private affair over the years, the season of deliverance was quite public.

The times in our lives when the change takes place is what proclaims the news that a battle has been silently fought and won. This season of change does not fall upon us, neither do we fall into it. Seasons of change take deliberate action, perseverance, and faith beyond measure.

The winter may be harsh, but springtime is surely coming, and after that, the warm days of summer. Stay with God through the winter season of your sickness, trust Him through the spring of your healing, relax in the summer of your deliverance and rejoice in the warm embrace of your autumn. Ensure that your final season is your best season.

Pastor Londy Esdaille (Nevis)

WEDNESDAY 23rd

...I have no one, when the water is troubled, to put me into the pool – John 5:7

THROUGH THE EYES OF SOMEONE ELSE – Reading: John 5:1-15

In today's lesson we read of a man who was, through sickness, immobile. As a result, he lay in one position for thirty-eight years.

I'm quite sure that I've only heard this text preached and taught by able-bodied people which may, to some extent, have influenced the delivery. I do understand though that there can be multiple sermons and revelations in any one passage of Scripture.

John 5 is sometimes presented as this disabled man being used to, and comfortable in his situation such that when Jesus asked him, *'Wilt thou be made whole'* (v6), the man did not simply say yes.

However, if we follow the text carefully, we will see that he did not know that it was Jesus talking to him (v13). As far as he was concerned, it was just an ordinary man kind enough to make time to have a chat. Is there anyone reading this page who has never given more than a yes/no answer to a closed question because they had a lot of feelings to vent? Personally, I would not suggest that he was making excuses in his reply of, '*Sir, I have no one, when the water is troubled, to put me into the pool...*' (v7). He was sharing years of pent-up frustration, he'd been in a situation for so long, and the system of being the first to get into the pool at the season of the troubling of the water, excluded him from any possibility of being healed.

I love that Jesus allows us to talk. He gives us space to say how it is, not how it should be or how it looks to others. He doesn't condemn us for doing less when others think we should do more. He doesn't say stand up when He knows we can only sit down, He does not say run, when He knows that we can only crawl. Jesus knew that if this man stayed at Bethesda for another thirty-eight years, he would never make it into the water. He was lame! How would he get into the pool without help?

Just like with the woman caught in the act of adultery (without the man!), and Jesus did not further embarrass her in front of the crowd, Jesus said to this crippled man, *'Take up your bed and walk'* (v8). Jesus changed the order; He did not tell him to make more of an effort next time, He took this man out of the queue for the pool and healed him on the spot.

For today, let's consider whether we are harsh in our judgment of others in their seasons of discomfort or distress. Do we see legitimate reasons as excuses? Do we make unkind, unnecessary comments about things we do not know much about and have not yet experienced? Try to see through the eyes of the one who is afflicted, and through God's eyes, not our own.

JEJ

THURSDAY 24th

...there was a woman which had a spirit of infirmity eighteen years – Luke 13:11

FREEDOM FROM BONDAGE – Reading: Luke 13:10-17

As I read the Scripture, the words of the chorus, *'Everywhere He went, He was doing good'* immediately sprang to mind. He is our sympathizing Jesus, our high priest who is touched by the feelings of our infirmities. He epitomized compassion when He walked the earth and to this day His compassionate nature remains the same.

Imagine being bent double for 18 years because of Satan's bondage. To be in such a state would present an extremely limited view of the surroundings. Enter Jesus, full of compassion as His gaze fell upon this unfortunate woman. His compassionate nature would not allow Him to let her remain in this state. Never mind it was the Sabbath, never mind that He was engaged in teaching, Jesus recognised a need that He could meet with immediate effect.

Thus, the Great Physician took action at once. He called her, He touched her and she stood up straight. She was no longer limited to staring at her feet and the ground. Now she had an opportunity to look up and see the beauty of her surroundings, the handiwork of the Lord. What a change in outlook for her in so many ways!

Jesus' compassion brought freedom from Satan's bondage. No wonder this woman was full of praise! With a heart of thanksgiving, she *'glorified God'* (vs 13). When God breaks our chains, the end result is always the same - an outpouring of praise and thanksgiving to the one who brings the change. Hallelujah! Hallelujah! Hallelujah!

Sis Barbara Hendrickson (Nevis)

FRIDAY 25th

The LORD shall fight for you, and ye shall hold your peace – Exodus 14:14

YOUR CHANGE IS GOING TO COME – Reading: Exodus 14:1-14

The Israelites, in leaving Egypt, were leaving an old season, and going into a new one. They were transitioning from slavery to freedom. Transitions are often times of uncertainty; the past, even though uncomfortable, is familiar, and the future, although full of potential, is uncertain.

One writer said: 'Embrace uncertainty. Some of the most beautiful chapters in our lives won't have a title until much later'. The Israelites were uncertain because they didn't know what the next chapters in their lives would be. You may be uncertain today, but know this: Your change is going to come!

In order to go through a change of seasons successfully, you must have the mind of Christ. You must listen to the Word that God has given for that transition period, and you must obey.

The Word to the Israelites was to, *'Fear not, stand still, and see' (Exodus 14:13).* The opposite of fear is faith. As you stand still, you must open your eyes and look with the eyes of faith. In standing still, you can fully focus on God, rather than focus on the next footstep.

With one season behind, and about to embrace the new season ahead, don't take the old season's mindset into the new. Rather, be full of faith, stand still, and see the salvation of the LORD. For in the new season, the 'Egyptians', i.e., those that have plagued you for so long, will be a thing of the past.

Believe that the battle is the LORD's and He will fight for you. Believe that there is a new season coming, and that your change is going to come!

Minister Jo Earle

SATURDAY 26th

Let no man despise thy youth... - 1 Timothy 4:12

LOVING THE YOUTH – Reading: 1 Timothy 4:1-16; 1 John 2:13-14

It is easy for generations to compare one another, for the experienced to look down on the less experienced.

Often the perspective we use for this Scripture, *'don't despise thy youth',* is given to the young. But a plea echoed by Jesus is for mature believers not to despise the children, to be patient with the children and the young. Perhaps in a time where the generational-divide is stark, the church can shine the kingdom of God and encourage and delight in one another, regardless of our age.

How can we encourage youth? We can do as was done in the Scripture, we can lay hands and pray for conviction, protection, development of their gifting and walk with God.

We can expect God to work powerfully in their lives. We can role model love in the way we live, by our pure faith and pure life. We can set an expectation that their lives will role model the same. We can honour young leaders and nurture their growth with wisdom.

God, unlike the world, brings His children together to work both experience and strength together in His kingdom, so that He may be glorified.

Joy Lear-Bernard

*SUNDAY 27th

The LORD...bringeth low, and lifteth up. He raiseth up the poor out of the dust...
1 Samuel 2:7-8

MORE THAN ENOUGH – Reading: 1 Samuel 2:1-10

If anyone can turn things around, God can. In 1 Samuel 1, we read of Hannah's sorrow at not being able to conceive. We read also of the provocation of Peninnah, Elkanah's other wife, who was the mother of several children for Elkanah.

After many tears and petitions, Hannah entered a new season. God opened her womb and she bore Samuel – future Judge, Prophet and Priest of Israel. Today's lesson from 1 Samuel 2 is a record of Hannah's prayer and song of thanksgiving to God for reversing her situation. We know about Samuel, but did you know that God blessed Hannah with three sons and two daughters (v21)? She would have been satisfied just with the one son she'd asked for (1 Samuel 1:11), but God gave Hannah more than...

God often gives us more than we ask for, He adds *'a little something'* as a divine bonus. He did it with the widow of Zarephath. She looked after God's servant, Elijah, and baked him a little cake first, expecting that afterwards she and her son would starve to death. But instead, her meal and oil were multiplied, and they survived the famine (1 Kings 17:12-16). When another widow did not have the means with which to clear her husband's debt, and the creditors were coming to take her sons away to be slaves, God gave her more than enough oil to clear the liability, she had extra to live off for the rest of her days (2 Kings 4:1-7). We move from having five thousand men, plus women and children hungry, to picking up twelve bags of fragments to take away after they were all fed (Matthew 14:13-20).

Pray with an open mind. God responds to our requests according to (out of) His riches in glory. He does not have to rummage around to see what He can find to help us out! Our prayers are limited because our finite minds don't have the capacity to ask God for what He's fully able to do. So, ladies, don't be timid, don't modify your requests*: 'Ask, and it shall be given you; seek, and you shall find; knock, and it shall be opened unto you' (Matthew 7:7).*

JEJ

Clocks go backward (GMT)

MONDAY 28th

I will restore to you the years that the locust hath eaten…Joel 2:25

MAKING UP FOR LOST TIME – Reading: Joel 2:12-27

As I sat on the bus
I noticed it was driven at an intense speed
My bus driver was trying to make up
For lost time.

The bus had been due in a few minutes
As the bus timetable had rightly indicated
It had to be earlier.

I felt the rattling of the bus
And from my back window saw the traffic that followed
Some vehicles were on time and some had lost time.

I know in many people's lives
There have been lost times
Bad situations, decisions, and people
Have robbed many of time
Whether or not they were saved.

But I can look forward
Leaving my lost times behind
Remembering that God is a restorer
The years that the cankerworm, palmerworm and locust have taken
Are over.

Praise God, as I look forward
My aim is to redeem the time
For the days are evil
But my God will recover all.

Sister Jennifer Henry

TUESDAY 29th

Come unto me, all ye that labour and are heavy laden, and I will give you rest
Matthew 11:28

TRUST HIM – Reading: Matthew 11:28-30

It is astounding to know that God, Creator of heaven and earth, reveals Himself to us and through us, through this world and through His Word. The redemptive revelation of God is of course in Jesus Christ, *'God dressed in His work clothes'*, as our dear Bishop Dunn once said. The finite mind then, cannot possibly fully capture this infinite God, but we can still know Him!

We know God through the Holy Spirit, which gives us personal relationship with Him, through faith. Revelation is the very structure of the Lord's church. It doesn't matter our level of knowledge, intellect or status we may have applied to ourselves or others; the fact is, knowing God can only happen through God's own disclosure of Himself and His plan.

Hebrews 1:1-2 tells us, '*[1] God, who at sundry times and in divers manners spake in time past unto the fathers by the prophets [2] Hath in these last days spoken unto us by his Son, whom he hath appointed heir of all things, by whom also he made the worlds*'.

As believers, God reveals Himself to us in the most magnificent ways, that's why there are so many names of God, for example:

- Elohim
- El Bethel
- Jehovah
- Adonai
- El Shaddai
- El Elyon
- Immanuel
- Jehovah Shalom

I have listed just a few above and say with confidence, that whatever you face today, God has a name to cover it and will reveal Himself as such, if you trust Him.

God can and will reveal Himself to you, even in during challenging times. Trust Him!

Latoya Foster

WEDNESDAY 30th

The LORD has done spectacular things for us. We are overjoyed – Psalm 126:3 (GW)

THERE'S JOY AFTER SUFFERING – Reading: Psalm 30:1-5; 126:1-3

In nature, seasons speak of four divisions within the year which are Spring, Summer, Autumn, and Winter. These weather patterns come as a result of the earth's changing position around the sun.

Seasons can be used as a metaphor to describe the conditions Israel were in. They had just overcome the winter season which consisted of spiritual storms when they were held captive in Babylon. They had now been delivered and in Psalm 126:1 they describe their experience of being like a dream.

There's a difference between happiness and joy. Happiness speaks of an outward expression and is earthly, whilst joy is longstanding even during times of hardship and difficult circumstances. To have true joy you must have a relationship with God (Romans 15:13; James 1:2-3), because joy comes only from God (Galatians 5:22).

Israel was about to embark upon a new journey which consisted of re-establishing their nation in the Promised Land of Israel, and with excitement they began to praise God as they acknowledged so many great things that He had done for them.

The church is the body of Christ and we too go through different seasons. This includes winter where we suffer light afflictions, but it's only for a season (2 Corinthians 4:17-18). My encouragement is that when churches or individuals are going through storms, we pray for one another; pray for restoration and healing. Remember that God allows painful situations as part of our preparation for a glorified experience which is everlasting and beyond anything we have felt on this earth. Without suffering there is no glory (Romans 8:17).

'May the God of hope fill you with all joy and peace as you trust in him, so that you may overflow with hope by the power of the Holy Spirit' (Romans 15:13).

Rachel Lewin

THURSDAY 31st

Before you made me suffer, I used to wander off, but now I hold on to your word
Psalm 119:67 (GW)

THE PURPOSEFUL AFFLICTION – Reading: Luke 15:11-24

There are some lessons which we can only learn in a season of affliction or trouble. These lessons cannot be taught in a classroom or by reading a book, experience is one of the best teachers.

Our Heavenly Father allows these seasons so that we can develop in Him. It is in the heat of afflictions that I discover who I really am and what material I am made of. It is then that I discover how honest I am - how much integrity I have or don't have - when circumstances arise where only I (and God) will know what happened, and I have to act as judge for myself. I may think that I am patient and good-natured, but afflictions could show me otherwise.

Afflictions, when used as a learning-curve, can have a positive outcome. They identify our weaknesses by bringing what is in us to the surface for us to deal with. It is the Word of God that acts as a plumbline and serves as the rod of discipline to bring me to order and straighten me up. Didn't the Prodigal Son learn more through affliction in the far country than he did when living at home?

Sometimes we won't hear the preacher or the teacher, and we refuse to listen to different voices of warning, so we end up in a self-inflicted night season. But even then we learn, mature, and move on.

JEJ

november
Give Thanks

FRIDAY 1st

In every thing give thanks: for this is the will of God…1 Thessalonians 5:18

NO LIMITS – Reading: 1 Thessalonians 5:12-28

37 and 32, are the ages of my daughters. Who could it be but God?

When we found out that we were expecting our first and second baby we were excited and, like any other expectant parents, went through the motions of what to eat, what to do and not do, watching my tummy grow not thinking of anything else but to see through the full-term to nine months, and deliver a bouncy baby.

But that's not how the story was for me. I had never heard the words preeclampsia, prem-baby, high blood pressure. However, at six months for the first baby, and six-and-a-half months for our second, this was my diagnosis. Both babies were delivered early and weighing only a few pounds – my first daughter weighed 1 lb 12 oz, my second daughter weighed 2 lb 12 oz.

We were devastated, emotional, and looked at these tiny babies wondering how would they survive - but God! I say, *'No Limits'* because all we were told is that, *'they won't be able to do…', 'they won't be able to…', 'they might have this problem or that problem'.* But the medical team did not realise that we served a God that has no limits. Both of my daughters grew and thrived like any other baby, they may have been small but they proved the God that we serve.

So, when I look at them, I remember how good God has been to us. Both of my girls were born early and expected to have permanent disabilities or long-term problems, but God kept them and is still keeping them. All I would like to encourage anyone is that God is limitless, so don't allow your situation or anyone's opinion to limit your faith in what God can do.

Blessings.

Sis P

SATURDAY 2nd

I am the living bread which came down from heaven – John 6:51

MY DAILY BREAD – Reading: John 6:47-59

Every child born into a Christian home has learned the famous prayer in the Holy Bible, *'Give us this day our daily bread' Matthew 6:11*. What does this really mean? What is our daily bread?

In John 6 :35 we read, *'And Jesus said unto them, I am the bread of life: he that cometh to me shall never hunger, and he that believeth on me shall never thirst'.*

Therefore, when we ask for our daily bread, let us move our focus away from the natural things of this world such as food, clothing, shelter, education, vacation, and other such things. Let us rather turn our focus unto a closer relationship with God.

Our daily bread must become synonymous with prayer, reading the Word of God, faith, hope, trust, worship, thanksgiving, and praise. Just as we have set times for our various meals throughout the day, likewise we must have set times for our meetings with God. It is through these times that we receive the 'nourishment' needed to take us through times of adversity, grief, pain and loss.

Our 'daily bread' is always sufficient to meet our needs. This is the promise of God.

Pastor Londy Esdaille (Nevis)

SUNDAY 3rd

For the LORD is a great God, and a great King above all gods – Psalm 95:3

SAME GOD – Reading: Psalm 95:1-6

My pregnancy was a dream!

Each Antenatal Appointment was full of positivity and my baby girl was growing lovely. Embracing my body changes, my husband would regularly take photos of me and bump to capture the moment (looking back, I'm so pleased we did that).

I never imagined my world turning upside down within a few short hours after delivery.

On Friday 4th February 2022, the little girl that we had prayed for had arrived. My daughter was born, alive, arriving on her due date. There were unexpected complications following her birth and the shock alone could have killed me, but God. Prayer requests were sent out worldwide for healing, but God decided to take her home, in complete perfection, on 5th February 2022.

I didn't expect my baby to die. The hurt and pain cut so deep because my love for my girl was and is so strong. We didn't understand what happened and once we received the medical outcome, all we really wanted was a God-answer.

In my lowest moments the devil would try and whisper fear, negativity and doubts into my spirit, but God! God, immediately told me who I am in Him. That I am His, He has positioned me, He loves me, He'll never leave me, and that He is coming soon!

A few months later, God blessed my womb again, and I was pregnant with my little boy, our Miracle Baby. Although I carried well, naturally this pregnancy felt different and I continually sought God and said, *'Lord, your will'*. It was God's will that my son would arrive on Friday 3rd February 2023, twelve weeks early, just twenty-three minutes before his big sister's birthday. My little boy has his own story and testimony of being in NICU for nine-and-a-half weeks. But through the hard times, the pushing and the fight for survival, we thank God for life, that we are at home together, that our Miracle Baby is striving and growing beautifully.

We may not understand why certain things happen, but we have to put our complete trust in God. Child of God, be kind to yourself and take it moment by moment. Ask God for renewed strength each day and He'll give just that.

'For I know the plans I have for you, declares the Lord, plans to prosper you and not to harm you, plans to give you hope and a future' (Jeremiah 29:11).

Sis Sharlene Wright

MONDAY 4th

...our God, we thank thee, and praise thy glorious name – 1 Chronicles 29:13

SOMEBODY TOUCHED ME – Reading: 1 Chronicles 29:10-25

I often heard people talk of back pain, from aches to debilitating pain.

Then I experienced this back pain that could barely be eased, I could only pray. I could not have imagined how it would progress, or how God would heal me.

A presence woke me one morning; I saw the figure at the end of my bed. Without fear, knowing that the Lord had sent my deliverer, I touched the painful area and cried, *'My back!'*.

The touch was warm, soothing, and I allowed my faith to trust this touch. I woke sometime later, sat up and had no pain, no discomfort.

With tears and a thankful heart, I could only give thanks, rejoice and tell of God's healing power.

Rose Morrison

TUESDAY 5th

Bless the LORD, O my soul – Psalm 103:1

THANK YOU FOR YOU – Reading: Psalm 103:1-14

Bless the LORD today with all your heart, with all your soul, with all your might, and with all your strength. He is worthy of your praise. Be encouraged by the words of this poem today:

My soul blesses you Lord
And this cannot be contained
I have a passion to praise you
I will not be ashamed!

It's your holy name I adore
It's to you I give my thanks
Thank you for your mercies and your grace
And your love that's so immense.

I give you thanks! source of my health
Your power I'll never forget
You give me hope, my great Redeemer
You loved me when I was a wreck.

My gratitude feels limited with words
Because you deserve more
But today I pour out my heart to you
And I promise to give you my all.

Let us pray:

Almighty God, King of kings and Lord of lords, you who are worthy to be glorified, honoured and praised, we give you thanks today. Thank you for your loving nature, thank you for your wisdom that is above all, thank you for your forgiveness of sin, thank you for your power to redeem and to save. Thank you for the example you set on how to love our neighbour and forgive others of their wrongdoings, because you first loved us. You've done so much for us, and we thank you for it all today. In Jesus' name. Amen.

Laylah Walker

WEDNESDAY 6th

...call upon his name, declare his doings among the people... – Isaiah 12:4

THANK THE LORD – Reading: Isaiah 12:1-6

One of the first principles we teach young children is to be thankful. When they receive something, we teach them to they say thank you, ta, or whatever they can verbalise. As children get older, some become ungrateful and expect to get whatever they want without showing any appreciation.

There was a recent social media organised shoplifting call to Oxford Street in London. Hundreds of young people gathered to participate in the looting whilst the police tried to disperse them, and some shops were forced to close and lock customers inside. What has happened!

We used to start the school day with assembly singing songs like, 'W*e plough the fields and scatter, the good seed of the land, for it was fed and watered, by God's almighty hand; He sends the snow in winter, the warmth to swell the grain, the breezes and the sunshine and soft refreshing rain. All good gifts around us are sent from Heaven above, then thank the Lord, oh, thank the Lord for all His love.'*

This instilled in us to be thankful to God. Isaiah 12:4-5 encourages us to exalt and celebrate the name of the Lord, to speak and make His name known to others causing His name to be remembered. Why? Because He has done excellent things in the earth. Our testimonies are evidence of the goodness of God and our praise of thanksgiving express our gratitude.

Let's remember, be thankful to Jesus and bless His name.

Name withheld

THURSDAY 7th

...(God's) power at work in us can do far more than we dare ask or imagine
Ephesians 3:20 (CEV)

GOD BROUGHT ME THROUGH MENINGITIS - TWICE! Reading: Ephesians 3:14-21

It is a period of my life that I shall never forget, a time when illness pushed me to the brink of existence testing the limits of my resilience and faith in God. It all began with a bout of food poisoning that left me drained and weak, barely able to walk. Little did I know that this was the initial sign of a life-threatening battle.

You see, back in 2017 I thought I had severe flu, not realising that I had contracted viral meningitis. I went to bed and could not be woken by my adopted sons. These two boys called the ambulance and this act helped save my life. But you can't get meningitis twice? Well, that's what I thought!

In early December 2021, I had spent the weekend sick with what I thought was food poisoning, a dodgy pizza! My sisters knew I had spent the weekend in bed recovering from the aftermath of diarrhoea and nausea. At one stage they thought I had contracted COVID, and advised me to take a lateral flow test, but this came up negative. *'It's the pizza - never again!'*, I declared, and went to bed that Sunday afternoon to rest. This is the last thing I remember until I woke up in hospital some weeks later.

My sisters and I have a daily routine of morning prayer on the Lifeline prayer line, praying from 6am onwards. One Monday in December 2021, my younger sister noticed my absence on the prayer line, *'I can't hear Jenny's voice. This is not like Jenny!'*, she thought; *'She is always online from 6am'*. Determined to find out where I was, she called my mobile and home number several times but could not get through. She then contacted one of our other sisters (who lives closer to me) and asked her to go to my house with her husband to see if I was okay.

So where was Jenny? There was no response from my mobile. When my sister and brother-in-law arrived at my house, my car was not parked directly outside as it usual. *'Oh, she has gone to work, her car is not here'*. However, my younger sister was not convinced. She demanded that they drive around and check my car was not parked at the other end of the road, *'sometimes she has trouble parking outside her house'*, my younger sister explained. As they drove around, they found my car parked at the other end of my road. Suddenly a moment of panic erupted, something has happened to Jenny!

On entering my house, they found me slumped at the top of the stairs, lying precariously with one hand up in the air, one leg folded under me. They tried to rouse me but I could not talk, and when I attempted to talk it was slurred and laboured. The ambulance was called and initial concerns were that it could be a stroke. Upon arrival at the hospital and having my sisters there to give information on my medical history, the diagnosis came swiftly – meningitis. The very word sent shivers down their spine, '*meningitis'*? - but she's had this already! How can she have it again? My condition deteriorated rapidly, and I was placed in ICU, surrounded by constant care.

The battle against meningitis was fierce, I drifted in and out of consciousness and concerns arose over my kidneys and liver. I was given blood transfusions and strong medications as the relentless assault of the infection had taken a toll on my vital organs. My body was struggling to cope and the possibility of organ failure loomed like a dark cloud. Whilst I drifted in and out of consciousness, the nurses reported hearing my calling out Jesus, Jesus, Jesus.

All the time the Lifeline prayer warriors prayed and interceded on my behalf. It was as if their collective faith created a shield around me, providing hope and strength during the darkest hours.

Miraculously, my condition began to improve. Then the day came when I woke up. The nurse came along and said she had to perform some neurological assessments because my brain had suffered from a massive infection and they needed to assess if there is any damage. She asked me my name, date of birth, if I knew what day it was, what day it was yesterday, etc. I asked her whether I had passed the assessment? *'Oh yes you have!'*, she replied. However, this was a short-lived sense of achievement. I was unable to walk and lost some visibility in my right eye. It was a gruelling journey of rehabilitation and healing, but the power of prayer played a pivotal role in my recovery. There were concerns I was immunocompromised, and I was referred to a specialist; after intensive testing I was given the all clear. The consultants were unable to say why/how I contracted meningitis twice as I did not display typical symptoms. However, they felt that it would be wise to take antibiotics for the rest of my life as a precaution. A prescription was sent to my local pharmacy and GP. I have chosen not to take those antibiotics but to stand on God's Word where He tells me, *'I am the LORD that healeth thee' (Exodus 15:26).*

Today, I stand as a testament to the unconquerable and incredible power of faith. My battle with illness taught me that even in the darkest moments, when all hope seems lost, the collective strength of prayers and unwavering support can lead to miraculous recoveries.

This is a chapter of my life that I will forever hold close to my heart. It is a reminder of the extraordinary power of God's Holy Spirit that lies within us.

Sister Jenny

FRIDAY 8th

Children are a heritage of the LORD: and the fruit of the womb is His reward
Psalm 127:3

STILL LOVE THEM – Reading: Psalm 127:1-5

When God entrusts us with children, we must love them but not make them into little idols.

God blessed me with some lovely children, and because of my upbringing, I vowed that they would never go through the same struggles that I did. I remember a church-mother once saying that moms should never leave their children while they go abroad. But, the kind of life I wanted for my kids, I could not earn that kind of money back in the place where I was born to sustain that lifestyle.

I came to England and worked so hard to give my children a better life. I had more than one job, trying to pay for school fees and nice clothes to send over to them. Instead of going to church on Sundays to worship God, I was always working. I now admit my biggest mistake - I didn't teach them that God is more important than education!

Today, those same children don't bother with me, and the enemy is using them against me. As I started to write this testimony, something came on my mobile phone in the news section. A father was saying that he genuinely doesn't love his son anymore.

I am extremely sad and broken hearted. I don't want to say that I don't love my children because I remember how my Heavenly Father has forgiven me so many times. I know that there are many other hurting parents who feel like I do, and how that father on the news felt, but try to recall God's love for you despite your faults. When Satan wants to get to us, he will use even our children.

Let us continue to pray for our children that they will one day yield their hearts to God.

Mothers, keep strong and keep praying for each other.

Name withheld

(I Arise! 2022)

SATURDAY 9th

Every good gift and every perfect gift is from...the Father of lights, with whom there is no variation or shadow due to change – James 1:17 (ESV)

GOD'S AMAZING GRACE – Reading: Acts 9:1-19

This is a testimony, on behalf of my late mother (Mamá) who passed in April 2022, and the faithfulness of Jesus Christ in answering my prayers.

I was the only light shining in my family, a witness of God's redemptive power. I introduced this love to Mamá, who resisted like Jonah in disobedience and ran the other way for many years.

In 2007, I met a Christian woman in London whilst working for a woman's refuge. She became a mother in the Spirit to me. Momma C and I enjoyed great times of fellowship. We fasted and prayed for Mamá's salvation for a number of years. The prayers intensified when Mamá became quite unwell. Despite her ill health, she still continued running.

Coincidentally, or Godcidentally, it transpired that Mamá and Momma C both lived in the same city. Many times Momma C would invite Mamá to church but to no avail...until that day!

One Monday evening, Momma C and her husband Papa T, were having their weekly Bible Study at their home when they heard a knock at the front door. Momma C opened the door to see Mamá standing there asking if she could come and be a part of the Bible Study. Momma C does not recall giving her the address, and assumed that I had asked her to come but that was not the case. It was an answer to a desperate daughter's prayer for her mother. Sunday night I had felt such a burden for Mama's soul that I made an urgent phone call to Momma C asking her to pray for my mother. She said she would contact her the following day. However, Momma C didn't get a chance to contact her on the Monday but the Lord Himself moved upon Mamá s heart and there she was, standing at the door, asking if she could come in and listen to the Bible Study.

She started attending church and continued Bible Study with Momma C and Papa T. Mamá came to the point of repentance and accepted The Master's invitation to become born again. She felt she now finally was ready to bury the *'old man'* and be risen in water baptism - in the name of Jesus Christ.

The week commencing the baptism had finally arrived. I came down from London to spend time with Mamá and we went to the city for some shopping therapy. The Holy Spirit had prompted me to fast, everything was going to plan. However, as we walked around the stores, I noticed Mamá's countenance and appearance had changed. It was apparent that an internal struggle was going on. No matter what I said, Mamá was convinced she was not ready. *'Another time would be better'*, she said, *'just not this time'*. She became angry, frustrated, and now confusion had joined our shopping trip. A grey cloud followed us around the shopping centre.

I sent an SOS to Momma C to pray. She replied quickly that she also was in the same shopping centre! Momma C was also fasting, uttering our heavenly language silently around the shopping centre. We then decided to go into a Christian bookshop looking for a particular book. As we entered into the bookstore the bookseller stood in awe when he saw Mamá. His name was Jeff. Jeff passionately confessed how he'd always been head-over-heels in love with Mamá at school. They reminisced, laughed, shared childhood memories of over 40 years or more. The cloud soon shifted. He encouraged her that getting baptised was the best decision she could ever make. The enemy of doubt and confusion was defeated right there and then.

On the day of the baptism, we arrived at the church to meet Jeff standing at the entrance, waiting for Mamá, holding her hand to witness her baptism in the name of Jesus Christ. Several months later she was baptised with the Holy Ghost with the evidence of speaking with other tongues, as the Spirit gave her utterance. Little did we know that her days were numbered.

So thankful to the Lord for His grace and mercy, that Mamá was given the time to make her calling and election sure.

Hallelujah!

Shantelle Smith

*SUNDAY 10th

In everything give thanks: for this is the will of God in Christ Jesus concerning you
1 Thessalonians 5:18

IN EVERYTHING GIVE THANKS – Reading: I Thessalonians 5:12-28

It is December 7th 2022. Travelling to England from the United States, a usual travel after Thanksgiving with the parents.

6:00am landed in England. After 10 hours detention, was being returned to United States!

Spoke to everyone I passed - from ticket counter, to escorts to the plane, *'Happy Holidays!'*.

The female officer shared, *'You were pleasant, so it worked for you'*. A free flight to America - *'Thank you, Jesus!'*.

December 26th, the Dr's Office called 911 during my father's routine appointment. I was able to spend time with my father in the hospital, then at the Rehabilitation Centre after the surgery where we said, *'we'll see you tomorrow'*.

My brothers, mom and I were together with my father.

He passed away February 8th, 2023.

Thank you, Jesus, that I was sent back to America on December 8th, 2022.

Lady Yolanda Edmund

Remembrance Sunday

*MONDAY 11th

For he satisfieth the longing soul, and filleth the hungry soul with goodness
Psalm 107:9

REBELLION – Reading: Isaiah 61:1-11

B was a girl who was raised quite privileged but was rebellious. She disappointed her stepmom upon graduating from high school, her father already being deceased.

Rebellion wreaked havoc in B's life, she ended up unwed and a mother of six; she daily experienced every named abuse from a dangerous and insecure partner. To escape this reality, B migrated from her homeland, leaving everything, inclusive of children, in her quest for new beginnings.

On arrival to her new environment, she found all the wrong crowds, general idlers, mischief-makers, drug-peddlers, and shoplifters. B attended parties, but felt misplaced and uncomfortable so moved to a different city, got herself gainfully employed and started to settle in.

One day a lady invited her to Church. Initially she was uninterested, however circumstances impelled her. When she attended the service, she was heavily convicted by the Word, and yielded; God called and she answered.

Upon being baptised, two other members of her household followed and were baptised too! B now lives a life void of abuse and has a fantastic relationship with her children.

I was B.

God's lovingkindness transcends circumstances and mistakes: *'Where sin abounded, grace did much more abound' (Romans 5:20).* God destroyed the power of sin that caused me to be in awkward situations abusing myself. Diamonds and gold come from the deepest recesses of the earth, covered in dirt, but process and time brings them to perfection, valuable and beautiful.

God promised beauty for ashes, and a garment of praise for the spirit of heaviness.
He hath made everything beautiful in His time.

Name withheld

***Armistice Day**

TUESDAY 12th

O LORD our Lord, how excellent is thy name in all the earth – Psalm 8:1

GOD BROUGHT US OUT – Reading: Psalm 8:1-9

I was meant to call him Judah, *'Praise'*, but instead named him Cordai. Judah was the name that kept on coming to me during my pregnancy, but instead I gave that to Cordai as his middle name.

Cordai was the youngest of my children and was crawling at the time of the accident. We had just boiled some water in the kettle. For some reason the kettle was at the edge of the counter and while my back was turned, somehow, Cordai managed to pull the kettle down on his face. I heard him scream! His face was white as a sheet. I quickly started to run cold water on his face. Some of his skin had come off and was on the floor. It was awful! I knew that only God could help.

At the hospital, I was the only one allowed to go in and see Cordai due to the risk of infection. He was wrapped in bandages. I had my Bible with me, but could not read it. I wondered how a loving God could allow this to happen to us. My whole district of churches was praying but I could not pray. In my head, I kept on hearing the screams of my baby; I felt his pain!

The consultant and plastic surgeon said that my son would have many keloids (raised scars) even after surgery. I went into depression and had to go into hospital. I felt that I couldn't cope with my son looking like this. I self-neglected and had to have a Mental Health Specialist.

One Sunday, a Church Sister came to the hospital and prayed for me. I felt God for the first time since the accident, and shouted out, *'JESUS'*! The walls of my depression were broken; I had an earth-shaking deliverance!

When the bandages were taken off my son, his face was now pink instead of as white as it was straight after the burn. Healing had begun. It was a long journey, but his face is now completely healed! The only scar remaining is on his shoulder and I believe it is there as a reminder that God is a deliverer! Everyone who heard of the burn, or saw him after the accident, when they see Cordai now, they give God the glory!

Sister Yvonne Hermit

(I Arise! 2022)

WEDNESDAY 13th

So will I sing praise unto thy name for ever – Psalm 61:8

TRUSTING GOD WHEN LIFE HURTS – Reading: Psalm 61:1-8

August 2020. I had found out that I was pregnant, but I wasn't sure how far I was into the pregnancy. My husband and I, we were so excited!

Whilst at work one day, I experienced cramps and bleeding. My husband met me at work and took me to the hospital who referred me to the Early Pregnancy Assessment Unit (EPAU). I had to wait a few days before being given an appointment. That added to my distress as I didn't know what was happening or what the outcome would be.

I had to keep going back to the EPAU so that they could frequently do repeat blood tests and monitor my HCG hormone levels; they're supposed to double every other day, but my levels were rising much more slowly. I'd had an ultrasound at my first appointment but they couldn't see anything at that stage because the baby would have been too small. Eventually, after around three weeks I was brought into a room with five professionals and told that I was having an Ectopic Pregnancy (EP).

An EP is a real pregnancy but the baby is growing in the wrong place. Mine was stuck in my left fallopian tube on its way to my womb. There is nothing that can be done to an EP to make it continue and the baby survive. If the baby had continued to grow, it would have burst my fallopian tube with severe or even fatal consequences for me.

I was given three options:

1. To wait and see if the pregnancy would dissolve itself
2. Take a medication to dissolve the pregnancy
3. Have surgery to remove it which would probably result in my left fallopian tube being removed

This whole experience was a real test of my faith because it was hard to see God in the situation. I was broken and knew that all of the choices presented to me would not result in the child which my husband and I had prayed for. All of this was happening during the midst of the COVID-19 pandemic, which was already a stressful time. On top of that I had to deal with this life changing experience.

I realised after speaking-out that so many women experience pregnancy loss, but many don't talk about it and go through it alone. It is important (for those who feel comfortable) to talk about our human experiences so that we can support each other.

I had to grab on to who I KNEW God was! I had to recall every example of His love for me. I had to remember that no matter what, He oversees and understands. Even now I don't know the reason why the EP had to happen, but I have witnessed enough of God to know that nothing I go through will harm me but make me stronger!"

Jessica Grizzle

(I Arise! 2022)

*THURSDAY 14th

I will not leave you comfortless: I will come to you – John 14:18

THANK GOD FOR THE COMFORTER – Reading: John 16:5-16

We are told when we come into the Church as newly baptised saints, that we must also receive the gift of the Holy Ghost. When I was first told about this it was perplexing; my first reaction was to ask what need do I have to be filled with the Holy Ghost? I was so elated and full of joy after baptism in water, that upon hearing about the need to be filled with the Holy Ghost, it did not immediately make sense to me.

In my mind I thought, *'Surely I am now joined to Christ as I have been made new by His Grace. What was this Holy Ghost that was being spoken of? What more should I want from this new life?'.* But as I continued my journey in Christ it became clear that I needed more of Him to help me develop beyond my first experience.

I sought earnestly through the Word and prayer to be filled with the Holy Ghost. St John 15:26 says, *'But when the Comforter is come, whom I will send unto you from the Father, even the Spirit of truth, which proceedeth from the Father, he shall testify of me'.*

My eyes were opened to why we all need the Holy Ghost to live holy; without the Holy Ghost in me I was not able to do God's will; I could not be transformed and conformed into His image (Romans 8:29). The Holy Ghost, i.e., The Comforter, the parakletos, is our helper or advocate, needed to guide us in His ways. I give thanks to God for the infilling of the Holy Ghost.

SSP

World Diabetes Day

FRIDAY 15th

...let us offer up a sacrifice of praise to God continually, that is, the fruit of our lips giving thanks to his name – Hebrews 13:15

GIVING THANKS TO HIS NAME – Reading: Hebrews 13:8-15

Each and every day there is something to thank God for.

This is so easy to say, *to read*, when in reality it can feel difficult to praise or give thanks while our heart is breaking – when we have lost a loved one, when nothing is going right, when the children are playing up again, when a relationship is broken, or we don't get the job or assignment we had desired.

But know that God is greater than our circumstance, even when it doesn't feel that way. He holds all power in His hands, we need only to have confidence in Him and allow His sovereign will to rule in our lives (*yes, I know, always easier said than done*). No matter what, God is worthy of our thanks, our praise; of our worship. Even through tears and pain, as we continue to offer Him our lives, we offer up our praise. Not for the hardship, but for who He is, for what He has done, what He is doing and what He can do. He holds our past, present and future in His hands.

Look what He has already brought you through and take courage. Recognise His glory, dominion and power. Hope in Him always and give thanks.

Regardless of what your day may bring, trust Him in all things and be thankful. Life may not look the way you'd planned, but trust in His sovereign will and raise up your 'Sacrifice of Praise'.

Christine Knight

SATURDAY 16th

I will praise thee, O LORD, with my whole heart... - Psalm 9:1-2

I'M THANKFUL – Reading: Psalm 9:1-10

I proved God.

After having a child via a successful pregnancy, it was followed by four miscarriages over four years.

Prayer and faith moved God to grant me another child, proving that nothing is impossible for God.

'I will praise thee, O LORD, with my whole heart; I will shew forth all thy marvellous works. I will be glad and rejoice in thee: I will sing praise to thy name, O thou most High' (Psalm 9:1-2)

Rose Morrison

(I Arise! 2022)

SUNDAY 17th

Hitherto hath the LORD helped us – 1 Samuel 7:12

MY TIME WITH GOD – Reading: 1 Samuel 7:3-17

Dear God,

I just want to say thank you for all your help in my life.

Lord Jesus I am grateful for the good, the bad and the ugly things life has thrown at me. I'm grateful for the small things, big things, and everything in between. In all things I give you thanks.

I have been disappointed by many and have disappointed many. Lord, I will pray for those that hurt me and bless those who hate me, for it is better to give than to receive.

Lord Jesus, I will make every effort to live a blameless and pure life with your help. Thank you for your goodness, grace and mercies.

Lord, when distractions and temptations come, let me be encouraged to keep going. Lord Jesus, you bring me peace and I am so grateful for the peace you give me. Thank you, Heavenly Father.

Lord, I thank you for the people you have placed in my life that pour into me, pray for me and encourage me.

Thank you, Lord, for loving me when no one else would. Lord, so many gave up on me but you never did. Lord Jesus I am forever grateful that you died for me. I am forever grateful!

Just like that stone in 1 Samuel 7:12, let my gratitude be a memorial forever of your goodness.

Name withheld

MONDAY 18th

Every day will I bless thee; and I will praise thy name for ever and ever – Psalm 145:2

ECHO HIS PRAISE – Reading: Psalm 145:1-21

This psalm of David is the first out of the final six poems of praise concluding with the doxology of Psalm 150.

This is known as an acrostic poem; each verse was written in sequence of the Hebrew alphabet, from Aleph to Tav. This psalm gives the A-Z reason to bless and praise the Majestic Sovereign One!

This psalm conveys a message of desire and passion to bless and praise God. In Latin, it reads as: *'Exaltabo te Deus meus rex' – 'I will extol thee, my God, O king; and I will bless thy name for ever and ever'.*

David was the King of Israel, chosen by God from following sheep to be ruler over the people (2 Samuel 7:8). He reverenced God and acknowledged Him to be The King over his rule. He communed with himself to rise, to lift and continually bless God.

Imagine, every day to bless His Majesty for ever and ever, every day to praise His Majesty, for ever and ever. This continuation of adoration to God is to be enraptured from the natural to heaven's realms!

Further on in this psalm, David mentions the unsearchable greatness of God, declaring the greatness of His power and mighty acts, the majesty of His everlasting kingdom.

To the eternal God, glorious in power, let us remember His great goodness.

Bless His holy name for ever and ever!

CDP

TUESDAY 19th

To him who is able to do immeasurably more than all we ask or imagine…to him be glory in the church – Ephesians 3:20-21

KEEP ON PRAYING – Reading: Ephesians 3:14-21

April 2012

One Sunday morning at around 5am, my husband found our son, Shaun, on the floor of his bedroom groaning in pain. We phoned for the ambulance and contacted some of the brethren to pray.

At the hospital, one of the doctors asked: *'Who is Shaun's mother?'*. Shaun had given the Dr a message: *'Ask mommy to pray!'*. Shaun had had a stroke. Shaun's brain was swollen, we were told that he'd have to have an emergency operation but he said to me: *'Don't worry mom; I'm going to be alright'.* I had to attend a funeral service. On the way to church I received a phone call to say that Shaun had been rushed into theatre. The funeral service was put on hold and the church prayed.

Shaun had only been married for around eight months when he had the stroke. The prognosis was that Shaun would be in a wheelchair forever. Every day we were at his bedside praying. Eventually, when his condition began to improve, again one of Shaun's doctors asked me, *'Are you Shaun's mother? In all my years in medicine, I have never seen anyone recover from this kind of stroke! Whatever you're doing, keep on doing it. Keep on praying!'.*

When Shaun made his first steps, I cried like a baby. At times when we were going through this, it felt like more than we could bear, but God…! I've proven that God is real. After Shaun was discharged from hospital, one of the nurses saw Shaun in a supermarket. They came over and asked Shaun for his name. The nurse thought that he looked like Shaun but they couldn't believe what they were seeing, so they asked him to confirm his name.

I give God all of the praise, He alone is worthy.

Mother Dorcas Campbell

(I Arise! 2022)

*WEDNESDAY 20th

Let everything that hath breath praise the LORD – Psalm 150:6

INVITATION TO PRAISE: LET EVERY BREATH – Reading: Psalm 149:1-9

We all enjoy the great expressions and exuberance of David the psalmist, the writer of songs, poetry and hymns. In Psalm 150, he implores every one that has breath to praise the LORD.

How complex have become many of our worship ceremonies! Services of such beauty and harmonic balance and glorious resound. But let's not forget that the breath in our lungs is the prerequisite for praise. Simply put, David says if you are alive, if you're breathing then you are invited to praise. Praise (to God) by definition means to focus on things that He has done - to focus on the goodness of God. It's to give testimony to the acts or works of the Mighty God and in this simple yet profound verse, David points out the mighty act of God is you! Breathing. The breath in our bodies comes from God and gives every human on earth a reason to praise.

Your beating heart is the decision of the everlasting God. It was in His mind that you should be here today in this moment. David knew that the heart of God loves and moves in the worship and praise pouring out from His creation, and David's invitation is to you and I today.

Whether alone or in a service full of other worshippers. For you there may be so many things wrong and so few right it can seem. But God has given you reason right there in the intake and exhale of your breath as a reminder that you came from Him. Praise and thanksgiving are acknowledgements that the breath in my body comes from you, belongs to you and is for you, God. It is an honourable announcement of God's goodness with every breath we take that we are giving praise to God.

Joy Lear-Bernard

World Children's Day

THURSDAY 21st

Continue in prayer and watch...with thanksgiving – Colossians 4:2

GRATEFUL – Reading: Colossians 4:1-6

There are days when I just want to curl up and hide myself from the world. Not just family, or colleagues or my neighbourhood but just, The World. These are days when I feel I have lost my will even to live. Am I normal? What is wrong with me? Was this how Elijah felt when Jezebel threatened his life?

I AM BETTER THAN THIS!

Woman of God, when life has you cornered; shift your focus! Leave your problems at the feet of Jesus and focus on the 'I AM THAT I AM'.

We're no longer a slave to sin, therefore when negative thoughts come to captivate the mind, break free using the Word of God, *'For the Word of God is quick and powerful, and sharper than any twoedged sword' (Hebrews 4:12).* It cuts and heals at the same time. Open your mouth and declare the Word of God over your life, *'Is there anything too hard for God? (Genesis 18:14)'*; therefore, have faith in God!

Why should I feel discouraged, when Jesus is the answer! In Thee O Lord do I put my trust, let me never be ashamed. *'Thanks be unto God who giveth us the victory…' (1 Corinthians 15:57)* again and again.

I am grateful because, *'I am fearfully and wonderfully made…' (Psalm 139:14)* in the image of God. I am thankful that, *'the LORD will perfect that which concerneth me' (Psalm 138:8)*. So, lift your head up, Woman of God! You are blessed and highly favoured.

GRATEFUL!

MinE

FRIDAY 22nd

...consider how great things he has done for you – 1 Samuel 12:24

GOD'S FOOTPRINTS – Reading: 1 Samuel 12:20-25

God has always left footprints in my life. He would take me to different places before I understood the significance of why I was there. These steps have led me to the next steps. This testimony begins when I met who is now my husband. To cut a long story short when we met, we found that we both had a desire to reconnect with the Lord although we were in a backslidden state. After our initial meeting we found we were compatible, spent a lot of time together, and after about a year of being together we went out to Singapore to meet his parents. While I was there, I attended a Pentecostal Church which was something I wasn't familiar with, and was surprisingly filled with the Holy Spirit.

Given my Seventh Day Adventist background, this was something I did not expect or even know about. At the time, I was working in the casino dealing roulette, black jack and stud poker. I was also smoking cannabis and cigarettes but I knew immediately that my lifestyle had to change. After leaving Singapore and coming back to the UK I started feeling uncomfortable in my job. The day came when I found myself running out of the door and I ended up going to meet my husband and my mom on a road in London; It wouldn't be until I went looking for a new job that I realised the same road that I ran to meet my husband and my mom was the road that my new job was located. That was the step that enabled me to get away from the casino and develop my relationship with the Lord.

As I reflect, I can see how elements of footprints has been consistent with my life. I was born two months premature and spent the first weeks of my life in an incubator, but God kept me. Apart from a lazy eye, I didn't have any kind of disability to correlate with.

After having a healthy son, I lost three babies consecutively over the course of about 10 years and I couldn't understand why I couldn't carry another baby. I started looking for answers outside the conventional options that were available to me. One of my mom's friends knew of someone who was a health practitioner that did health screening identifying issues in the body. I met with her and she made certain recommendations.

Not long after beginning my training in colon hydrotherapy, I discovered I was pregnant. While carrying my daughter, and even before that, God sent messengers to tell me what was going to happen and to encourage me that everything was going to be okay. Everything was going fine in the pregnancy until I was 26 weeks and then I started to see signs that were concerning. I refused to go the hospital for about two weeks, however, it came to the point where I could not ignore the symptoms any longer and went to see the doctor. To my utter dismay he said I had to have bedrest. After many tears I finally agreed. I remained on bedrest for two weeks and God used me to encourage other ladies while on stay there.

At 28 weeks, early in the morning my daughter, Lael, was born. She cried in the delivery suite. All I did was worship God, thanking Him for bringing forth my daughter. After having my daughter, I continued my studies and qualified as a hydrotherapist and as a nutritional therapist.

All I can truly say is that God orders footsteps in ways that we cannot ever imagine, if we allow him to lead us.

Alethia Lee

SATURDAY 23rd

And one of them, when he saw that he was healed, turned back, and with a loud voice glorified God – Luke 17:15

THE REAR-VIEW MIRROR OF GRATITUDE – Reading: Luke 17:11-19

In this lesson we see that one encounter with Jesus Christ changed not just the life of this former leper, but also his position. The leper turned back and fell down on his face. When you encounter Jesus Christ and He heals you, He changes your position and status in life from who you used to be, to who you are now. The spirit of gratitude causes you to turn back.

It is said that you can't move forward whilst looking in the rear-view mirror, but gratitude works differently! You can't fully appreciate where you are going in your new healed life without looking in the rear-view mirror of gratitude. Every journey you make in your car you can't make successfully without a rear-view mirror, in the same way gratitude must be a part of every journey, season, and situation in life.

Gratitude also has the profound effect of keeping us humble. The former leper fell on his face as an expression of worship, humility, and thankfulness. When we look back at our lives, we are grateful to God for what He has done. But when we change our position and fall on our face, and all we see is the ground and the feet of Jesus, we become very conscious of the fact that if it wasn't for the mercies of God that rescued us when we were, *'torn up from the floor up'* we wouldn't be here.

How can we not be humble and grateful? The heady mix of humility and gratitude flows out of us like the oil from Mary's alabaster box; the perfume of our worship fills the air between us and the throne of God. An encounter, a change of position, and a grateful heart make for a beautiful life.

Minister Kay Dawkins/MinK

*SUNDAY 24th

...by prayer...with thanksgiving let your requests be made known unto God
Philippians 4:6

AN ATTITUDE OF GRATITUDE – Reading: Philippians 4:1-9

Did you know that thanksgiving is a key component of prayer? Thanksgiving is not only an occasion celebrated in the United States in November, but also an expression of gratitude to the Lord to acknowledge different things.

This may include, but is not limited to, God's awesome being, His many blessings, or specific testimonies. It's not just when you pray that you should give thanks but also when you make a petition. You should take the time to reflect on His goodness towards you and be grateful for your answered prayers and supplications.

Philippians 4:6-7 reveals what shall be rewarded to you when these things are taken into consideration. An internal and supernatural peace that can only come from God and is beyond our human understanding. It is something you cannot explain but you feel it intensely. The peace of God will fill your heart and thoughts when you seek the Lord with a heart of thanksgiving. Whether it be to pray or to praise Him or when making a request, always be sincere.

Let us pray:

Heavenly Father, thank you for your mighty power, eternal love and endless grace. I come to you on behalf of your daughters today, thanking you for all that you have done in their life. You know the challenges they are currently facing, but we thank you for the overwhelming sense of peace you provide that none can comprehend. Please guide their steps today and strengthen them for what lies ahead. In Jesus' name. Amen.

Laylah Walker

***Buy Nothing Day**

MONDAY 25th

Enter into his gates with thanksgiving, and into his courts with praise...
Psalm 100:4

A THANKFUL WORSHIPPER – Reading: Psalm 100:1-5

We, the Church of the living God, were created to worship God, and Him alone.

Rocks and stones can cry out in praise, but only those who are able to reflect on the goodness of God, can give God thanks and worship. Thanksgiving is necessary for true worship. Only a heart of gratitude can be thankful. We have to cultivate a lifestyle of thanksgiving. When we give thanks, we cannot complain, it's one or the other.

A thankful person is a joyful person. A joyful person is wonderful to be around, and their thanksgiving is attractive. It's infectious! When one worshipper starts to praise God, another worshipper cannot help but join in!

Even the angels who worship God, day and night, stop in wonder as they watch us give thanks and worship - for our worship is fuelled by thanksgiving. We are thankful for the love of God, our life from God, and our liberty in God.

Have a wonderful day today and every day, just being thankful.

Min Jo Earle

TUESDAY 26th

O give thanks unto the God of heaven: for his mercy endureth for ever
Psalm 136:26

GOD'S MASTER PLAN – Reading: Psalm 136:16-26

Don't lose hope, God has the Master Plan…

As a young wife of only two years embarking upon the whole new marriage-journey, I found out the most life changing news which most wives want to hear…I was going to have a baby! I was 'over the moon' and so excited for what was to come that I began to embrace the change.

But my joy was short-lived; my excitement soon began to change to fear and disappointment. This is because I began to experience pain and, following a routine check-up, I was told that I was having an Ectopic Pregnancy. I didn't know much about this, neither did I know how much that my life was weighing in the balance!

Another blow was about to hit me. I was told that I would have to have an emergency operation and, as a result, I would not only lose my unborn baby but also one of my fallopian tubes. I was devastated! I had so many questions, even for God: *'Was I not good enough?' 'What did I do wrong?' 'Why me?' 'Do you really love me, God?'* These, and so many other questions, led me down a very dark path. I was told that it was going to be very difficult for me to conceive again because my other fallopian tube appeared also to be damaged. I lost hope.

Fast forward to the future. I have been blessed to have children and favoured to have healthy pregnancies, including a multiple pregnancy, without medical intervention. Who could it be but God?

So, it's with my testimony that I encourage someone reading this not to lose hope in their present circumstances. God has the final say and He has the Master Plan! Trust Him, He knows what He's doing even when we can't see and understand why.

Name withheld

(I Arise! 2022)

WEDNESDAY 27th

...thanks be to God, which giveth us the victory through our Lord Jesus Christ
1 Corinthians 15:57

MY SON WAS COVERED – Reading: Psalm 92:1-5

God has kept my heart from breaking beyond repair on numerous occasions, more than I can ever record. He has taught me that one should always pray, even when you feel like fainting.

The year was 1991 when I dressed my skinny, funny, happy-go-lucky 11-year-old son in his new school uniform, ready to start his new school. He looked so happy and was very excited. This was the first time Mickel was going to travel on the bus by himself. I was nervous, but told myself that I needed to let go, he is a big boy now.

Earlier that morning, at around 5am, the Spirit of God woke me up with an urgency to pray for Mickel. Three times the Holy Spirit spoke to me; I got up and prayed. As I waved my son off, looking at him walking down the road, I felt no alarm. The time came for my son to come home, and I prayed that he had caught the correct bus.

Mickel came bursting through the front door looking like he had conquered Mount Everest! *'Mom!'*, he blurted out, *'Guess what happened when I was walking under the underpass?'.* I stopped what I was doing and looked at my son. Mickel continued to tell me how a man with mental health challenges chased him the length of the underpass, and didn't stop until Mickel reached the zebra crossing lady. He said that he was scared then happy when he saw her. This same man went on to attack two women in the underpass before he was apprehended by the police.

I can only give God all the glory for His many mercies towards my family and I. That morning God disappointed the enemy's plan. PRAISE THE LORD.

Heather Dawn Simpson

*THURSDAY 28th

Having therefore obtained help of God, I continue unto this day… - Acts 26:22

THANKS BE TO GOD – Reading: Psalm 136:1-26; Acts 26:22

I am so thankful to God for His strength in my life because it is impossible for me to make it on my own. When I think about the things that we as believers of God must endure, I understand that it has only been through the love and power of God that has helped us every step of the way.

One of the amazing things about God is that He empowers us to fulfil our earthly assignments. God gives us everything we need to finish the work He has given to us. This is why the more that I serve Him is the more that I realize this journey really isn't about my wants and desires, but it is about fulfilling the purpose that God has for my life, and then reaching back to tell others about our Great God and how they can experience His saving and miraculous power for themselves.

When we obey His Word, He opens doors and windows and pours out blessing and favour. We can rest assured that although the process may be difficult, it was the process that developed us into who we are today. Think about the things you had to face like pain, trials, insecurities, abandonment, betrayal, disappointments and for some of us grief, but we've made it through to encourage others that they can make it too! Every day we ought to give thanks to God for His goodness and grace towards us.

Pastor Chelly Edmund (USA)

***Thanksgiving Day, USA**

FRIDAY 29th

I will sacrifice unto thee with the voice of thanksgiving…Jonah 2:9

GOD GAVE ME ANOTHER CHANCE – Reading: Jonah 2:1-10

I was raised as a believer, was baptised in the name of Jesus Christ at the age of 5 years old, and received the Holy Ghost at 11 years old. But I left the church to do my own thing.

One evening after putting my baby to bed, a man forced his way into my house and ordered me to my knees and into my living room. Another two came in. They said that I knew why they had come, but I didn't know!

I later realised that I was guilty by association with someone they knew. One of the men put the kettle on and threatened to burn me with the boiling water. They let in another three men. I had a gun pointed at my head and a knife at my neck. Although I was backslidden, I called for Jesus!

I had been shaking uncontrollably with fear and shock but when I called for Jesus, in that moment, His presence was more than I had ever felt before. I sensed His protection and peace surrounding me. If I had ever doubted that God is real, I knew then that He is real!

My baby was upstairs crying and my hands were tied. God intervened and spared my life. I would encourage anyone who is on two opinions about living for God, stay with Him.

Get to know Jesus!

Sarah McFarlane

(I Arise! 2022)

SATURDAY 30th

...with my mouth will I make known thy faithfulness to all generations
Psalm 89:1

THERE'S POWER IN JESUS' NAME – Reading: Psalm 136:13-26

I've had diabetes for 38 years.

Whilst travelling abroad some years ago, my insulin pen would not work for me to administer my insulin. I was worried that I would go into a Hyperglycaemia state.

I called to my God in my heart. In the stillness, I heard Him say: *'For every drop of Insulin, you need to call my name, **JESUS**!'.*

For that entire period of two days and one night, God preserved my pancreas!

Every time I get a chance to praise Him, I will!

Missionary Sandra Collins

(I Arise! 2022)

december

God is With Us

SUNDAY 1st

...thou hast been...a strength to the needy in (their) distress, a refuge from the storm, a shadow from the heat...- Isaiah 25:4

FROM TRAGEDY TO TRIUMPH – Reading: Psalm 40:1-17; Isaiah 25:4

My life had been so full of blessings. My husband Jack and I were involved in missionary work along with our youngest son Adam, building God's Kingdom and creating wonderful memories.

Then in July 2020 tragedy struck: our son Adam and his wife Sarah were tragically killed in a fatal car crash a week before their daughter Adalyn's 1st birthday. Both of their children were injured. In an instant our lives were changed.

I felt completely devastated the evening before their double funeral; I stood in the hallway of my home sobbing the loss of our youngest son and daughter-in-law. It was in the midst of my grief that I heard my Father's still voice, *'Daughter, why do you weep as those who have no hope?'* *'Because my heart is shattered into a million pieces'*, I replied. *'It's not the end'*, He said, '*it's the beginning of their life in eternity'*. Hope arose, *'Yes'*, I responded, *'that's right, we do have a Blessed Hope; it's not the end'.*

The following day was also their daughter Adalyn's first birthday. She spent it in ICU on life support. We were told that, if she survived, she would be a vegetable as she had severe brain damage. Her 12-year-old brother, Zylan, had head trauma and spent several days in the hospital. It was overwhelming. This was supposed to be a day of celebration for Adalyn.

We made it through by the Grace of God. We managed to get full custody of Adalyn. However, we were not able to obtain custody of Zylan who was our son's stepson. It was heartbreaking going through the court system as we wanted Zylan and his sister Adalyn to be raised together in a Christian home. It did not happen. We almost lost our home during this same time frame. We had lost so much. Jack, who had always been healthy, became ill with bone cancer. He had fought the good fight of faith and went on to his eternal reward in February 2022.

It seemed that everything that I loved was being taken from me. Except for my little brain damaged angel, Adalyn. I was buried under and in a dungeon of despair when, as our Lord called Lazarus out of the grave, I heard my Father's voice again, *'Come out Sally Chadbourne, I have an abundant life for you. I am not finished with you. You have a child to raise!'.*

Yes, I was called out, and I want you to know that He is in the Restoration Business! He has been blessing me beyond my wildest dreams. He has taken our cup of suffering (trembling) out of our hand, and replaced is so that our cup is running over with so many blessings. When Psalm 23:6 says *'Surely goodness and mercy shall follow you for the rest of your life*', it is true, yet only if you trust Him!

It is easy to praise and worship Him while you live on the mountaintop and life is good. What about when you are fighting the worst battle of your life? Do we really believe Him to the very core of our soul? All things work together for the good of those who are the called of the Lord, who love the Lord according to His purpose for each us. Never stop being grateful, keep making melodies in your heart. Never cease to worship Him, He will make a way for you. He is a rewarder of those who diligently seek Him. His Word and promises are true.

Adalyn and I are living testimonies of what our God can do. Adalyn is so full of joy. She is 4 years old now. Her brain is functioning as well as any child her age. Her motor skills haven't caught up yet, but she is improving in leaps and bounds. I know she will never be normal because she is extraordinary. I am getting healthier and younger. I am 70 going on 40!

Praise God! He turns our trials into our TESTimony!

Sally Chadbourne (USA)

MONDAY 2nd

Therefore the redeemed of the LORD shall return, and come with singing unto Zion; and everlasting joy shall be upon their head... - Isaiah 51:11

REDEEMED – Reading: Isaiah 51:1-23

Isaiah =Yahweh saves, Yahweh is salvation.

A major prophet, positioned first of the four main larger books of prophecy. A man of noble birth married to a prophetess who bore him children: Maher-shalal-hashbah - *'destruction is imminent'*; Sherajashub - *'a remnant shall return'*. Their names related to future events.

As the LORD's spokesman Isaiah, the eagle-eyed prophet, prophesied to the Northern and the Southern kingdoms. His time in ministry spanned a period over 50-60 years.

The death of King Uzziah was the turning point for Isaiah (chapter 6). From judgment and condemnation in chapters 1-39, hope is inserted in chapter 40, *'Comfort ye, comfort ye my people…' (Isaiah 40:1),* following with consolations and reassurance.

God has given the children of Israel hope, they will be brought back once they have passed under the rod (Ezekiel 20:37).

We as the church have also been given promises and hope. Although the hope is guaranteed, the onus is on the seeker; the call has gone out, the invitation is still open. There's a compilation of songs for the redeemed, the people rescued and delivered from the death penalty of sin.

The gift is salvation. The bride waits for her Lord. A chosen people that are overcomers, dressed in the righteousness of God. Redeemed when our burden of sins was high, redeemed when our soul was condemned to die.

Let us invite others to the celebration, call from the east and west, north and south.

Beloved of God, we will sing songs of praises, there is a better land in view.

We are the redeemed in Lord Jesus' precious name!

CDP

*TUESDAY 3rd

When thou passest through the waters, I will be with thee...Isaiah 43:2

MY REFUGE, SHIELD, BUCKLER & SHEPHERD – Reading: Isaiah 43:1-13

Our walk with the Lord can be described as a journey with the Rock of Peace where we say, *'Thank you Lord: my Refuge, my Shield, my Buckler and my Shepherd'*. Or it can be a tumultuous storm with an, *'Oh, I didn't sign up for this! Where is this going?'*. I need to know, but I also need to put my hand in the hand of the One who can still the water. My heart agrees that this is what I must do whenever I feel anxious and am walking hand in hand with fear.

When problems come, they can be like an avalanche! I remember singing an old hymn called, *'When the Sea Billows Roll'*. I have travelled across the water to France on a huge ferry with the sea billows rolling. We were not allowed to go up on deck due to the height and ferocity of the waves and all the physical symptoms which can be attached to that. This is a fantastic analogy for life. But with all the extreme storms we experienced on the ferry, the ups and downs, yet somewhere in between all of that we reached our destination!

On the return journey we rolled on to the ferry, and yes, with fear and trepidation recalling our outward voyage, but also with assurance that God created us and is always in control, He is never taken by surprise. See, we had a peaceful and extremely pleasant journey home. Up on deck with my then young boys, and remembering the sea billows rolling last time, and just simply sliding my hands into the hands of my Father in Heaven knowing He would get us home. Whether that is our home on earth, or when the time comes our home in heaven, He gets us home.

Let me remind you, the Lord is our Refuge, Shield, Buckler and Shepherd. Hallelujah!

Sandy Hemus

International Day of Persons with Disabilities

WEDNESDAY 4th

And the glory which thou gavest me I have given them…John 17:22

YOU HAVE A PRESENT & A FUTURE – Reading: John 17:20-26

'Father, I will that they also, whom thou hast given me, be with me where I am; that they may behold my glory, which thou hast given me: for thou lovedst me before the foundation of the world' (John 17:24).

As a believer in Christ, we do not only have a fulfilling day-to-day experience in Him, but also, we are guaranteed a glorious future.

Jesus' prayer in John 17 is quite revealing on what the present and the future holds for every true believer. The glory which Christ shared with his Father, He has also graciously and freely given to us to enjoy as His dear children.

Christ expects us to start enjoying the heaven kind of life from this very moment. Most exciting of all is the fact that we have been granted the nature of Christ by the indwelling of His Spirit within us.

Mother Joycelin Griffiths

*THURSDAY 5th

The LORD himself goes before you and will be with you…Deuteronomy 31:8 (NIV)

GOD WHERE ARE YOU? – Reading: Deuteronomy 31:1-8

If you have ever felt like you're alone, it was just a feeling rather than a fact. Our feelings will deceive us, that is why we have to look to God and not rely on ourselves.

We stumble through life, *'groping for the wall like the blind, feeling our way as if we had no eyes:' (Isaiah 59:10 - NIV).* So I am thankful that I trust in the one who knows the end from the beginning (Isaiah 46:10), and will guide us if we are open to His leading, *'Your word is a lamp for my feet, a light on my path' (Psalm 119:105 - NIV).*

God promises us in Deuteronomy 31:8 (AMP) that, *'It is the LORD who goes before you; He will be with you. He will not fail you or abandon you. Do not fear or be dismayed'.*

Though we don't know what tomorrow brings, our trust needs to be in the Lord because, *'The LORD Himself…'* has promised that He will always be present, therefore we need not to be afraid. Fear will cause us to doubt, and doubt leads to anxiety which can take a hold of our heart and mind. I have been through many challenges where I've trusted in others and been disappointed, e.g., at work where I trusted in employers; in relationships where I've been let down by the decisions of others. Then I've had health challenges where only God…

Jesus understands our human weaknesses and is with us in every situation. Hebrews 4:15 (NIV) reminds us, *'For we do not have a high priest who is unable to empathize with our weaknesses, but we have one who has been tempted in every way, just as we are — yet He did not sin',* and that is the example we need to follow.

Joan Philip-Bayliss

International Volunteer Day

FRIDAY 6th

Thou art my hiding place; thou shalt preserve me from trouble – Psalm 32:7

I WILL NOT LEAVE YOU – Reading: Psalm 32:1-11

There is something unsettling about feeling alone, particularly when there is a great need. Whether it is a financial matter, sickness or the need for comfort after a bereavement; there are times in our lives when we need others around us.

A well-known song by FJ Crosby, says:

I must have the Saviour with me
For I dare not walk alone
I must feel his presence near me
And his arm round me thrown.

Then my soul shall fear no ill,
Let Him lead me where He will
I will go without a murmur
And His footsteps follow still.

Here's the thing - the Lord has a way of instructing and comforting us, even in when He appears silent. He has a way of bringing back to our remembrance previous occasions of deliverance and healing. When our mind is taken back, it is then that faith comes forward and joins with our brother, Job, and says, *'I know that my redeemer liveth' (Job 19:25) … 'But he knows the way that I take: when he has* ***tried*** *me, I shall come forth as gold'* (Job 23:10).

Jesus promised that He would not leave nor forsake us. We can rely on His words because His promises are true and, '*by two immutable things, … it is impossible for God to lie…' (Hebrews 6:18).* It is His will that we draw close to Him in order for a beautiful relationship to be formed and maintained. This is often by the hard things we must go through.

Deveen Smith

SATURDAY 7th

Can a woman forget her sucking child…yea, they may forget, yet will I not forget thee
Isaiah 49:15

I CAN'T FORGET YOU – Reading: Isaiah 49:13-19

Many of you reading this page will have at some time or other experienced a feeling of being forgotten. I'm not referring to you being someone who needs to be Centre Stage or loves attention, I simply mean feeling abandoned or forsaken, wondering does anybody care.

Isaiah 49 is a good chapter to read when in that frame of mind. It confirms that, at its extreme, even a mother can forget the child to whom she gave birth and nursed at her breast. But God is quick to assure His people that, even if the woman who incubated you in her womb for up to 40 weeks should at any point forsake you, I, God, will not and cannot forget you.

Our Father remembers the sparrows
Their value and fall doth He see
But dearer to Him are His children
And He'll never forget to keep me.

He'll never forget to keep me
He'll never forget to keep me
But dearer to Him are His children
And He'll never forget to keep me.

The words of the Lord are so priceless
How patient and watchful is He
Though mother forget her own offspring
Yet He'll never forget to keep me.

He'll never forget to keep me
He'll never forget to keep me
Though mother forget her own offspring
Yet He'll never forget to keep me.
(He'll Never Forget to Keep Me – FA Graves)

JEJ

SUNDAY 8th

As soon as you hear…move quickly…that will mean the LORD has gone out in front of you – 2 Samuel 5:24 (NIV)

FOR THOU ART WITH ME – Reading: 2 Samuel 5:17-25; Psalm 23:4

W*hen I can't see or feel you, 'Thou art with me'*
I am never alone, for 'Thou are with me'
I will make it, for 'Thou art with me'
I can do all things, for 'Thou art with me'.

Though troubled on every side, yet not distressed;
Perplexed, but not in despair;
Persecuted, but not forsaken,
Cast down, but not destroyed (2 Corinthians 4:8-9)
For 'Thou art with me'.

Awake or asleep, when I am up and when I'm down
When I'm encouraged and when I am discouraged
When I am sick, and when I'm in good health
In joy or in sorrow, in a crowd or in a solitary place
In times of plenty, or experiencing a famine
I shall not want, for 'Thou art with me'.

So my soul shall fear no ill,
You can lead me where you will,
I will go without a murmur,
For, 'Thou art with me'!

(From Me to You – Jackie Jacobs)

JEJ

MONDAY 9th

the Lord himself shall give you a sign; Behold, a virgin shall conceive, and bear a son, and shall call his name Immanuel – Isaiah 7:14

OUR BESTIE – Reading: Genesis 28:10-22; Isaiah 7:14

Imagine walking into a room with a crowd of people who you don't know, and they're making no effort to get to know you either, how do you feel?

Now imagine being in that same room and in walks your best friend who comes and stands with you and you start chatting away as you do with a bestie, how do you feel now?

Being where people are doesn't mean that there is any connection, intimacy or fellowship between yourself and them, and life can be lonely without meaningful connections. God designed us perfectly but recognised that it wasn't good for us to be alone. We know God is always with us wherever we are, He is the best friend who walks into the often-crowded room of life when we feel alone and comes alongside us in fellowship and love.

God has promised to be with us, and we too should ensure that we are with Him in relationship too. Let's not walk into a church service and go through the motions, but really connect with our God who longs to be with us. The same way He avails Himself to be near us, let's endeavour to always be in His presence and not just in the buildings where services are held.

We feel loved, supported, and confident when our best friend shows up in whatever circumstances of life, but why? Because they are not just with us, but they are also for us. What a blessing it is to have God our best friend with us and for us.

Minister Kay Dawkins/ MinK

TUESDAY 10th

...Bethlehem Ephratah, though thou be little...yet out of thee shall come forth unto me that is to be ruler in Israel...Micah 5:7

GOD IS FAITHFUL – Reading: Micah 5:1-9

In the midst of life's trials and afflictions, we find solace and comfort in the words of Psalm 119:50, *'This is my comfort in my affliction, for your word has given me life'*. These words remind us of the unchanging presence of our Heavenly Father, who is with us always, offering His eternal word as a source of life and strength.

God's Word is not merely a collection of letters on pages, but a living testament of His love, faithfulness, wisdom, and guidance. When we face adversity, we can turn to the Scriptures and find reassurance that God is with us. His promises remain unwavering, and His words breathe life into everyone one of us.

Through the trials we encounter, we experience the truth that God's Word is our refuge. It provides comfort, understanding, and direction, guiding us through the darkest valleys and the stormiest seas. Just as a lighthouse guides ships to safety, God's Word lights our path and illuminates the way forward.

The assurance of God's constant presence empowers us to endure afflictions with hope and courage. Remember, the same God who walked with the people of Israel, walks with us today. He will never depart from us, and His promises stand firm.

So let us cling to God's Word in times of trouble, finding comfort in its truth and life in its promises. May we be encouraged to meditate on His Word day and night, drawing strength from its eternal wisdom. For truly, God is the word, and His word is life. Let us anchor our faith in this unchanging reality and find solace in His abiding presence.

Amen.

Name withheld

WEDNESDAY 11th

Lord, thou hast been our dwelling place in all generations – Psalm 90:1

NO PLACE LIKE HOME – Reading: Psalm 90:1-12

This psalm starts the 4th division or group of psalms and was written by Moses.

Upon reflection, we may have ideas for our ideal home; a dwelling where we can put our mark of style and design. Where creativity can have freedom! We cash-out to alter our residence according to our preference of taste. Whether it's one room or a mansion it's a personal space. If it's good space and a haven, then there's no place like home.

From the encounter of Moses with the burning bush (Exodus 3), to seeing the Promised Land before his death. Moses understood that God was in fact their dwelling place for all generations.

Called to lead Israel out of bondage and oppression from a country that was once a safe place under Joseph. With fulfilment of time and prophecy (Genesis 15:13-16), the exodus of about 600,000 men on foot, not including women and children in the count (Exodus 12:37) brought out the covenanted people (and others that joined them) from the land of Egypt, a place that had become perilous.

We have sung hymns; '*This world is not my home'*, and many others as we believe for *'a better land in view, Jesus has gone to prepare a home...'.*

*Today generations have since been labelled by society as: *'The builders'* (born before 1946), *'Baby boomers'* (born 1946-64); then there's *'Generation X'* (born 1965-79); *'Generation Y'* (born 1980-94); *'Generation Z'* (born 1995-2009) and the current *'Generation Alpha'* (Born 2010-2024).

But God has ***'a chosen generation'***, (1 Peter 2:9), selected from the world. We live in an earthly house waiting to be rehoused (2 Corinthians 5:1-2). Our life span is 70 years, anything over is by reason of strength.

As we consider our mortality, the passing time of each generation, we look to our immortal Lord. May we not forget He is our spiritual location, also our refuge.

He is our dwelling place.

CDP

The generations defined- mccrindle

THURSDAY 12th

...What manner of man is this, that even the winds and the sea obey him!
Matthew 8:27

HE'S ALWAYS THERE – Reading: Matthew 8:23-27

God desires relationship, i.e., connection with His people. This has been true from the beginning – it's relayed throughout scripture, and is true to this very day. An example of this can be found in Exodus 25:8; Moses was instructed to build a tabernacle so that God could dwell among them.

In the midst of your storm, hold fast to the one with whom you have a Divine Relationship, who has all power – the power to calm and take control; to give the help you need; to lift you up and carry you through. Trust Him during the difficult days and times that can sometimes call for more strength than we feel we have. But it is in our weakness that we see His strength.

There's a song that says, '*Standing somewhere in the shadows you'll find Jesus. He's the only one who cares and understands. Standing somewhere in the shadows you will find Him, and you'll know Him by the nail prints in His hands'.*

Know that God is always there, always willing to stand with us, to cover us and to love us. He is there waiting for us to call on His precious name, to seek a peace and a joy that comes only from Him. God never said that life would be easy, but He has promised never to leave us nor forsake us.

No matter what you are going through, or what today holds - laughter or pain, know that God is there with you. He cares about every detail of your life, and He loves YOU.

Christine Knight

FRIDAY 13th

Fear thou not; for I am with thee; be not dismayed; for I am thy God – Isaiah 41:10

NEVER FORSAKEN – Reading: Isaiah 41:10.

When we were growing up, for most of us, our parents were the ones we looked to when we were afraid. To us, they were super heroes, able to fight our battles and give us that sense of assurance that all would be well. As we grew older, we recognised their limitations and that there were some fears they could not allay.

The children of Israel had a wonderful Saviour and deliverer whom they did not always appreciate. They wanted to follow their own will. What folly at times, for He was the one who could indeed calm all fears. But God never gives up on His people. In a time when they may have been oppressed, His words came to encourage them, *'I am your God'*. He assured them that He was with them so they needed not to be afraid. He said, *'I am with thee…'* (Isaiah 41:10) What words of comfort and assurance! What a reminder that the relationship was still intact! Hallelujah! He was their helper and the one who would strengthen them. His victory would be their victory.

We who are also children of God, find a similar assurance in His words. When we go through difficulties, when we need that anchor for the soul, we hold to God's words of assurance – *'Fear thou not; for I am with thee'*. He supersedes our parents whose limitations we acknowledge even though we love and respect them. By contrast, our God is omnipresent, omnipotent and omniscient. He has promised never to leave us, nor forsake us, so we can hold to His unchanging word, His undisputable promises and His boundless love. Bless the Lord!

Sister Barbara Hendrickson (Nevis)

SATURDAY 14th

...but the LORD was not in the fire: and after the fire a still small voice – 1 Kings 19:12

NEVER ALONE – Reading: 1 Kings 19:9-18

I am come that you might have life
Why then is all this pain and strife?
In Eternity the Almighty reigns
Our salvation is by no means in vain
Jesus came to save His people from sin
We are alive today by His power within
No need for emptiness, feeling lost or undone
No need to declare the battle is not won
Jesus reigns supreme! Lamb upon the throne
Rise up Woman of God, you're never alone!

The Holy Script declares I will never leave
You nor forsake you
No other words could read so true
The King of kings and the Lord of lords
Left the splendour of heaven
Let's sound all alarms!
He saw you and me and called us to Him
Our imperfections did not deter His perfect will
With arms outstretched He gave us Himself
He gave us heaven and all its wealth
So why the long faces and doubt in our minds
We must be resolute all of the time
Jesus reigns supreme! Lamb upon the throne!
Rise up Woman of God, you're never alone!

Such preparation for us, such zeal He displayed
Our God cares for us in Royal Detail
There's nothing mediocre about our King
Angels do His bidding, Yes! the seraphim!
So, lift up feeble hands in praise to our God
He watches over us and gives us His Word
Yes, Jesus reigns! Lamb upon the throne
Hallelujah! We're never alone!

MinE

SUNDAY 15th

…he shall save his people from their sins – Matthew 1:21

THE SIGN – Reading: Matthew 1:21-25

The above well-known scripture for today's reading fulfilled an Old Testament prophecy found in Isaiah 7:14, *'Therefore the LORD Himself shall give you a sign, Behold, a virgin shall conceive and bear a son and shall call His name Immanuel'*. This prophecy has one meaning but two applications. The meaning is that *'God is with us'*, and that we shouldn't fear what anyone can do to us.

The first application is for Ahaz's day. King Ahaz was a man of unbelief. He was told to ask for a sign (Isaiah 7:11) to prove God's presence with him. He refused, choosing to trust in his own works for deliverance. His disobedience however, did not stop the prophet from speaking of the sign that will come. The second application is for us today in that we should not look to ourselves for deliverance like King Ahaz did, but look to the One who was born of a virgin in Bethlehem who came to save us from our sins. God is with us.

Matthew begins his gospel with the promise of God's presence with us in Jesus Christ. He ends with Jesus' promise to be with us as we share the gospel, *'Go ye therefore and teach all nations …I am with you always even unto the end of the world. Amen' (Mathew 28:18-19).*

O that the world would know this glorious truth; Jesus is more than a baby in a manger but as the angels told the shepherds, He is the Saviour of the World, Christ the Lord!

Our great Creator became our Saviour and all God's fullness dwelleth in Him (Colossians 2:9-10).

The LORD Himself did this (Isaiah 7:14). This act was God-ordained, God-accomplished.

CP

MONDAY 16th

...they presented unto him gold, and frankincense, and myrrh – Matthew 2:11

WHAT DID YOU BRING? Reading: Matthew 2:1-11

As a child, I noticed that whenever we were going to visit anyone at their home or in hospital, we always brought something. That's a principle that I've continued into my adulthood.

The wise men (the Bible does not report how many), in all of their excitement and packing to go to see Jesus, made sure that they brought something to leave behind: gifts of gold, frankincense and myrrh. They joyfully opened up their treasures as soon as they entered into the house where the child Jesus was with his parents. I don't believe that Mary had to say, '*Did you bring anything for Jesus?*'; or, *'Where's what you brought?'* or *'Open up your luggage and give the King a gift'*. Yet these are some of the prompts it's felt necessary to give the congregation in some of our worship services, i.e., *'lift up your hands'*, or, *'open up your mouth'*, - do this, do that.

Worship to God that has to be forced or provoked in any way is not really worship, and is unlikely to be accepted by Him. Worship is totally voluntary in acknowledgement of who God is. As our overflow of love and adoration for Him spills out of our heart, it changes the atmosphere of our homes, our church services and everywhere we go.

If you've brought something for Jesus, you will always want to give it to Him freely as soon as you see Him!

JEJ

TUESDAY 17th

The LORD is nigh unto all them that call upon him, to all that call upon him in truth
Psalm 145:18

AN ANSWER WITH NO DISTANCE - THE MAGNETISED TRUTH
Reading: Psalm 145:1-21

If you're upstairs and you call someone who is downstairs it's only polite to answer them. They often reply with a shout so you can hear them from upstairs, but often that's all we get - an answer with distance between.

Growing up this was one of my mother's irritations and I was told *'Kay, when I call you, I expect you to come to where I am, to hear face to face what I'm calling you for'*.

How loving and kind is our God that when we call on Him, He is not distant but closes the gap between us by coming near to us. What love is displayed that God is so attentive to our call that He doesn't just holla down the halls of our situations, struggles, or trials but He comes near and is present with us.

When we call on God our calls are magnetised by truth. The truth of a sincere heart crying out in desperation. The truth of a heart that knows only God can help. The truth that says, *'I've messed up God, but forgive me'*. The truth of knowing that I have the right as a child of God to call on my Father to help. The truth that declares *'I'm loved'*.

Prayer time:
Thank you LORD for closing the gap between my call with not just a response but your presence ever near. Thank you that when I call out to you in truth you are attracted to my call like a magnet. What an awesome God you are, and what a privileged position I am in to have the King's ear and presence.

Minister Kay Dawkins/ MinK

WEDNESDAY 18th

...call his name Emmanuel, which being interpreted is, God with us
Matthew 1:23

MEANING MATTERS – Reading: Matthew 1:22-25

What's in a name? My name is Laylah which in Arabic is interpreted as, *'night beauty'*. There are different ways to spell Laylah – Layla, Leila, Laila, etc., but no matter the variation, the meaning of the name remains the same.

Some people in the Bible had a name transformation and their new name held a powerful meaning. For example, *Abraham* (once Abram) means *'exalted father'*, *Israel* (once Jacob) means *'God perseveres'*, and *Paul* (once Saul) means *'small/humble'*. When you read the stories, you will understand the importance of their new names. With this in mind, when we hear the name *'Emmanuel'*, also translated as *'Immanuel'*, the power of the name's interpretation should not be taken lightly. When you shout aloud with praise and thanksgiving, *'Emmanuel!'* meaning *'Our God is with us!'*, you are acknowledging the meaning of His name that reminds you that you are not alone on this journey.

Be keen and eager to know more about your ever-present Saviour and Friend today. What does the interpretation of Emmanuel mean to you?

Let us pray:

Dear Lord, thank you for the promise you made that you will always be with us and for sending your Son, the Saviour of the World. You have reminded us today that names are important, and when we speak of the name Emmanuel, we are welcoming your presence into our midst. We ask for a covering from you today as we go about our day. In the name of Jesus. Amen.

Laylah Walker

THURSDAY 19th

And both Jesus was called, and his disciples, to the marriage – John 2:2

A SPECIAL GUEST – Reading: John 2:1-12

Today's lesson looks at Jesus, His mother and His disciples attending a wedding feast.

It seems that there was a significant under estimation of the number of guests expected when ordering the wine. At some point during the week of celebration, the servants realised that the wine was finished. Thankfully Jesus was there. Although Mary didn't know what Jesus would do to spare the bride's family from embarrassment, she was quietly confident that Jesus would intervene. She told the servants, *'Whatsoever he saith unto you, do it' (John2:5).*

A songwriter long ago said, *'I must have Jesus in my whole life…'*. There's nothing that I should do and nowhere that I should go that He should be unhappy to accompany me, or I put up a No Entry sign to Jesus. As a guest at a table, Jesus was enjoying the festivities just like everyone else but like a committed doctor, who never ceases to be On Call, Jesus saved the day.

Invite Him into every plan that you're making. Although God is omnipresent (everywhere at the same time), omniscient (knows absolutely everything) and omnipotent (is all powerful), yet He forces Himself on nobody. His name needs to be at the top of all of our plans, every idea, every guest list. Let Him know that He's welcome and you want Him to be there.

JEJ

FRIDAY 20th

The LORD, he is the God; the LORD he is the God – 1 Kings 18:39

CONFIDENCE IN THE LORD – Reading: 1 Kings 18:16-40

If you know that God is with you then you should act like it!

Elijah was not afraid to prove to evil prophets of Baal who God was, because God had never failed him. Elijah was so sure that the presence of God was with him that he was a little smug when the Baal worshippers were calling on their false god who did not come through for them.

When it was time for Elijah to make an offering, he knew that if he prayed the power down, his God would reveal His true nature to the people, for His own name's sake. Elijah's faith is truly admirable as he demonstrates how to seek the Lord with certainty that **He will turn up**!

Following Elijah's steps of faith, you should:

1) Recognise the sovereignty of the God whom you serve

2) Come before His presence with humility and lowliness of heart

3) Make your petition known to Him

You have to stand up for the Lord with confidence, especially in these trying times. He will deliver you.

Let us pray:

Dear Lord, thank you for the reminder of your amazing love today. Thank you for your omnipresence and your Holy Word that always reminds us that you are near. We understand that we are nothing without you. Help us to be more like Elijah, steadfast in faith and assured in what you can do. Give us a spirit of humility. In Jesus' mighty name. Amen.

Laylah Walker

SATURDAY 21st

...Let us now go...and see this thing which is come to pass – Luke 2:15

DON'T JUST TAKE MY WORD FOR IT – Reading: Luke 2:15-16; Acts 8:26-40

The joy of the shepherds is easy to feel and observe after they received a personal visit from angels to announce the birth of Jesus Christ.

Try for a moment to imagine the scene that night at this unexpected and awesome visitation.

After you have in your mind captured the surprise and delight of these shepherds, you will then understand why they would have probably signed-off work early for the night to go and see the *'...Saviour, which is Christ the Lord'* (Luke 2:11). This was not an everyday event!

Can you remember who first introduced you to the Lord Jesus Christ? What was your initial response? You may have taken a long time to be convinced while you tried to work out and understand the Message of Salvation, or you may have been like the shepherds - instant in their faith and acceptance as true the tidings which they heard – rushing and gushing to see more. This is not too dissimilar to the eunuch from Ethiopia who, after just one Bible study in the desert with Philip the Evangelist said, *'See here is water; what doth hinder me to be baptized' (Acts 8:36).*

There is something about when the Word pricks the heart to conviction and you want to move on quickly to the next stage. 'Now' starts to feel like a long time to wait!

JEJ

SUNDAY 22nd

So they hurried off and found Mary and Joseph, and the baby, who was lying in the manger – Luke 2:16 (NIV)

GOD REMEMBERS THE LOWLY – Reading: Luke 2:8-20

In Luke 2:16-17, it stands out to me, that the 'they' mentioned are shepherds who lived in the fields and are regarded at the time as the lowest of the Jews. Yet, they are the first to receive the Good News about the Saviour's birth, from none other than an angel of the Lord.

At the time, shepherds would have been the least likely group chosen to be the first responders. If the Lord had left it to local authorities the Pharisees would probably have been the group expected to hear the news first. God's ways however are the highest authority, and He always remembers the lowly. The humble surroundings of Jesus' birth were not the expected beginnings of a Saviour, just like His first visitors weren't from the most recognised of society.

God always rejects man's loftiness and promotes the lowly. Luke 19:10 reminds us that, *'the Son of Man came to seek and to save the lost'*. These shepherds received an angelic visit and hurried to see about what they heard. Verse 17 translated into Greek means that they did more than *'see'*. *'Seen'* translated is the Greek word *'Eido'* which means *'to come to the fulness of knowledge, without a doubt'*. What a revelation! What an honour! God tells them and shows them exactly who Jesus is.

Two thousand years later we still sing about these shepherds in December when reflecting on the birth of Jesus Christ. They represented the lowly and their place in history is immutable. This story should encourage us that, regardless of our status in the earth, it's our relationship with our Saviour that counts. Let's humble ourselves before Him and trust His plan for our lives. His plan is always greater!

Latoya Foster

MONDAY 23rd

***...while (Joseph) thought on these things, the angel...appeared...in a dream
Matthew 1:20***

A DIVINE INTERRUPTION – Reading: Matthew 1:18-25

Mary and Joseph were already betrothed when Mary became impregnated by the Holy Ghost. In Bible days, a betrothal was the first part of marriage, a legal and binding commitment between a man and woman. They would at the stage of betrothal be considered married and referred to as a husband or a wife. However, consummation would not be until after the wedding ceremony and celebration took place about a year later, i.e., part two of marriage formalities.

Try and picture then the difficult conversation they would have had as Mary attempted to convince Joseph that, although she was pregnant, she had not been sexually intimate with another man. I would fully understand if Joseph not only thought that Mary was lying but also that she was going mad! *'Erm, Joseph, the Holy Ghost (the what?) came upon me, and the power of the Highest overshadowed me (what are you talking about!) …' (Luke 1:34-35).* Let's be real, this was no ordinary tale to be digested just because Mary said so!

God being aware of Joseph's hurt and disappointment at Mary's news, intervened. Although Joseph did not tell Mary he was going to put her away (meaning divorce her since as I said betrothal was as binding as marriage), God read Joseph's thoughts and arranged a Divine Interruption in the form of a dream.

Not every dream means something so we must be very careful how we share and interpret them. Dreams can cause havoc! **Note**: If a dream contradicts God's Word, **please ignore it**! But what God does sometimes is, when He doesn't get our attention whilst we're awake, He arrests us in our sleep with a dream. All of what Mary had tried to say in a very muddled way became clear during the interruption. God told Joseph to cancel His plans about putting Mary away.

A Divine Interruption can be very inconvenient. You may have planned to marry a particular man and God interrupted days before the wedding. You may have planned to buy a particular property and at the last minute it fell through. You may have just finished decorating your house to your standard then God said move. But somehow thank God for interrupting and capsizing your plans, even if you never get an explanation of why!

JEJ

*TUESDAY 24th

...Simeon (was) waiting for the consolation of Israel: and the Holy Ghost was upon him – Luke 2:25

WAITING ON THE LORD – Reading: Luke 2:21-35

Simeon was a devoted man of God. He was waiting, like most Jews, for the Messiah to come. Whilst he was waiting, Scripture says in Luke 2:25, *'...the Holy Ghost was upon him'*. This means that the Holy Ghost (God) was with him.

Today, the Holy Ghost is not upon us, but dwelling within us (the believer). Whilst we await Jesus' return, we must ensure the Holy Ghost is in us helping us to be patient, teaching and guiding us so that in our waiting we will not be deceived by false doctrines and teachers.

If the Holy Ghost isn't dwelling in you, then today seek God and ask Him for the infilling of His Spirit. God was with Simeon and led him to the temple on that special day to see Jesus. Ensure that the Holy Ghost is in you and with you so that one day it will lead you to meet Him in the air.

Waiting isn't always easy, but remember, in your waiting God has not forgotten you, but is right there with you.

Lady Pam Lewin

***Christmas Eve**

*WEDNESDAY 25th

...God so loved the world that he gave his only begotten Son – John 3:16

YOU WON'T PERISH – Reading: John 3:1-21

Despite the Divine Directive not to look back at the destruction of Sodom, Lot's wife in Genesis 19 chose to look back, and she was instantly transformed into a pillar of salt.

Today, in the New Testament, John 3:16 speaks of belief in Jesus Christ - if we believe in Him, we will not perish:

For God so loved the world, that he gave his only begotten Son, that whosoever believeth in him should not perish, but have everlasting life. For God sent not his Son into the world to condemn the world; but that the world through him might be saved (John 3:16-17).

The outward man/woman may perish. The spirit man/woman (our soul) will have life eternal.

Choose to believe on Jesus.

Lady Yolanda Edmund

***Christmas Day**

*THURSDAY 26th

And in that day thou shalt say, O LORD, I will praise thee: though thou wast angry with me, thine anger is turned away... - Isaiah 12:1

A CHANGE IS COMING – Reading: Isaiah 12:1-6

A *change is coming*
Do you feel it in God's atmosphere?
God has finally heard you
There's no need to fear.

You've counted the hours
The minutes too
You've counted the seconds
Don't you know God has not forgotten you?

Will you believe what you have read?
Will you believe the words Jesus said?
Your special individual change
Is waiting for you.

Our God has a brighter horizon for you
You were overlooked
Many things in your life
As a Christian seemed to go wrong.

But don't worry my sister
Just keep your faith
Never let go
Nothing that is not God-ordained
Will the Master allow.

Jesus loves you!
Wait for that change is coming
Some of my favourite words:
'Look out and Wow'!

Sister Jennifer Henry

***Boxing Day**

FRIDAY 27th

My help cometh from the LORD, which made heaven and earth – Psalm 121:2

WE ARE ALWAYS IN HIS PRESENCE – Reading: Psalm 121:1-8

Psalm 121 acknowledges that our help comes from the LORD which made the heaven and the earth.

God, our Father, watches over us at all times. He does not grow weary or tired as we do, neither is He busy doing meaningless things, but is fully taking care of all of His children.

In times of trouble, many choose to turn to friends and family, self-help or even crystal balls, but they cannot help. God is more than able to support and sustain us. He is a big God and none of us will lack, *'Have I not commanded thee, be strong and of a good courage, be not afraid, neither be thou dismayed for the LORD thy God is with thee whithersoever thou goest?'* (Joshua 1:9).

When we take hold of the truth that God is for us, we have nothing to fear. God is always there. We are strengthened by the words of Psalm 40:17, *'I am poor and needy, yet the LORD thinketh upon me'.* God always provides hope and consolation for His people in whatever state, challenges and rough terrain we may find ourselves.

Though we may not see Him physically, God tells us this promise which is that He will never leave us nor forsake us (Hebrews 13:5).

Thank you, Jesus.

Missionary M Fraser

SATURDAY 28th

Do not fear what you are about to suffer…I will give you the crown of life
Revelation 2:10 (ESV)

THE FORMER THINGS SHALL PASS AWAY – Reading: Revelation 2:8-11

God promised in His Word that He will never leave us or forsake us. He did not promise that we would never suffer but Apostle Paul said, *'…the sufferings of this present time are not worthy to be compared with the glory which shall be revealed within us' (Romans 8:18).*

1st Thessalonians gives hope to the children of God; it reminds us that there is life after death. The dead in Christ shall arise first and those who are alive and remain shall be caught up together, in the clouds to meet Jesus, our bridegroom, and we shall forever be with the Lord (1 Thessalonians 4:13-18); then we shall receive the crown of life (James 1:12).

God understands the severity of the pain you experience, and understands that your afflictions have been for many years. Sometimes there seems to be no way out of your oppression and it's one spiritual attack after another. But remain faithful unto death because, *'God shall wipe away all tears from your eyes; and there shall be no more death, neither sorrow, nor crying, neither shall there be any more pain: for the former things are passed away' (Revelation 21:4).*

Rachel Lewin

SUNDAY 29th

...this woman was full of good works and charitable deeds which she did
Acts 9:36 (NKJV

A GREAT WORK – Reading: Acts 9:36-42

Here we have a woman, Tabitha by name, who may have appeared to be so insignificant to some, but to others she was a great woman of God.

Why was this? The Bible tells us that she was FULL of good works. Her works were so highly regarded that when she died the brethren refused to accept it.

Sisters, what are your God-given gifts and talents?

Shine, press through in spite of adversity! It is only then that we can join with Nehemiah and say, *'we are doing a great work and we **cannot** come down' (Nehemiah 6:3).*

Deveen Smith

MONDAY 30th

...my reward is with me, ... - Revelation 22:12

NO IOUs – Reading: Revelation 22:1-14

I think that most of us have at least once experienced someone taking credit for work which we did or an idea that we had. Depending on that person's character, they may have passed back the compliment and admitted that it should really go to you.

Working for Christ is so much easier than working for man because He keeps an accurate record of what we've done, we cannot fool Him.

You may have been labouring for the Lord for years, and maybe feeling a bit tired now, but continue to be faithful. God does not only reward those whose ministry takes them on the frontline where what they do is seen, He also observes those 'offline' ministries between only you and another person. He sees you busy caring for the poor and needy in the community, being a carer for a sick or elderly relative, those prayer calls made to anyone who God lays on your heart.

You will be paid in full. It can be annoying if you do a job for somebody and when it's finished, they say that they can't pay you right now – they offer you an IOU until the end of the month or even later. We won't have that problem when Christ returns. Our pay is already sealed with our name written in His handwriting, and He'll be bringing it with Him.

JEJ

*TUESDAY 31st

So, what do you think? With God on our side like this, how can we lose?
Romans 8:31 (MSG)

GOD IS WITH US & FOR US – Reading: Psalm 124:1-8; Romans 8:31

Where would we be if the LORD was not on our side. Each moment of each day is made that more tolerable because we are confident that all things are working for our good. If He was not with us, we would not have been able to cope with the many setbacks we have both experienced and witnessed.

Not only is God with us, but He is also for us and as such He will defend us, prosper us, heal us and deliver us. Let the theme of our praise be the never-failing love of God, let our worship forever resonate with the sounds of gratitude.

Lift up your voices, women of God, be no longer silent! Daniel's God is able to deliver. No matter what the problem, our God will always come through for us.

Another year has come to an end. As we reflect upon the past 365 days, no doubt there will be many things for which we are grateful. Like me, there will be uncompleted projects and assignments that you will no doubt complete at some point in the future.

Nevertheless, be strong in the Lord and in the power of His might; proclaim the good news that through the storms and the rain of another year we are victorious, we are overcomers because, *'greater is He that is in us, than he that is in the world'*!

Dexter E. Edmund
Presiding Bishop, BUCJC Apostolic UK & Europe

***New Year's Eve**

SUPPORT DIRECTORY

Please contact one of our professionally qualified Bethel UK Counsellors if you have been emotionally affected by any of the subjects covered in ***I Arise! 2024***: **Bethel Counselling Initiative 07783 046250.**

Alternatively, please see the list below which includes independent agencies in the UK who will be able to offer you support:

Child Bereavement UK
https://www.childbereavementuk.org/
Helpline: 0800 02 888 40
Email:helpline@childbereavementuk.org

Provides support for children and young people up to the age of 25 who are facing bereavement, and anyone impacted by the death of a child of any age. They offer support sessions for individuals, couples, families and children and groups for families, parents and young people. Also provides a helpline and guidance for professionals.

Cruse
https://www.cruse.org.uk/
Helpline: 0808 808 1677 (Monday to Friday 9am to 9pm)
Email:helpline@cruse.org.uk
Cruse Chat live online chat also available

A national charity offering bereavement support, information and campaigning. Cruse offers up to six sessions of one-to-one counselling support, usually on the phone / online, as well as a free helpline and chat support. The website includes guides to understanding grief that are written by bereavement specialists, and information about what to do after someone dies.

Dementia UK
Tel: 0800 888 6678
Carers Direct - helpline for Carers: 0300 123 1053
John's Campaign: 01245 231898 (support to be able to sit with /support loved ones whilst in hospital). Contact Julia Jones julia-jones@talk21.com or Nicci Gerrard nicci.gerrard@icloud.com
Admiral Nurse Dementia Helpline 0800 888 6678
Age UK National Helpline 0800 6781602

Hope Again (Cruse)
https://www.hopeagain.org.uk/
Tel: 0808 808 1677 (Monday to Friday 9.30am to 5pm)
Email:hopeagain@cruse.org.uk

Trained volunteers are available to speak on the free helpline or by email. The website includes parental / guardian advice, videos and resources for families on how to support a child or young person who is grieving.

MIND
http://www.mind.org.uk/
Info line (Tel.): 0300 123 3393 (open 9am to 6pm, Monday to Friday)
Legal line (Tel.): 0300 4666463 (open 9am to 6pm, Monday to Friday)

Mind's Info line provides information and signposting about mental health problems, where to get help, treatment options and advocacy services. Legal Line is a telephone service offering legal information and general advice on mental health related law e.g., on being detained under the Mental Health Act ('sectioned'), mental capacity, community care, discrimination and equality.

National Association for People Abused in Childhood (NAPAC)
https://napac.org.uk/
Tel: 0808 801 0331 (helpline open Monday to Thursday: 10am to 9pm, Friday: 10am to 6pm)

Email:support@napac.org.uk

A registered charity providing support and information for adult survivors of any form of child abuse.

National Domestic Abuse Hotline
https://www.nationaldahelpline.org.uk/

Tel: 0808 2000 247 (free and 24/7)
Live chat also available through the website Monday to Friday, 3pm to 10pm.

Run by Refuge, this national helpline provides emotional and practical support, including helping individuals to find a refuge or other place of safety and access specialist services in their locality.

National Stalking Helpline
Tel: 0808 802 0300
https://www.suzylamplugh.org/am-i-being-stalked-tool

The National Stalking Helpline is run by Suzy Lamplugh Trust. They provide information and guidance on topics including:
•The law in relation to stalking and harassment in the United Kingdom
•Reporting stalking or harassment
•Effective gathering of evidence
•Ensuring your personal safety

Rape Crisis
https://rapecrisis.org.uk
Tel: 0808 802 9999
Live chat available through the website.

Rape crisis is a charity working hard to end sexual violence and abuse. They provide support after rape, sexual assault, sexual abuse or any form of sexual violence.

Relate
https://www.relate.org.uk
A national charity offering support for marriages in crisis

Shelter
https://england.shelter.org.uk/
Helpline: 0808 800 4444
Live chat available through the website.
National charity providing one-to-one, personalised help with housing issues and homelessness, a free emergency helpline and free legal advice for people who have lost their homes or who are facing eviction.

Silverline
www.thesilverline.org.uk
Helpline Tel: 0800 470 80 90

Silverline is a national, free, confidential helpline for older people offering friendship, advice and information. It is open 24 hours a day for anyone who feels alone or wants to talk about something. As well as the helpline, they offer telephone friendship (a weekly 30-minute call between an older person and a Silver Line Friend volunteer), Silver Letters (a fortnightly exchange of a letter between an older person and a volunteer), Silver Circles (a call between a group of older people on a shared interest or topic, taking place each week for 60 minutes) and Silver Line Connects (help with informing and connecting an older person with national and local services).

The Daisy Chain Project: Domestic Abuse Legal Advice Charity
https://www.thedaisychainproject.com
Email:info@thedaisychainproject.com

A charity based in Worthing with a UK-wide reach that aims to help fight domestic violence by providing pro bono legal advice, educating people about what constitutes domestic abuse. The Daisy Chain Project legal team consists of qualified and regulated barristers and solicitors who offer free legal support to men and women experiencing, or fleeing, domestic abuse. All barristers and solicitors are regulated by the Bar Standards Board and Solicitors Regulation Authority respectively.

Victim Support
https://www.victimsupport.org.uk/
Helpline: 0808 1689 111 (24/7)
Webchat available through the website

Provides free and confidential support for people affected by crime and traumatic events, regardless of whether they have reported the crime to the police. Services include information and advice, immediate emotional and practical help, longer term emotional and practical help, advocacy, peer support and group work, restorative justice, personal safety services, help in navigating the criminal justice system.

Young Minds Crisis Messenger
https://www.kooth.com/
For urgent help text YM to 85258

Provides free, 24/7 crisis support across the UK if you are experiencing a mental health crisis. All texts are answered by trained volunteers, with support from experienced clinical supervisors. Texts are free from EE, O2, Vodafone, 3, Virgin Mobile, BT Mobile, GiffGaff, Tesco Mobile and Telecom Plus.

Contact us at: bethelwomen@bethelunitedduk.org.uk

Printed in Great Britain
by Amazon